INS

INSECTS

by ROSS E. HUTCHINS

Illustrations by STANLEY WYATT

PRENTICE-HALL, Inc., Englewood Cliffs, N. J.

Insects
by Ross E. Hutchins

© 1966 by Ross E. Hutchins

Copyright under International and Pan American
Copyright Conventions

First PRISM PAPERBACK edition, 1972

Published by arrangement with Prentice-Hall, Inc.

ISBN: 0-13-467423-5

Library of Congress Catalog Card Number: 66-13038

Printed in the United States of America

10   9   8   7   6   5   4   3   2   1

Prentice-Hall International, Inc., London
Prentice-Hall of Australia, Pty. Ltd., Sydney
Prentice-Hall of Canada, Ltd., Toronto
Prentice-Hall of India   Private   Ltd., New Delhi
Prentice-Hall of Japan, Inc., Tokyo

Other books by Ross E. Hutchins

Insects: Hunters and Trappers
Insect Builders and Craftsmen
Wild Ways, A Book of Animal Habits
Strange Plants and Their Ways
This Is A Leaf
This Is A Flower
This Is A Tree
The Amazing Seeds

G OD must have loved the insects he made so many of them—just how many nobody knows because new ones are being found and named every year; perhaps even every day. The number of distinct, named species runs into the hundreds of thousands and that is several times as many as there are different species of all the other kinds of animals put together.

Not all human beings share God's preference. To most, a "bug" is merely something to be swatted, poisoned or stepped on. Even among professional entomologists there are those to whom the only important questions are how to get rid of the harmful insects and how to encourage the beneficial. But there are other scientists and laymen to whom the endless variety, complexity and incredibility of insect ways of life are fascinating—partly because insects are, of all animals, the most completely "inhuman." They represent a solution to the problems of living more radically different from man's than that of any other kind of living creature.

Naïvely observed, insects seem far more ingenious, efficient and successful than we. They seldom hesitate and they seldom blunder. The spider spins his astonishing web, the bees employ their astonishing "direction finder" with almost perfect skill. And yet we know that their patterns of behavior are fixed, inherited and almost unmodifiable; their remarkably successful way of life proceeds, it would seem, with little or no consciousness of what is being done or why it should be done.

Millions of years ago one group of living creatures took one road, a different group, another. The first, to which man belongs, came to rely more and more upon some sort of awareness, the other more and more upon fixed instincts.

In our case what we learn is far more important in our lives than those instincts which we inherit. In the case of the insects the reverse is so profound that if they can learn at all it is to an almost insignificant extent. Because our society is becoming so tightly organized and the techniques of "conditioning" human beings so refined, the insect is sometimes held up to us as an awful warning against what we might come to resemble. The difference is between techniques which can be learned and techniques which are inherited. We—at least so we like to think—embody the triumph of the first tendency, the insects certainly embody that of the second.

Ross E. Hutchins is a renowned world authority on insects. In this book he meets a challenge which most of his fellow professionals would have refused to accept: to survey in one volume the whole field of entomology, displaying a viable method which is neither that of merely broad generalization nor that of random example. He tells us what is true of all insects; he describes the most important of the types of insects and he illustrates these types with specific accounts of their behavior. I know of no other book which will tell the reader so much and tell it so interestingly.

—Joseph Wood Krutch

Contents

Introduction   xi

one   The World of Insects   3

two   Instinct, Intelligence and Behavior   25

three   The Songs They Sing   45

four   The Aerialists   63

five   Insect Migration   77

six   The Water Realm   95

seven   The Hunters   117

eight   The Farmers   143

nine   The Builders   165

ten   The Paper and Tent Makers   187

eleven   The Nectar Gatherers   207

twelve   The Carpenters, Miners and Gall Makers   225

thirteen   Plant Curiosities   247

fourteen   The Pollinators   261

fifteen   Chemical Warfare   273

sixteen   Of Size and Strength   287

seventeen   Of Light and Color   297

eighteen   Insects and the Future   311

Index   315

Introduction

THIS is a book about the strange and remarkable realm of the insects. Insects are an ancient tribe with habits which parallel our own. The human race is of relatively recent origin with a social structure that is just now evolving into ever-increasing complexity. By contrast, the social habits of such insects as the termites, bees, hornets and ants have been fully formed for millions of years. Their social structures are highly functional and amazingly complex and have survived in a world that has changed slowly but continuously down the eons.

To best understand and appreciate the insects one must know something about their past history, what their ancestors were like and how they lived. They are a diverse animal group and have evolved in such divergent ways that within their ranks are found almost every habit that the human mind can conceive. Millions of years ago, insects "invented" jet propulsion, air-conditioning, humidity control, cold light, chemical warfare, and they solved many of the complex problems of aerodynamics, celestial navigation and communication. Many of the skills evolved by insects compare with human accomplishments; they fabricate paper of excellent quality, construct structures of clay, stone and other materials, drill through hard substances and, by special chemicals they secrete, cause plants to build homes for them. All these things they do by instinct or "inherited knowledge" passed down through their generations. Their evolution followed a path different from our own; insects have only limited capacities for learning, they are hatched from the eggs with all the skill they will ever have.

Many of the facts presented here have never appeared in a popular volume; they are to be found only in technical publications, buried in the terminology of science, which often makes dull reading. The writer is indebted to numerous biologists, both past and present, who have, in many cases, spent their entire lives probing into the secrets of one insect or insect group and recorded their findings in scientific journals. Unfortunately, in a popular book it is impossible to give all of them the credit they are due.

This book does not deal with the details of classification, though an effort has been made to give as much helpful information in this regard as possible. For those who wish to identify insects there are manuals available that are devoted to the various groups. No one manual will be found that covers all the groups in detail; the class Insecta is so large that, in a lifetime, a person can become familiar with only a small portion of it. In this volume we are concerned with the living insects and their habits, not with dead specimens in museum cases. This is the story of the potter wasp building her clay masterpiece; of the dragonfly with its bright wings flashing over pond and stream; of the *Pepsis* wasp dueling to the death with the tarantula; of the insect clan, the hunters and the hunted, and of the builders and the craftsmen that toil in the summer sun.

INSECTS

chapter one

The World of Insects

THE story of insects is truly a success story. Once launched on their evolutionary careers, the insect tribes multiplied and expanded in amazing diversity. They are now found in almost every conceivable location and inhabit every continent including Antarctica, where many collembola or springtails were found at 6,000 feet above sea level on Mount Gran. Nearly a million distinct species have been described and catalogued, and more than 6,000 new species are being recorded each year. At present, about 80 percent of the world's known animals are insects, but the proportion of insects will no doubt increase. Insects are small and easily overlooked whereas most other animals are larger and more apt to be found by zoologists. In many tropical lands, such as the central portions of South America, there are probably numerous, as yet unknown, insects. Some entomologists believe that the total number of insect species may eventually reach several million.

The insects are an ancient tribe; they were already old when the dinosaurs roamed the earth. Their origins stretch so far back in time that we can only guess at the nature of their remote ancestors. As with other animals, the clues to their past history are buried in the earth as fossilized remains, but there are vast gaps in the fossil record covering millions of years, and when we go beyond the Carboniferous period, which began about 300 million years ago, the trail fades completely.

Insect origins beyond that point are shrouded in mystery. It might almost seem that the insects had suddenly appeared on the scene, but this is not in agreement with accepted ideas of animal origins. The insects were certainly there, but they left no fossilized remains. This may seem strange until we recall that about the only fossils left by very ancient insects were wings. The remote, wingless ancestors of the insects that crept over the rocks and through the archaic vegetation perished and their delicate bodies soon disappeared; they formed few fossils.

Insects' bodies are covered with shells composed of a hard substance called *chitin,* which is resistant to acids and alkalies but is slowly dissolved by water. Thus, it was chiefly their wings that settled into the clays and sediments of the ancient ponds and lakes and left impressions or imprints that became immortalized in stone. The chitinous substance of the wings slowly disappeared and only their prints remained as proof that they had been there.

Further back in time, beyond the winged insects, the little-known wingless types lived and gradually developed, following the slow processes of evolution. The oldest true insects known were springtails, tiny insects that are still abundant in damp places today. Geological time moves slowly, and millions of years passed during which new insect species and types were evolved and then passed away; only the fittest survived.

The sea-inhabiting trilobites and crustacea and, later, the land-dwelling scorpions, centipedes and millipedes preceded the insects and were their remote ancestors. All these lived during the Silurian period, a time of moist, warm climates about 400 million years ago. The great invertebrate clan was on the rise, leaving the sea and invading the land. Insect life was like a slowly flowing stream that meandered through the eons, gradually taking on new characteristics and discarding old.

Fossilized insects belonging to six different orders have been found in late Carboniferous stone, but most of these became extinct. One of these insects was *Palaeodictyoptera,* a mayfly-like insect that probably became the ancestor of all modern flying insects. It is probable that all winged insects have a common ancestry, since the veins in their wings all have certain similarities. Once wings were developed, the destiny of the insect clan was practically assured. The ability to fly is an important milestone in the development of any animal group.

Insect wings did not arise fully formed. At first there were probably ancestral forms that sailed through the air on flat, wing-like extensions from the sides of their bodies. They were like gliders. The next logical step was the addition of flight muscles, and powered flight became a reality. The wings of the first flying insects did not fold; they were like dragonfly wings, held straight out from the body. Later insects developed the ability to fold their wings like fans. This is the condition found in grasshoppers and beetles, which fold their hind wings beneath the protective front wings. There is an unusual feature about insect wings that deserves mention: of all animal wings, insect wings are the only ones that were developed as special structures; the wings of all other flying animals —bats and birds—are merely modified legs. Flying insects became a reality about 50 million years before the reptiles and birds took to the air, and for those 50 million years the only flying creatures were insects.

During the late Carboniferous and early Permian, the primitive dragonflies made their debuts. These were the *Protodonata* and they closely resembled the types we see flying so gracefully over ponds and streams. But, whereas modern dragonflies are never very large—hardly over four inches —many of the ancient types were giants. Fossils of these large dragonflies have been found in France, Kansas and Oklahoma; some of them measured 30 inches across. The cockroaches have been with us for a long time; huge cockroaches crept through the dank vegetation of the ancient world and, little changed, their smaller descendants have followed the slow course of history down to the present.

Insects have left their remains as fossils in ancient shales. This cranefly fossil came from the Florissant beds of Colorado. (Specimen, courtesy of General Biological Supply House, Inc.)

While most of the ancient insects are known only from wings or fragments imbedded in shales and other types of rock strata, many prehistoric insects were often preserved in amber. Amber is actually the fossilized resin of trees that flourished many millions of years ago. This resin oozed out of ancient species of pine trees, and while it was sticky, like fly paper, it entrapped and preserved numerous insects and other small creatures. At an early date it was noticed that within many of the pieces of amber there were well-preserved insects—flies, gnats, ants and so on. Nearly a thousand different kinds of ancient insects have been catalogued from Baltic amber alone. Insect-bearing amber has also been found in other parts of the world, including Sicily, Romania, Burma, Zanzibar, Indonesia, Mexico, Canada, Alaska and the Philippine Islands. In the United States, it has been found in Tennessee and in ancient lake beds in the Mohave Desert. On Columbus' second voyage to the West Indies he reported the discovery of amber in the Dominican Republic. Recent collections of amber from this location have shown that about one out of every 15 to 20 pieces contains insects or other things which became imbedded in it. Besides insects, these include spiders, flowers and leaves.

Much of our knowledge of the insects that existed from 50 to 100 million years ago comes from those preserved in this resinous material, which is really ideal as a preservative. Insects trapped in it show all the minute details of their structure and appear as if they had lived only yesterday, instead of many millions of years ago. Strangely, many of these ancient insects resemble very closely those that live today. At least six different species of ants found in amber are so closely related to modern types that they cannot be distinguished from them. Insects have changed very slowly with the passing millennia. Dr. C. T. Brues of Harvard University has placed pieces of fly paper in a forest and recorded the kinds and numbers of insects trapped. By comparing these data with similar data from insects found in amber, he has come to the conclusion that insects are, at present, just about as abundant as they were 70 million years ago. Altogether, about 13,000 species of fossil insects have been formally described.

It is difficult for the human mind to visualize the vast expanses of geological time. Years, in astronomical numbers, are almost meaningless. It is estimated that living things have existed on the earth for about 500 million years, or since the advent of the Cambrian period. Beyond the Cambrian, the rocks seem barren of life. It may help to visualize geological time if we compare the period of time since life began on earth

A fly preserved in amber. It became entrapped in the resin of a forest tree forty million years ago during the Oligocene period in East Prussia. It resembles modern flies very closely.

to the distance from New York City to San Francisco. If we had started on a trip across the country from New York at the time when life seems to have originated and had traveled at the snail-like rate of about one-third inch a year, we would have arrived at San Francisco this year. If we had observed the insect life along the way, we would have encountered the first dragonflies in the vicinity of North Platte, Nebraska, after 250 million years of travel. We would have seen our first beetles at Cheyenne, Wyoming. Continuing at the same slow pace, we would have entered the Age of Reptiles as we crossed the border between Utah and Nevada. Here we would also have seen our first primitive grasshoppers. Near Ely, Nevada, we would have encountered bees and flies, and somewhere in western Nevada we would have entered the Age of Mammals.

Here, for the first time, we would have seen colorful flowers, and butterflies and bees sipping nectar from them. Somewhere beyond Sacramento we would have seen small, three-toed horses scampering through the forests. When we at last arrived at San Francisco Bay and could see the city only a few miles away, we would have caught up with primitive man, a late-comer on the world scene.

If we delve into the question of the actual number of individual insects, the figures become astronomical. If we were to count the insects on an acre of meadow or in a forest, we would certainly find that the population reached into the millions. Insects have many enemies, but this hazard is offset by their tremendous reproductive capacities. A queen honeybee may lay up to 2,000 eggs a day and live for several years. If we assume that a queen bee lays eggs at this rate for six months out of each year and lives for three years, she would lay more than a million eggs. The queen of an East African termite, *Macrotermes bellicosus,* is probably the champion egg layer. These large queens have been found to lay eggs at the rate of an egg every two seconds or 43,000 a day! How long these queens live is unknown, but estimates range from 15 to 50 years. This fantastic egg-laying rate is apparently necessary to maintain the population of workers, which reaches into the millions.

The squash bug has piercing and sucking mouthparts and is a serious pest of squash. Here a female is seen in the act of laying eggs.

One often reads estimates of potential populations of insects based on the reproductive capacities of the females, but such estimates are not based on actual probabilities; they merely represent theoretical possibilities. For example, it has been stated that the descendants of a pair of houseflies, if they all lived and did well from April to August, would total 190,000,000,000,000,000,000 individuals. Fortunately, the balance of nature, in the form of natural controls, limits such population explosions among insects just as it does among other animals and among plants.

The insect tribe is quite well defined, it may be characterized as being made up of backbone-less animals (invertebrates) having their bodies divided into three regions—head, thorax and abdomen. There are three pairs of legs and, usually, two pairs of wings, all attached to the midsection or thorax. The flies are the exception with respect to wings; they have but one pair, the hind pair being modified into gyroscopic navigational organs. In some groups, such as the beetles and grasshoppers, the fore wings are hard and sheathlike, the hind wings being folded, fanlike, under them. Some of the more primitive insects, such as the bird lice and fleas, are wingless.

Insects are often confused with other small creatures such as pillbugs, spiders, ticks and mites. While all the above animals, as well as insects, are classed as *Arthropods* or joint-legged animals, only those with certain well defined characteristics may correctly be called insects. Of all the Arthropods, only insects have their bodies divided into head, thorax, and abdomen, and possess *three* pairs of legs, all attached to the thorax. By contrast, pillbugs have their bodies divided into many segments and have many legs. Spiders have only *two* body regions; a front portion called the *cephalothorax* and a hind portion called the abdomen. They have *four* pairs of legs. Ticks and mites are a little more difficult to identify but, in their adult stages, they almost always have four pairs of legs. A creature classified as an insect must have a body covered with a hard shell and divided into three sections, and three pairs of legs attached to its middle body section. However, the above characteristics serve to distinguish only *adult* insects. Thus, caterpillars, beetle grubs, fly larvae and other immature insects are more difficult to identify as insects.

During the long evolution of insects, nature was continually experimenting with new models. Some of these were improvements and survived, others were discarded along the way and are known to us only as fossils. At the present stage of world history there are about 25 orders or

HYMENOPTERA
ANTS
BEES
WASPS

DIPTERA
FLIES

COLEOPTERA
BEETLES

LEPIDOPTERA
MOTHS
BUTTERFLIES

ORTHOPTERA
GRASSHOPPERS
CRICKETS
COCKROACHES
ALLIES

HEMIPTERA
HOMOPTERA
THE BUGS

ISOPTERA
TERMITES

ODONATA
DRAGONFLIES

This is the family tree of the insects. It shows, in a general way, how the major orders or groups evolved from cockroachlike ancestors hundreds of millions of years ago. The insects at the bottom of the family tree are thus the most primitive, while those at the top are the most advanced.

major groups of insects, but many of these are of minor importance and seldom noticed by the average person. Ten of the insect orders may be considered of major importance and are listed below along with the approximate number of known species.

Odonata—dragonflies and damselflies; 4,870 species.
Orthoptera—grasshoppers, crickets, katydids, cockroaches, mantids and walkingsticks; 22,500 species.
Isoptera—termites; 1,717 species.
Hemiptera—"bugs" such as stinkbugs, water bugs, water striders, squash bugs and chinch bugs; 23,000 species.
Homoptera—cicadas, leafhoppers, aphids and scale insects; 32,000 species.
Coleoptera—beetles; 276,700 species.
Lepidoptera—butterflies and moths; 112,000 species.
Diptera—two-winged flies; 85,000 species.
Siphonaptera—fleas; 1,100 species.
Hymenoptera—ants, bees and wasps; 103,000 species.

There are ten other orders that, while deserving mention, are of minor importance. These are:

Thysanura—silverfish and firebrats; 700 species.
Collembola—springtails; 2,000 species.
Ephemeroptera—mayflies; 1,500 species.
Plecoptera—stoneflies; 1,490 species.
Dermaptera—earwigs; 1,100 species.
Mallophaga—bird lice; 2,675 species.
Anoplura—sucking lice; 250 species.
Thysanoptera—thrips; 3,170 species.
Neuroptera—antlions; dobsonflies and lacewings; 4,670 species.
Trichoptera—caddisflies; 4,450 species.

The insect orders are phylogenetic groups, that is, each one contains insects that followed the same line of evolution. Thus, the insects in each order are quite closely related to each other. In most cases these relationships are obvious; most all beetles are beetlelike, and the relationships between the butterflies and moths are easily seen. Less obvious are the connections between the grasshoppers, mantids and cockroaches. Over the years there has been some question among entomologists as to the division of the bug clan; usually these insects are separated into two orders, Homoptera and Hemiptera. All Hymenoptera look pretty much

The bull-dog ants (*Myrmecia*) are found in several tropical lands. They are vicious biters.

alike, except for ants which are wingless in the worker caste. The similarity of winged males and females to bees and wasps is obvious, however. On the other hand, there are wingless wasps (*mutillids*). Although most lice are wingless, a few possess wings. Based on general appearance, some insect relationships are a little difficult to understand; sheep ticks, which are completely wingless, are classified in the Diptera or two-winged fly tribe, and the beaver louse, believe it or not, is a parasitic beetle. The fleas, classified in a separate order, the Siphonaptera, are quite closely related to the Diptera from which they branched off many millions of years ago. The caddisflies, Trichoptera, that live on the bottoms of streams and construct pebble cases, are related to the butterflies and moths.

The insect legions, as we have seen, are very old, so they have had sufficient time to adapt themselves to almost every type of life. Probably no other animal group has so perfected and refined the living habits of its members. For example, the 17-year cicadas dwell underground for exactly 17 years and then, as if at a given signal, they all emerge within a few days. The honeybees have no audible language, yet they are able to communicate very precisely the location of choice nectar-bearing flowers to their sisters. The great *Thalessa* wasp alights on a dead tree and knows, by instinct, that her prey—an insect grub—is boring deep within the wood. The potter wasp fashions a graceful clay jug, lays an egg in it and then stocks it with caterpillars. She then seals the neck with clay. Her young will develop within the confines of the clay vessel, feeding on the supply of food. But the potter wasp that works so skillfully never saw a clay jug before she began constructing her small masterpiece. Instinct alone guided her actions as surely as if she had followed a blueprint. *Hydropsyche,* a caddis, weaves a silken seine at the bottom of a stream to trap food from the passing water. All these abilities were acquired as instincts over millions of years of trial and error. Time was the teacher in nature's school.

The body structure of insects differs considerably from that of higher animals. In our bodies the hard skeleton is on the inside, with the muscles on the outside. In some ways this makes for more flexibility of the limbs and other parts, yet the insects with their shell-like skeletons on the outside get along very well. This outer shell, or *exoskeleton,* has a number of advantages. It furnishes protection for the internal organs and, apparently, enables muscles to work more efficiently. Such a skeleton seems ideal for small creatures, but in larger animals its weight would be out of proportion to its other advantages. Insects are all of small size, and it is probable that this weight problem is one of the limiting factors. Long ago nature experimented with large animals covered with heavy outer armor. There were once, for example, enormous turtles, but these seem not to have been very successful in the struggle for survival and they soon passed out of the picture, victims of their own evolution.

Insects' exoskeletons are composed of several substances, the most important of which is *chitin.* This is hornlike material, ideally suited to its function. Chemically, it is a nitrogenous polysaccharide having the formula $(C_8H_{13}O_5N)_x$. It is resistant to concentrated acids and alkalies. Actually, the chitinous walls of insects' bodies may be hard or flexible depending on whether another substance, *sclerotin,* is present.

The relatively enormous loads which many insects are able to carry is partly the result of the efficiency of their enclosed muscles. Insects'

Some of the tree-hoppers are of unusual form. This one (*Thelia*) has its pronotum prolonged into a hornlike projection. It has piercing mouthparts and feeds on plant juices.

muscles do have great leverage, and almost unbelievable powers of endurance. These muscles look similar to our own, even under the microscope, but they are anchored to the insides of their skeletons and are usually straplike or ribbonlike in form. They are not spindle-shaped as are mammal muscles. Some of them are attached to chitinous tendons which, in turn, are anchored to the body wall. In other cases there are projections from the inner surface of the body wall for muscle attachment. Even though insects are of small size, they have an enormous number of muscles and their musculature is very complex. A caterpillar, for example, has about 2,000 separate muscles. In general, insect muscle is quite similar to our own, both in microscopic structure and in chemical composition.

The presence of a hard exoskeleton poses a number of problems, one of which is the matter of growth. As an insect grows, its exoskeleton gradually becomes "too tight." When this occurs, a *molting fluid* is secreted which dissolves the inner layer of the exoskeleton. The outer layer then splits down the back and the insect crawls out. At first the newly exposed skeleton is soft and flexible and expands to allow for the insect's increase in size. During the growth of a caterpillar, for example, there are about half a dozen of these molts. Thus, there is not a gradual increase in body dimensions as in our own case; rather, there is a step-by-step growth. This method of growth has been compared to that of a small boy whose clothes gradually become too small and must be periodically replaced by larger sizes.

Since insects' bodies are enclosed in exoskeletons, their limbs must be hinged or jointed to allow freedom of movement. Thus, the insects, along with their relatives the Crustacea, are in the class *Arthropoda,* meaning "joint-footed." But whereas the Crustacea (crabs, crayfish and lobsters) are aquatic and breathe by means of gills, the insects obtain air through a system of tracheal tubes. Along the sides of an insect's body there are breathing pores, or *spiracles,* one pair to each of the posterior body segments. Inside the body these air tubes, or *tracheae,* branch and rebranch into a complex system that conducts air directly to all organs and muscles of the body. Blood plays a secondary role in insect respiration. If you will observe a grasshopper at rest, you will notice that its abdomen pumps in and out like a bellows. In a number of insects there are saclike expansions of the tracheal system that help to increase the efficiency of air intake and exhaust. In flying insects these air-filled spaces increase the insects' buoyancy, as does the system of air sacs found in most birds.

The insect's respiratory system is more efficient than might be supposed. For example, it has been found that at each deep respiratory movement of a grasshopper, there is a 20 percent renewal of air in its hind leg. This is better efficiency than that achieved by our own respiratory system. In some insects it has been found that air is drawn into the tracheal system through some spiracles and exhausted through others; thus, there is a directed flow of air through the tracheal system. In the grasshoppers of the genus *Chortophaga,* air is drawn into the spiracles on the thorax and forced out of those on the abdomen. Strangely, however, the direction of air flow is reversed now and then. In tests it was found that this air was under considerable pressure, that there was sufficient pressure to support an 8-inch column of water.

So far we have talked only about the respiration of nonaquatic insects. The respiratory systems of aquatic insects have many adaptations to enable them to exist in their special habitat. These will be discussed in a later chapter.

In insects, the blood has little to do with carrying oxygen and carbon dioxide. In our bodies blood flows to the lungs where its carbon dioxide is exchanged for life-sustaining oxygen. Thus, our blood actually functions as a gas transportation system between the lungs and body organs. The insect's respiratory system is much more direct, and there is no "middleman." The air, as we have already seen, is carried directly to the tissues and organs. The exoskeleton has been discussed as a limiting factor in insect size, but it seems likely that the method of insect respiration is of even greater importance. It is a mathematical fact that as an animal's body increases in outside size its internal volume increases much faster. Thus, there is a delicate balance between body size and the insect's direct method of respiration. Seemingly, a large animal body cannot be efficiently aerated by a tracheal system.

If you examine a living caterpillar, one with a semitransparent outer covering, you can probably see its heart beating—or at least what passes for a heart. The heart of a typical insect is tubular and extends along the upper portion of its body just beneath the body wall. In a caterpillar, the beating of the heart can be seen as waves of contraction moving forward from the rear portion of the abdomen and into the thoracic region. This "heart" is actually a tube having a pair of *ostia* or slitlike openings in each body segment. These ostia have valves which allow blood to enter but prevent it from escaping as the waves of contraction move forward through the heart. Thus, blood is sucked into the ostia and forced forward through the thorax and on into the head through a small tube or *aorta*. Here the brain—what there is of it—is continually bathed in fresh blood. From the head the blood flows backward through the body cavity, bathing and nourishing the tissues and organs as it goes. It then reenters the various ostia along the sides of the heart. This, in brief, is the basic plan of insect blood circulation, but in its details, it is actually more complicated.

While it is true that insect blood flows backward through the body cavity among the organs, there are certain special structures that help to direct this flow so that it will reach all parts of the body and the appendages. In most insects there are two membranes, one above the digestive tube and one below it, which help to distribute the blood uniformly. These membranes are muscular and they undulate, forcing the blood backward. To make sure that the legs and wings are supplied with nourishing blood, most insects have pulsating organs which cause the blood to circulate through the appendages. The number of pulsating organs varies in different insects; in the housefly, for example, there are four to each wing. It is odd that the flow of blood often reverses itself, and instead of flowing forward toward the head, it may flow backward for a few seconds. A similar reversal of flow occurs in the wings of some insects, such as the American cockroach. No one knows why this takes place, but it has been suggested that the flow reverses itself when the ostia become blocked. Thus, it is possible that this is a safety mechanism, which enables the heart or pulsating organs to clear themselves of any obstructions.

The blood of insects differs considerably from our own. It rarely contains *hemoglobin,* the red pigment found in our red blood cells. This substance has the ability to absorb oxygen where it is abundant, as in the lungs, and to give it off where it is needed, as in the organs and muscles. Among insects, hemoglobin is found only in certain chironomid (midge) larvae that live in water, but in this case, it is dissolved in the blood plasma or fluid instead of in special cells. These midge larvae are known as "bloodworms." Insect blood, or *hemolymph,* is usually colorless or tinged with green or yellow. In it are a number of substances, including proteins, sugars, fats, salts and uric acid. Contained in the blood there are also a number of cells of various types. While some of these cells circulate freely in the blood, others normally rest on the surfaces of the internal organs. The work of these blood cells may be roughly compared to our own white blood cells; their function is phagocytic, that is, to remove foreign particles and organisms that enter the body. During molting these cells increase tremendously in number and are involved in the removal of solid particles that appear in the blood. They also increase in number at the time of pupation when the insect's larval tissues are being broken down and rebuilt into organs and structures more suited to adult, winged life.

The insect digestive system is, in a way, similar to that of higher animals. Basically, it is a hollow tube extending through the body from mouth to anus. Connected to the mouth are salivary glands which secrete enzymes and fluids which moisten and begin the digestion of foods. In some insects, such as caddisfly larvae, caterpillars, silkworms, cocoon-spinning wasps and leaf-rolling grasshoppers, the salivary glands are modified into silk-secreting organs.

Leading backward from the mouth is the esophagus, followed, in most insects, by the crop where food is stored. Behind the crop is the *proventriculus* which, in some insects, is modified into a thick-walled grinding organ or gizzard. Part of the digestion takes place here, and the food then passes on into the midgut where digestion continues and where nutrients are absorbed. The remaining waste material then passes on into the hindgut and out of the body.

The digestive enzymes of insects are similar to those of mammals, which is not surprising when one considers that they eat quite similar foods. Generally speaking, the enzymes present in the digestive systems of various insects are closely related to the type of food normally consumed. For example, the blow-fly, *Calliphora*, that feeds on sweet substances, secretes carbohydrate-dissolving enzymes, such as amylase, invertase and maltase; the African tse-tse fly, *Glossina*, which feeds upon blood, secretes protease, a protein-dissolving enzyme. On the other hand, omnivorous insects, such as cockroaches, secrete an assortment of enzymes to aid in the digestion of their varied foods.

Insects' alimentary canals are either straight, or coiled to permit increase in length. As a general rule, the length of an insect's digestive system is closely related to its food habit, and those feeding on diets rich in proteins have shorter digestive systems than those that feed on starchy materials.

There are many specializations and variations in insect digestive systems, brought about by special foods and feeding habits. In the case of the cockroach, there is a well-developed, muscular gizzard equipped with six powerful teeth. In the case of the flea, the proventriculus is armed with minute spines that pierce and break up ingested blood corpuscles so that they can be more easily digested. The larvae of mason wasps live and develop in sealed clay cells which were previously stocked with paralyzed spiders. In these larvae the alimentary canals are incomplete; there is no connection between the mid and hind intestine and, thus, no excrement is voided during larval development. This same adaptation is found in the honeybee. This is an obvious advantage when one considers the confined living quarters in which larval development takes place.

One of the most interesting of these special adaptations is found in the honeybee, whose crop is used as a storage tank. As the worker bees fly from flower to flower collecting nectar it is stored in the crop, but the nectar is prevented from passing through the digestive system by muscular valves which do permit the passage of pollen grains. When the workers return to the hive, the nectar in the crop or "honey stomach" is regurgitated into wax cells for storage.

As in the higher animals, most insects are faced with the serious problem of water conservation. As food passes through their digestive systems the contained fluids are gradually absorbed out through the intestinal walls so that by the time the waste is voided it is almost dry. In some insects, such as those that feed on dry, starchy foods and those that bore through dry wood, the waste emerges as a dry powder. Some insects obtain very little moisture from their foods in the form of free water. For example, the larvae of certain stored food pests, such as *Tribolium* and *Dermestes* beetles, obtain their water from the breaking down of carbohydrates during digestion. Thus, their water is obtained as a side product of metabolism and is called "metabolic water." Some seed-eating rodents that live in desert regions are also endowed with this ability. On the other hand, insects such as the Homoptera, or sucking bugs, that siphon large quantities of watery sap from living plants are faced with the problem of eliminating excess water. Many of these insects have complex filter systems that allow water to bypass the midportion of their alimentary canals where the main digestion and food absorption takes place. In this water filtration system, loops of the foregut are placed in close contact with the hindgut and water passes readily through the separating walls and on out of the body by way of the hindgut. In the meantime, digestible food passes into the midgut where it is digested and absorbed. Waste materials are then emptied into the hindgut where they join the water that was "short-circuited." The fluid material that is finally discharged from the alimentary canal varies in composition; in some cases it contains considerable sugar. This is the origin of the so-called honeydew produced by plant lice or aphids that is so eagerly sought by ants and, sometimes, by honeybees.

Insects do not have kidneys as such, but they do have organs that serve the same purpose. The most important of these are the *Malpighian* tubes which lie in the body cavity and usually open into the midgut. These excretory tubes vary greatly in number. There are two in the scale insects and more than 150 in grasshoppers and honeybees and they are always in pairs. As the blood flows among the body organs, it also bathes the Malpighian tubes, which absorb waste materials and carry them out of the body by way of the intestine. These tubes are in a more or less constant state of movement and show violent contracting and relaxing movements like coiled springs. This movement probably helps them to absorb waste materials from the blood and perhaps stimulates the flow of these materials through their hollow passages. We know that the salivary glands of insects are often modified into silk glands, so it is perhaps not surprising to find that the Malpighian tubes, too, often serve dual purposes. For example, in some leaf beetles (Chrysomelidae) these tubes secrete a glue which the female uses to cover her egg mass. Spittle insects dwell in foamy masses on plant stems and this foam is a product of both intestine and Malpighian tubes. In several insects, such as the lacewings (*Chrysopa*) and certain beetles, silk for spinning cocoons is also secreted by the Malpighian tubes.

As might be expected in a "mechanism" as complicated as an insect, there is a central control system. This is basically quite similar to our own nervous system, consisting of a small brain located in the head and of a pair of parallel nerve cords running lengthwise of the body just beneath the digestive canal. This is analogous to our spinal cord, but instead of being above the digestive system, it is beneath it. The relative location, however, is unimportant and is merely an anatomical detail. A telephone cable works just as well underground as it does when attached to poles overhead. Insects and all their relatives followed this line of evolution.

An insect's brain functions as a control center. It controls and coordinates the reflexes of the body with information received from the sensory organs, such as the antennae and eyes. It consists of two enlarged *ganglia* or nerve centers, one pair just above the esophagus and the other pair below it. The one above the esophagus—the larger—is connected with the eyes. This ganglion is joined to the one below the esophagus by two nerve cords that extend downward around the esophagus like a collar, one on either side. The lower ganglion is largely in control of the mouthparts. The paired ventral nerve cords previously mentioned are attached to the rear portion of this latter ganglion. These structures, brain ganglia and paired nerve cords, make up the central nervous system, which is connected to the various muscles and sensory organs by means of branching nerves as in our own bodies.

While the young of some of the more primitive wingless insects, such as silverfish and springtails, look very much like the adults, most young insects do not resemble the adults at all. The young are often so different that the uninformed might believe them to be entirely different kinds of insects. Would a visitor from Mars suspect that a creeping caterpillar had any relationship to a butterfly? In a way, the life histories of insects follows the sequence of changes that occurred during their evolutionary development. The first insects were creeping types like caterpillars; later, they acquired wings.

The life story of an individual insect is called its life history or *metamorphosis*. Characteristically, most insects do not become gradually

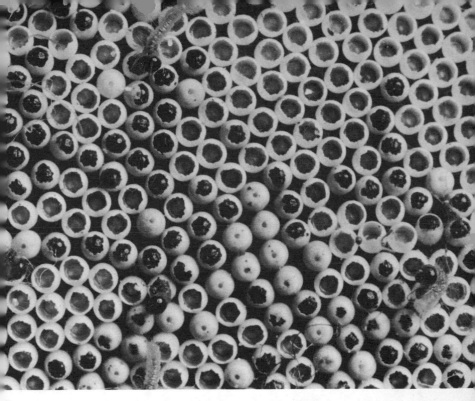

Moth eggs in the process of hatching.

larger as they grow; rather, there are major developmental stages through which they pass. For example, the butterfly lays eggs which hatch into creeping forms with chewing mouthparts. These are called caterpillars or larvae. Incidentally, the word caterpillar is derived from two Latin words, *catta pilosa,* meaning "hairy cat," which is quite descriptive of some kinds. During this stage the insect feeds and grows. As a matter of fact, it is only during this stage that actual growth occurs, and a caterpillar's only aim in life is to feed and store up food. As it increases in size, however, the number of cells in its body does not increase; they merely become larger. When full grown, the caterpillar sheds its skin and transforms into a *pupa.* This is called a *chrysalis* in the case of a butterfly. When this transformation occurs, the larval cells begin to die and clusters of adult cells, which have so far been quiescent, are stimulated into growth by hormones or chemical regulators secreted by glands in the head and thorax.

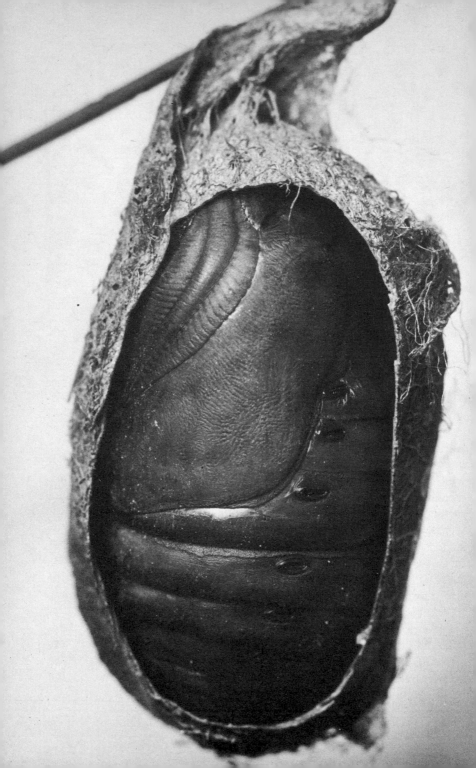

During the pupal stage the larval tissues are torn down and slowly rebuilt into organs more fitted for aerial life. These changes are roughly comparable to what might occur if an automobile were to be torn down and then rebuilt into an airplane.

When the chrysalis is mature, the wings and legs of the future butterfly can be seen through its transparent skin. It is usually in this stage that winter is passed, but with the coming of spring the back of the chrysalis splits open and the butterfly crawls out. At first its wings are mere fluid-filled sacs, but these rapidly expand and harden, and the adult winged butterfly is ready for flight. It no longer has mouthparts fitted for chewing leaves; they are now tubelike and are used only for siphoning nectar from flowers. There is no growth during the adult stage.

This life cycle is typical of many insects—moths, bees, wasps, ants, beetles and flies. All these insects have four stages as in the case of the butterfly and are thus said to have a *complete* life history or metamorphosis. In some insects, such as beetles, the larval stage is often called a "grub."

In many insect groups there are only three steps or stages in their life histories; the pupal or resting stage is absent and the larval stage is called a *nymph* instead of a caterpillar or grub. Insects having this type of life cycle include the dragonflies, bugs, mayflies, grasshoppers and cicadas. In some insects, such as the grasshopper tribe, the young or nymphs resemble the adults except for the absence of wings, but in others, like the dragonflies and cicadas, the young do not resemble the adults at all. Young dragonflies are wingless, crawling creatures that live in ponds and streams; sometimes they are called *naiads*. When these are fully developed, they crawl up above the surface of the water, attach themselves to plants and the winged adults emerge from them. This is called an *incomplete* life history or metamorphosis, since there is no inactive pupal stage.

This cutaway view of a Saturnid cocoon shows the pupa. From this cocoon will emerge the adult moth.

chapter two

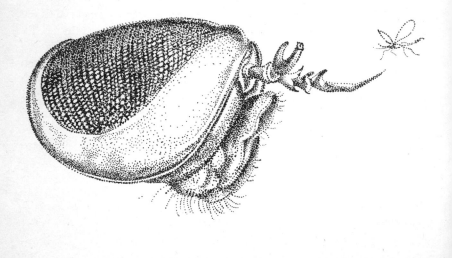

Instinct, Intelligence and Behavior

FOR hours on end I have watched mud-dauber wasps at their labors. The female carries out her work in a set pattern. First, she selects a suitable site for nest construction, then a source of clay. Perhaps it is the other way around, no one really knows for sure, but in any event, she begins carrying loads of clay and forming them into cells with amazing skill. Many trips are made and the work progresses as if with purposeful intent. If I get too close to her while watching her work, she looks at me with concern, then, apparently deciding that I constitute no hazard, she continues her work. After a cell is finished she goes spider hunting and fills it with paralyzed spiders. When the cell is stocked with spiders and an egg is laid, she flies again to the margin of the stream or pond and brings more clay to seal the cell. This is the final act. She then begins work on another cell.

In the process of watching these activities I gradually found myself thinking that the wasp was working with intelligence and skill, that she decided when she would gather clay and when she would hunt spiders. It is only natural, of course, to endow the creature with our own mental processes, to assume that her "mind" works the same as ours. There are good reasons for this anthropomorphism on the observer's part. The mud-dauber builds her cells with such consummate skill that it is difficult to believe that inherited instinct alone guides her actions. It is probable

The *Ammophila* wasp uses a pebble to tamp down the earth over her nest burrow. This is one of the few instances among animals in which a "tool" is used. Is this an "intelligent" act?

that she never saw a clay cell before she set out to build one. She will never see her offspring and, if she is building her cells in autumn, she will perish before her young emerge in the spring. She has never had an opportunity to learn her trade. These things we must continually tell ourselves if we are to understand the ways of wasps.

Actually, the minds of men and wasps function in entirely different ways. The mind of a man grows and develops, gradually learning new skills and capabilities that are almost without limitation. The wasp has but little ability to learn new tricks; all her skills were inherited from past wasp generations and she is a slave to her instincts. Her mind is like a tape recorder that, once started, must continue to the end. Only when the tape is finished can she go back and play it over again. Always she must build a cell, stock it with spiders and seal it in the proper sequence. She is an automaton, an unreasoning machine that, seemingly, knows no happiness, sorrow or anger. Although as she works she buzzes with apparent satisfaction and, at times, shows fear, we cannot assume that these reactions parallel our own. We do not know how the wasp feels about her surroundings, we can only watch her reactions to factors in her environment and try to interpret them as best we can. We often say that a bee buzzes in anger, but this is merely a convenient way of stating an observation, since the bee's reaction may or may not be the same as our own.

Insects, like other lower animals, react by instinct, inherited behavior carried out without conscious thought. Instinct is not unique, however, to the lower animals—fear, anger, mating and eating are examples of instinctive acts in human beings.

In their simplest forms, the reactions of insects to factors in their environment are called *tropisms*. These include responses to such things as light, temperature, chemicals, touch and wind, as well as to water and air currents. Depending on the instinctive reactions to these factors, an insect's responses may be either negative or positive. For example, a housefly is attracted to sugar, a response that is said to be a *positive chemotropism*. In this case the chemical is sugar. *Drosophila* flies are attracted to fermenting fruits as a result of this same tropism. Here the insect is attracted by the odor of alcohol. In the same way a butterfly lays its eggs only on certain plants because these have the proper odor and will serve as food for her young. I once watched a swallowtail butterfly laying eggs in a tropical forest. She flitted about among the dense vegetation pausing now and then to deposit eggs on wild lemon bushes. To my eyes the foliage all looked similar, but the chemical sense of the butterfly was never fooled. In each instance where she alighted and laid an egg, I found that it had been attached to a lemon bush leaf. On the other hand, many substances repel insects and their reactions are said to be negatively chemotropic. For instance, moth balls are used to protect woolens because clothes moths are repelled by naphthalene.

In insects there is apparently no sharp line between taste and smell and their sensory organs for perceiving chemical substances may be located almost anywhere on their bodies. They may be on the antennae, on the mouthparts, or on the feet. Many butterflies have olfactory organs on their feet, as do the blow-flies. It was found that the red admiral butterfly could distinguish sugar in solution at dilutions 200 times greater than could the human tongue. Similar results were obtained with honeybees, which have their chemoreceptors on their antennae. It has been found, however, that these bees cannot perceive the odors of some chemicals as well as we can.

Chemotropic responses enable insects to find mates as well as food. Moths are often attracted great distances by odors of prospective mates. For example, some research workers liberated marked male moths a mile away from females and found that they returned within 10 to 12 minutes. Odors also serve social insects, such as hornets, bees and ants, in identifying individuals of the same colony. Those that do not "smell right" are not usually admitted to the nest. Sensitivity to odors is thus of use to insects in locating the proper foods, finding mates and identifying each other. But there is still another, and very interesting, use for this odor sense. It is used by many ants in following trails. Many of us know there are ants that quickly locate sources of food, such as dead insects or animals, and that there is soon a string of ants hurrying out to dismember and carry in the booty. How is such information conveyed to the ants back in the nest? When the scouting ants locate food supplies they hurry home, and as they walk along they lay scent trails by periodically touching their abdomens to the ground and releasing a chemical substance called a *pheromone*. This substance is secreted in minute amounts by Dufour's gland, located near the tip of the abdomen at the base of the sting, and it is through the sting that the substance is ejected. It is quite volatile and its chemical nature is as yet unknown. The pheromone thus blazes the trail, making it easy for others to follow. It is interesting, too, that these chemical trails are often directional—the ants can tell in which direction they point. Apparently, this is determined either by the shape of the scent spots or by their gradient since the scent trails slowly fade away. The truth of the directional nature of these trails can be demonstrated by allowing a column of ants to cross a chip or a sheet of paper and then rotating it 180°. The ants will be confused since the trail is going in the wrong direction. Soon, however, they reestablish the trail and the column moves on as before.

There is apparently a difference in the intensity of the scent trails. If the source of food is large, the trail laid by the finders attracts many ants. On the other hand, the column of ants rushing out to carry in the spoils tends to dwindle as the food source is depleted. The scent trails actually convey a variety of information.

The trails laid by various kinds of ants do not all last the same length of time. Sometimes—perhaps in most instances—they are short-lived. Those laid by *Pheidole* ants, for example, last only about six minutes.

Trails that are much used tend to become more or less permanently marked. There is an advantage to the fading away of trails to temporary food sources. If the trails were more permanent, there would soon be confusing networks of blazed paths leading nowhere.

Not all ants use scent trails. Like wasps and bees, some ants orient themselves by visual observation of conspicuous landmarks. The harvester ants (*Pogonomyrmex*), for example, do not depend on scent trails at all. This is probably because of their food habits and their habitat. The seeds upon which they feed are scattered about on the ground among the vegetation and there would usually be little use in trails being laid. Too, harvester ants, in most cases, live in dry areas of shifting sand where scent trails would soon be obliterated. When an ant finds a seed, she carries it back to the underground grain bin and then sets out to hunt seeds again, perhaps in a different direction. Ant trails are also specific as to the kind of ant laying them, and different kinds of ants do not follow each other's trails. Each species of ant has its own special pheromone or chemical language. When the trails of two kinds of ants cross each other there is no confusion; each species goes its own way. Perhaps we might compare these specific ant trails to those made by American Indians who could identify the tribe of an Indian by his moccasin tracks.

Phototropism is the reaction of an animal to light, which may be either negative or positive. In its simplest form an insect is either attracted to light or repelled by it. Fly maggots (*Lucilia*) crawl away from a source of light and are thus negatively phototropic, while other insects are attracted toward light sources. There has been a great deal of research on insects' reactions to light rays. It has been found that there is considerable difference in their attraction to rays of different wavelength or color. As a general rule, insects are attracted more to light rays of short wavelengths, that is, to colors at the blue end of the spectrum. Most insects are colorblind to yellow or red. On the other hand, butterflies are strongly attracted by some red flowers. Ants, being blind to red, can be observed by red light and their reactions are the same as if they were in total darkness. We humans are blind to infrared rays, a fact that was taken advantage of in World War II in the use of the Sniper-scope. This piece of equipment was attached to a rifle and emitted an infrared beam of light which was reflected back to a sensitive screen, making human targets visible in the darkness without them knowing that they had been seen.

Although bees are red-blind, they can often distinguish between two red flowers if one of them reflects ultraviolet rays. It is of interest in this connection to consider the case of the flowers that depend on humming-birds for pollination. There are no hummingbirds in Europe and there were originally few red flowers. Hummingbirds are very sensitive to red and most of the flowers they pollinate, especially in tropical America, are red. European flowers did not develop red colors because the bees, upon which they depended for pollination, were red-blind. As most flying insects are not strongly attracted to yellow lights, yellow light bulbs are often used in outdoor lights since they attract few moths and gnats.

Insects' reactions to light are quite complex. We say that a moth is attracted to a light, but this statement does not explain why or how. The moth is not consciously attracted, it simply flies toward the light because it must. When a light appears in its vicinity the nervous controls of the moth automatically orient its body in flight so that the illumination of both its eyes is equal. This, of course, causes it to fly toward the light, often with fatal results. This can be easily proven by blinding one eye of the moth with an opaque coating of paint. When this is done the moth no longer orients itself toward the light. Thus we see that a moth does not fly toward a source of light out of curiosity but "automatically," help-lessly under the control of its own reflexes. Insects are also sensitive to light intensity. Moths are repelled and butterflies are attracted by brilliant sunlight. So we see that moths are attracted to lights up to a certain in-tensity, then repelled. This explains why a moth does not "attempt" to fly toward the sun during the day or toward the full moon at night. The light of the moon is of too low intensity to arouse any reaction at all. It is an interesting fact, too, that some insects' reactions to light change as the need arises during their life histories. Maggots of the black blow-fly (*Phormia regina*) are negatively phototropic while they are feeding in decaying matter, but, when mature, suddenly become positively photo-tropic. It is then that they crawl out to the light looking for places in which to pupate.

Insects' eyes differ considerably from our own. We have two image-forming eyes with optic nerves running to the brain. It is in the brain that the images are "put together" so that we perceive depth. In the case of insects there are many eyes, each with its own separate lens and sensi-tive visual unit, all connected with the brain by nerves. This is called a *compound* eye and, due to its curvature, each individual eye points in a slightly different direction. This results in *mosaic vision*. In other words, each individual eye sees a slightly different portion of the visual field. The separate images are all put together into a composite "picture" in the brain somewhat as the two images from our two eyes are combined. Just how distinct is the vision of insects is not as yet known, but it does seem to be admirably suited to perceiving rapid movement. Slowly moving objects apparently do not disturb insects. I once proved this to my own satisfaction. I saw a robber-fly alight on a stump. These hunting insects are extremely alert to movement, yet I was able to pick this specimen up between my fingers by approaching very slowly, only moving my fingers when they were almost touching the insect. This technique can be used on other insects if one has the patience. If you have ever watched a lizard in the act of stalking an insect, you have observed this slow approach being put to practical use. The praying mantis is also very skilled at stalking its insect prey. It moves toward its intended victim with slow, machinelike precision, lashing out with its raptorial front legs only after it is very close.

Most insects have an enormous number of facets or units in their compound eyes. The housefly has about 4,000, the water-beetle (*Dytiscus*) 9,000; the worker honeybee has 6,300; the queen, 3,900; and the drone, 13,000. Seemingly, the drone needs a large number of facets to find the queen during the mating flight. Nor are the eye facets of all insects' eyes always all the same size. Examining the eyes of a horsefly under a lens reveals that the facets on the upper portions of the eyes are much larger than those on the lower portions. We might say that they wear bifocals. In the whirligig beetles (*Gyrinus*) the upper and lower portions of the compound eyes are entirely separated. The upper portion of the eye rests above the surface film of the water while the lower portion is adapted to seeing beneath the surface. This beetle is thus enabled to perceive food or enemies both above and below the water's surface.

The eyes of insects are remarkable structures and in addition to their use as instruments of vision are used in navigation. This is a subject that has mystified scientists for hundreds of years, but it is only in the last few years that some of the mystery has been dispelled. This has sometimes revealed other, and even more interesting, puzzles. It has been known for a long while that insects such as ants use the sun as a coordination point just as we do in marine and aerial navigation. Crawling ants can maintain a straight path by moving at a fixed angle to the sun, and this angle remains fixed in the insect's eyes or brain. The compound eyes of insects with their individual "eyes" or *ommatidia* radiating through almost 180° are especially well fitted to sun navigation, since each lens is focused on a small portion of the sky.

In 1923 a zoologist named F. Santschi noted that ants (*Cataglyphis albicans* and *Monomorium salomonis*) living on the barren desert areas of North Africa could maintain straight courses even though there were no guiding landmarks. He discovered that if he placed a dark box over the ants and then removed it a couple of hours later the ants started off on their safari again but in a slightly different direction. This new direction, it was discovered, was at an angle to the old trail equal to the distance the sun had moved while the ants were imprisoned under the darkened box. The angle of the sun had remained fixed in the ants' brains. Santschi also found that by using a mirror to reflect the sun's image, he could make the ants crawl in any direction, even away from the nests to which they were attempting to return. He also made another test, the results of which he was unable to explain. He placed a deep box, open at the top, around the column of ants and found that they continued in the proper direction even though they could not see the sun. Santschi believed that the ants oriented themselves by the stars even though the tests were made during the day when stars are not visible, at least not to human eyes. It was only after Dr. Karl von Frisch, many years later, discovered that honeybees could distinguish polarized light that the phenomenon was explained. The ants were apparently orienting themselves by polarized light from the sky.

The insect that has been studied more than any other in respect to navigational ability is the honeybee. In the process of gathering nectar and pollen these bees fly almost continuously, except at night or during unfavorable weather; thus, they have need for a means of rather precise navigation. Honeybees orient themselves in two ways: if there are conspicuous landmarks they use these, but if no such navigational guides are present they use the sun. Bees' memory of places is really quite remarkable. If a hive is moved some distance during the winter and nothing is placed in front of the hive to call attention to the fact that a change has occurred, most of the bees will return to the old site in the spring. It is standard practice among beekeepers to place a tree branch in front of a moved hive to make the inhabitants aware of their new surroundings.

The human eye cannot distinguish polarized light, but the honeybee, like Santschi's ants, can do so and takes advantage of this ability in navigation. If you will obtain a piece of polaroid film or a photographic polarizing filter and, while looking at the horizon through it, rotate your body around, you will find that the sky darkens at right angles to the sun. It was found that bees could properly orient themselves if they could see only a small portion of the sky. The exact mechanism by which this is done is as yet not fully understood.

For many years it has been known that scout honeybees leave their hives and go out seeking good nectar sources. When they return they engage in so-called honey dances. In these dances the scout bees execute tail-wagging promenades on the combs. Until recently it was thought that this dance—called in Germany a *Schwänzeltänze*—meant, "I have found nectar-bearing flowers, go out and find them."

The first mention of these "honey dances" in the literature dealing with bees was probably that of M. J. E. Spitzner in Germany, who wrote in 1788, "When a bee finds a good source of honey somewhere, after her return home she makes this known to the others in a remarkable way. Full of joy, she waltzes around among them in circles, without doubt in order that they shall notice the smell of honey which has attached itself to her; then when she goes out again they soon follow her in crowds."

It remained for a dedicated observer of honeybee behavior in Austria, Dr. Karl von Frisch, to discover that these dances are actually much more complicated than had been believed. After more than 40 years of careful research, von Frisch proved that these so-called dances are a type of charade in which the scout bees give their hive mates very precise information, not only as to the direction and distance of the flowers but the kind as well. Information as to *kind* of flower is simple; the scout bees give away free samples of collected nectar. Their mode of conveying the other information is much more complicated, as Dr. von Frisch demonstrated.

Karl von Frisch's research has become a classic of the twentieth century and is probably the most important and remarkable work ever done on animal behavior. His results were so astonishing that he couldn't believe them himself. However, other scientists have now corroborated his work in every detail.

Dr. von Frisch used glass-sided hives which allowed him to watch the bees going about their normal routine. Next, he baited the bees with a saucer of honey placed some distance away. Dr. von Frisch then remained by the source of food and waited until scout bees located it and filled their honey stomachs. He marked the bees by daubing them with colored paint. Returning, then, to the hive he watched the scouts' actions through the glass wall. Upon their return they began their waggle dances with a few of the other bees following them. Gradually, the "word" seemed to spread among the bees that there was a source of food available. There was great

It has been found that scout honeybees convey information regarding the location of nectar-bearing flowers to their sisters by means of charadelike dances performed on the combs within the hive. The workers then go out and gather the nectar.

DANCE ANGLE

When a scout honeybee locates nectar-bearing flowers at distances of farther than 100 yards it returns to the hive and does a figure-eight dance on the comb. The angle of the promenade or waggle run across the waist of the figure eight indicates the direction. Within the dark hive the angle is indicated with respect to gravity, and this is the angle the bees must follow with respect to the sun when they leave the hive.

excitement and shortly there began a flow of bees out of the hive to the new food source. In time the saucer of honey was emptied and the bees settled down again. This was a simple experiment which had been done many times before. But von Frisch believed that there was more to the dances than met the eye, so he began placing his little saucers of honey at different distances and in different directions from his observation hive. Thousands of tests were made and the results checked and rechecked. Gradually, a pattern appeared and von Frisch realized that he had at least had a glimpse of an amazing discovery. He found that when a scout bee finds a nectar source, whether it be a saucer of honey or a field of flowers, she returns to her hive and goes into a "dance." However, this performance follows a definite pattern, it indicates both direction and distance. He found that if the food was more than 100 yards away the scout bees indicated this fact by figure-eight dances on the comb. The waggle run forming the "waist" of the figure eight indicated the direction with respect to the sun. Within the hive it was dark of course, so gravity was used here in place of the sun. The angle of the central promenade with respect to the vertical indicated the angle from the sun. Nectar sources less than 100 yards from the hive, he found, are indicated by another type of dance. When the nectar source is closer than about 10 yards the scout bees dance in circles, but as the distance increases these circular or "round" dances assume a sickle-shaped form which is gradually transformed into the typical figure eight. A glance at the accompanying diagrams will help in understanding the forms of these charade-like dances.

Since honeybees may range as far as 3 miles in harvesting nectar, they must have an additional means of communicating distances beyond 100 yards. This is done by varying the speed of the waggle runs across the waist of the figure eight. For example, 20 runs a minute means that nectar is to be found a half mile away; 12 runs across means that it is two miles away. Beyond two miles there is but little decrease in the speed of the waggle dances.

The direction, as we have already seen, is indicated by the promenade across the waist of the figure eight. An upward wagging run indicates that food is in the direction of the sun; a downward run indicates the opposite direction. Angles between are indicated by runs to either right or left. The bees evidently have a delicate sense of feeling for gravity and can transform this into a bearing on the sun when they emerge from the hive. They thus have all the information they need in locating the source

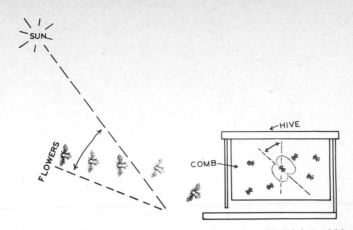

This diagram illustrates how the bee substitutes gravity (right) within the dark hive for the sun's angle (left) outside the hive.

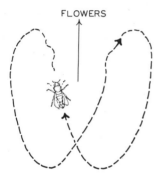

When flowers are located at distances of from 55 yards to 100 yards from the hive the scout bees indicate the fact by a dance of this form. Beyond 100 yards the dance takes on the typical figure-eight form.

When scout honeybees locate flowers very close (about six feet) to the hive they indicate the fact by a dance of this type.

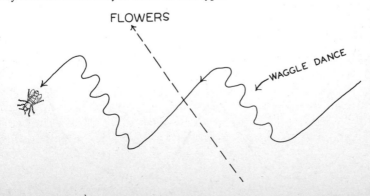

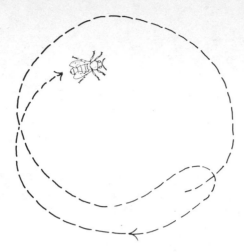

A round dance by the scout bees indicates that flowers are about 10 yards away. As the distance becomes greater the dance assumes the so-called sickle shape (see next picture).

This so-called sickle-shaped dance indicates that nectar-bearing flowers are to be found within a distance of from 15 yards to 55 yards.

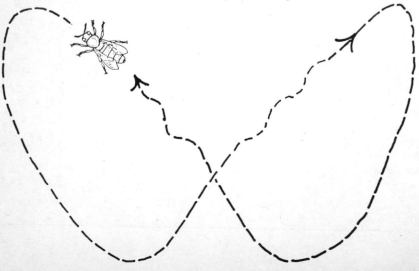

of food. They know the distance and direction and have been given samples for identification.

To properly tie up the research, von Frisch placed the combs in his observation hives in horizontal positions, which is, of course, abnormal. The bees, by the way, were observed by red light, to which they are blind. With the combs in this position the bees were confused and could no longer communicate information since they could not indicate, by their dances, nectar sources in relation to gravity. This, then, is the remarkable story of Karl von Frisch and his dancing bees.

Like most scientists, Dr. von Frisch continued his studies and discovered other remarkable facts about the language of bees. His original research was conducted on the black Austrian variety of the honeybee, *Apis mellifera carnica*. When the Italian variety was studied it soon became evident that these bees (*Apis mellifera ligustica*) exhibited somewhat different dance patterns in relation to the distances they indicated. For example, the Austrian variety uses the round dance to indicate distance up to 275 feet, and beyond that distance the tail-wagging dance is used. The Italian variety, however, switches to the tail-wagging dance at about 120 feet. One of Dr. von Frisch's associates, Dr. Martin Lindauer, traveled to India to study the dance behavior of other species of the genus *Apis,* including *A. florea, A. dorsata* and *A. indica*. Here also it was found that there were differences in the dialects of the bees' "languages." From these studies it is evident that, like humans, bees develop different languages and dialects in different localities.

The swarming of honeybees is the natural process by which new colonies are established. When conditions within the hive become crowded, new queens are produced and at the time of swarming the old queen leaves, taking with her a sizable cluster of workers. This swarm flies out and settles, usually on a tree limb. Scouts are then sent out in search of new quarters. Upon their return these scouts engage in dances very similar to the honey dances. By their enthusiasm the scouts indicate the relative desirability of sites they have located. The dances continue for some time, with the scouts that have located questionable sites gradually giving way to those that have found better sites as indicated by the liveliness and length of their dances. Some of the scouts that have previously found poor locations go out and check the supposedly better places found by other scouts. Eventually, all the scouts appear to agree and the swarm flies off to the chosen site. It may occasionally happen that the scouts cannot agree, in which case the cluster simply remains on the limb and is killed by frost when winter weather comes. It is fortunate that such instances are rare.

While the communication of information to each other by honeybees has been known for some years and has been quite thoroughly studied, recent research by Dr. Adrian M. Wenner and his associates has shown that these bees also communicate extensively by means of sounds. These sounds consist of buzzes and pipings having modulations and variations that seem to mean different things. For example, when a hive is shaken the bees emit a certain buzzing sound, followed by faint beeping sounds. Apparently this latter sound has a soothing effect on the inmates of the hive. Dr. Wenner recorded this beeping sound and then played it back to a hive of disturbed bees with the result that they were quieted. How these sounds are produced is still being investigated, but they appear to originate in the wings and not, as was once thought, from air expelled through the spiracles. Here again is evidence that we have much to learn about these remarkable insects.

As noted previously, honeybees perceive colors much the same as we do. This is natural when one considers that they are continually harvesting nectar from colored flowers. This has led some beekeepers to paint their hives in contrasting colors so the bees could find their way home to the proper hive. While this makes for a very pretty apiary, research indicates that little good is derived from the practice.

In addition to the abilities recounted above, bees also have a well-developed time sense. If a dish of honey is placed where they can find it at a certain time each day, the bees quickly learn to visit the spot at that time. They can also be trained to visit a specified place several times a day, provided that these visits are at least two hours apart. This time perception seems to be tied to a 24-hour cycle and the bees cannot be trained to respond to a longer or shorter "day." Whether this rhythm is brought about by external influences or by some internal physiology is unknown, though there are strong indications that it is related to their internal metabolism. When bees are fed certain substances their sense of time is changed. This is also true of ants. For example, when salicylic acid was fed to ants their metabolism was speeded up and they visited feeding places sooner than usual. Perhaps this is a clue to the time sense of both honeybees and ants. It has been proved that honeybees are not governed entirely by external influences. Experiments were conducted in Paris in which bees were kept in a room continuously illuminated by artificial lights. Even under such conditions the bees could still be trained to come to food at certain hours. Under Dr. von Frisch's direction these bees were later flown to New York where, still in a continuously lighted room, they came to food at the regular time. This, however, was Paris time, not New York time. Moving them to a new time zone had not changed their internal clocks.

So far in this chapter we have considered, briefly, several of the factors in insects' environments and the ways in which they react to them. There are many other stimuli to which insects react and to which they must respond properly if they are to survive. These include such things as reaction to touch, *thigmotropism;* the reaction to water, *hydrotropism;* and the reaction to temperature, *thermotropism*. There are many others.

Do insects have the ability to learn? We tend to regard them as being mere slaves of their inherited instincts, but let us see if this is always true. In the competitive world, insects, like most other creatures, must be adaptable if they are to survive. A creature that learns nothing by repeated errors does not live long, for the laws of survival of the fittest soon eliminate it from the struggle. Instincts, then, must be flexible to a certain degree. When young ants and honeybees first emerge from their pupal cases, they serve an apprenticeship within the nest or hive. Having learned this "trade" they then begin making short exploratory trips in the vicinity, learning the topography of the territory in which they will forage for food. The prominent landmarks are soon fixed in their brains. This is information that could not be inherited. We cannot peer into an insect's brain and tell what goes on there any more than we can tell what goes on in the brains of our human friends; we can only submit them to tests of various kinds and try to interpret the results. One technique that has been used in studying the learning abilities of insects and other animals is that of placing them in complicated mazes and determining how quickly they solved the problem of finding their way out. Many such experiments have been carried out with *Formica* ants since these ants do not lay scent trails, depending on visual stimuli in finding their way. These mazes are designed in such a way that there are a number of "choice points" at any one of which the wrong choice leads the test animal into a blind alley.

Dr. T. C. Schneirla of the Department of Animal Behavior at The American Museum of Natural History has contributed much to our understanding of insect behavior. Among the noteworthy tests he has carried out was that of placing eight *Formica* ants and eight rats in mazes of the same design. That is, both mazes had six blind alleys and the same number of "choice points." They differed from each other only in size.

All the rats mastered the maze within twelve runs; in other words, they learned to pass through the maze without error in twelve attempts. The ants, by contrast, required thirty runs to master it. Now you may say that the ants were pretty stupid in needing so many trials in learning the maze. It must be admitted that the ants did not show as much ability as the rats, but considering the relative sizes of their brains, the ants did exceedingly well. It was of interest, too, that when their paths through the mazes were reversed the rats showed a saving in learning time while to the ants it was an entirely new problem and had to be learned over again.

It was found also that the ants relied somewhat on light direction in finding the correct path through the maze, since they became confused if the position of "sun" was changed while they were passing through it. This would seem to indicate that the ants were navigating by sun compass. However, when the "sun" was moved the ants then relied on their antennae and were successful in finding their way without help of the sun. This shows that they are adaptable and can substitute one sense for another if one fails. It is of interest, too, that there are "smart" ants and "stupid" ants, since some individuals scored much better in the maze trials than others.

Some nest-building insects, such as mud-dauber wasps, also show more skill than others. Some of the clay cells built by these wasps are well constructed and beautifully finished, while others are sloppy. As might be expected, insects low in the evolutionary scale score poorly in maze tests as compared to ants, which are highly advanced. The lowly cockroach, for example, won the booby prize when pitted against an ant. It has also been found that there are differences in insects' memories. In spite of their apparent stupidity, cockroaches seem to have good memories and can remember a simple maze for about a month. On the other hand, *Formica* ants can remember a rather complicated maze for only three weeks. There is still another facet to insects' memory responses. When they are confronted with the same problem in different situations they react as if it were an entirely new one. For example, if a maze that has previously been mastered by an ant is placed in its path as it returns to its nest, it does not recognize it at all and blunders through it as if it had never been in it before. Truly intelligent actions are rare among insects—if, indeed, they ever occur—and we must always be suspicious of statements made in this regard. Perhaps the closest to an intelligent act of any insect is that of the *Ammophila* wasp that uses a small stone to tamp down the earth over its nest tunnel. This is probably the only case in which an insect uses a "tool."

While few insects perform intelligent acts, there are many cases in which insects exhibit certain "human" characteristics. For instance, *Bembex* wasps excavate holes in the earth and then stock them with captured and paralyzed horseflies. It was noticed that in a sandy area of Florida where large numbers of *Bembex* wasps were nesting, they were not above stealing horseflies from each other to save the labor of hunting them. Here, certainly, is a characteristic, however reprehensible, shared by some other animals higher in the evolutionary scale, including humans.

chapter three

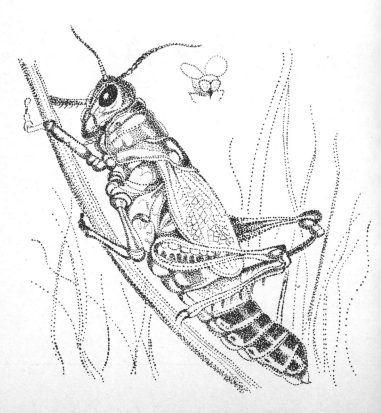

The Songs They Sing

THE ability to make sounds is one of the attributes of many insects. We are all familiar with the angry buzz of bees and wasps or the happy songs of katydids and crickets on summer evenings. While it is true that the songs of male katydids and crickets are mating calls and, as such, help in bringing the sexes together, some of these calls or songs seem to go beyond such mundane, instinctive objectives and to be sung for the sheer joy of being alive.

The first animal sounds were probably made by insects. This is not mere conjecture; the fossil of a large, primitive orthopteran having sound-making organs on its wings was found in Australia. This grasshopper ancestor lived about 200 million years ago, many million of years before the first birds arrived on the world scene.

There seems no doubt that the sounds made by insects are a form of communication, just as are our own voices. Insects make sounds by rubbing parts of their armorlike bodies together; only rarely are sounds produced by air or by drums. Human voice, of course, produces sound when air is forced between the vocal cords and the resulting sound is then modified by the mouth and lips. The howler monkey has resonance chambers on the sides of the neck which increase the volume of sound and give the voice great carrying capacity. Birds produce sounds or songs in still another manner. At the point where the trachea divides in the breast cavity there is an enlarged structure called the *syrinx*. This is actually the "voice box," and within it is a bar of cartilage called the *pessulus*. Air passing through the syrinx, from the lungs, causes the pessulus to vibrate. This is the origin of birds' voices. In some birds—swans, for example—the trachea is very long and coiled within the breast bone. This has the same function as the coiled tube of a trumpet. Thus, the voices of birds and mammals differ considerably from those of insects, which consist of squeaks, buzzes, hums, clicks and drumming sounds.

Most insects make sound by rubbing parts of their hard bodies or appendages against each other. This is called *stridulation*. Thus, insects should really be called "instrumentalists" rather than "singers." It is an interesting fact that we humans sometimes communicate with each other by similar means. We clap our hands to indicate approval, snap our fingers or whistle to gain attention, or stamp our feet in anger. On the other hand, there are a few rare cases where insects make sounds by forcing air from body openings. For several centuries it has been known that the deaths-head moth (*Acherontia atropos*) of Europe makes a sound by sucking or blowing air through its proboscis. The pharynx or "throat cavity" acts as a pump and the stream of air is rapidly interrupted in the epipharynx or "roof of the mouth" in such a way as to produce loud squeaks. Some insects also produce audible sounds by forcing air from the spiracles or breathing pores along the sides of their bodies. For example, lubber grasshoppers (*Brachystola*) force air out through the thoracic spiracles, making hissing sounds. Inside the thorax there are large, lunglike sacs filled with air. By contracting the body muscles, air is forced out of these sacs much as air from our own lungs is forced out through our throats. Under certain conditions queen honeybees make piping sounds, but whether these are made by air passing through spiracular valves or by a vibration of the wings is still uncertain. Most authorities seem to believe the sounds are produced by the wings.

Sound making is more widespread in the insect tribe than was once supposed, and it often occurs where least expected. For example, a number of aquatic insects have well-developed sound-making equipment. The water scorpion (*Ranatra*) has a scraping apparatus located at the base of the coxa of each foreleg. This makes a squeaking sound that can be heard either in the air or in the water; it is louder when made under water. Just what the purpose of this sound is has not been determined since it is made by both adults and nymphs or immature forms. If it were purely a mating call, it would be expected to be found only in the adults.

The backswimmers and water boatmen are also "wired for sound" and the sounds they make are of very high intensity considering the sizes of the insects. It is probable that these sounds are used to attract the opposite sex.

Recently, observations were made by Dr. Richard D. Alexander of an unusual sound-producing technique of a grasshopper named *Paratylotropidia brunneri*. This is a large grasshopper, and Dr. Alexander heard it making soft clicks on a prairie along the Mississippi River near Valmeyer, Illinois. After close observation, it was discovered that the sounds were made by the mandibles of the insect clicking together at the rate of six to seven times per second. The sound can be heard for some distance and is, apparently, a means of communication. Dr. Alexander was able to imitate the sound, and obtain a response from a nearby male, by striking two metal objects together. It seems probable that this method of communication was evolved from feeding sounds.

Some of those ancient insects, the dragonflies, have sound-making equipment in their larval stages. These consist of toothed areas on the sides of the abdomen against which the hind legs are rubbed, resulting in shrill tones. The sound is produced when the larvae are disturbed and may thus serve a defensive function.

Sound making is quite common among members of the beetle tribe. As a matter of fact, one authority has stated that sound equipment is apt to be found in any insect where one part normally rubs against another. The beetles all have hard, ridged bodies, so it is not too surprising to find that many of them have roughened areas that are capable of producing sounds when scraped by legs or other movable body parts. A number of long-horned beetles squeak loudly when held in the hand. Probably these may be interpreted as sounds of distress or alarm. Some beetle larvae, too, make sounds. For instance in the case of *Passalus* grubs, which are the larvae of betsy-beetles, the hind legs are greatly reduced in size and they function only as scrapers which rasp upon roughened areas near the bases of the middle legs. These large insects are semisocial, that is, they live in rotten wood in small colonies consisting of both adults and larvae or grubs. Their sounds are probably a form of communication or identification.

Of even more interest are the sounds produced by death-watch beetles that tunnel through wood. The adults make tapping sounds that can often be heard in old log cabins. In early days when most of our ancestors lived in such structures, the tapping or ticking of these insects was sometimes heard late at night when all was quiet. The superstitious believed that the sound was associated with impending death. In her delightful book, *Insect Fact and Folklore,* Miss Lucy Clausen quotes a piece of medieval poetry as follows:

> Then woe be to those in the house that are sick!
> For, sure as a gun, they will give up the ghost,
> If the maggot cries click when it scratches the post.

Actually, the clicking sound is made by the adult beetles and is believed to be a mating call.

To insects such as the death-watch beetles that dwell in dark burrows some means of communication is apparently desirable, so it is not too surprising to find that termites, too, use taps to telegraph information or to sound alarms. If a piece of wood containing a termite colony is broken open so that the inmates are exposed, the large-headed soldiers can often be seen in the act of tapping their heads against the floors of the galleries. The sound can be heard a foot or so away and resembles the ticking of a watch. These soldiers are probably sounding a rallying call to the others. In the case of some kinds of termites, *Leucotermes* and others, the insects hammer in unison, producing a faint drumming sound.

A number of species of ants, too, make sounds. Good examples are the leaf-cutters or *Atta* ants. Authorities are not in agreement as to the purpose of these ant calls, but it seems likely that they are alarm sounds. If an *Atta* ant is held between the fingers, its squeak can be heard several feet away. A number of other ants also make squeaking sounds. It has been found that these are produced by a stridulating organ consisting of a series of striations on the base of the gaster (abdomen) and a scraper on the petiole (waist). It is believed that some ants make tapping sounds like termites. One ant, *Camponotus mus,* a native of Brazil, nests in bamboo and when disturbed makes a metallic, whirring sound like a rattlesnake.

There are a number of insects that make humming sounds with their wings—for example, flies, mosquitoes and bees. In some cases these sounds are merely incidental to flight, but in other cases they are actually a means of communication. The male mosquito is attracted to the female by her high-pitched wing sounds. The wing rates of the *Aedes* mosquitoes range from 300 to 500 vibrations per second. There is some variation among different species and, in some cases, beat effects occur. Thus these female wing sounds probably are selective in attracting males of the same species. Male mosquitoes are attracted to tuning forks vibrating at the same pitch as the females' wings. The wings of the housefly vibrate 335 times per second or at the scale of F. A bee's wings match the sound of A while vibrating at the rate of 440 times per second. The vibration rates of insects' wings can be precisely measured by anchoring them with cement and placing them so that the tips of their vibrating wings just brush against the surface of a smoked kymograph cylinder revolving at a known rate.

From this brief discussion it is apparent that many insects use sound as a means of communication. Many insects have well-developed organs for the perception of sound waves. Insects' "ears" are located on various parts of their bodies. The sound receptors of the katydid are on the front legs and those of the grasshopper are on the sides of the thorax.

So far we have said little about those insects that are the real choristers of the insect world, the crickets, katydids, grasshoppers and cicadas. We have saved the best until last. Second only to the birds, these insects are the world's foremost singers. Their songs may not be as pleasing to most peoples' ears as those of birds, but they serve more or less the same purpose.

The katydids belong to the order Orthoptera, a large and important insect group which also includes the grasshoppers, cockroaches, crickets, mantids and walking-sticks. All the katydids and their close relatives belong to the long-horned grasshopper family Tettigoniidae, whose members have very long antennae and long, green wings. The group includes

In many places in eastern United States, summer evenings are enlivened by the song of the true katydid. The male produces the sound by rubbing a scraper on one wing over a file on the other.

the bush katydids, which are normally green but are occasionally pinkish; the cone-headed katydids, which have cone-shaped heads and powerful jaws; and the meadow katydids, which are of small or medium size and dwell in grassy meadows. The champion songster is the so-called true katydid (*Pterophylla camellifolia*) of the eastern United States, which usually inhabits trees. The green coloration of these insects makes them difficult to see when they are resting among leaves. They are also accomplished ventriloquists and are usually quite difficult to locate by their song, they never seem to be where one expects to find them.

The sound-making apparatus of the katydids is on their front wings and consists of a scraper on one wing, which is rasped back and forth across a filelike row of teeth on the opposite wing. This sound-making equipment is found only in the males; the females are silent but have hearing organs or ears on their front legs. While the songs of katydids may sound attractive to other katydids, to the human ear many of them sound like a pocket watch being wound. The true katydid sings only at night, though some related species are often heard during the daylight hours. They are called katydids because of a fancied resemblance of their calls to the words "katydid-katydid-katydid."

This is a close-up of the sound-making apparatus of the katydid. At the left is the file across which is drawn the scraper at the right. The sound is transmitted to the surrounding air by the drumlike mirrors.

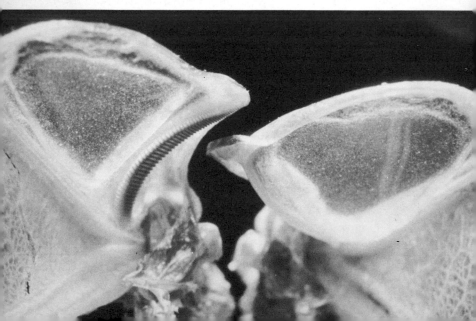

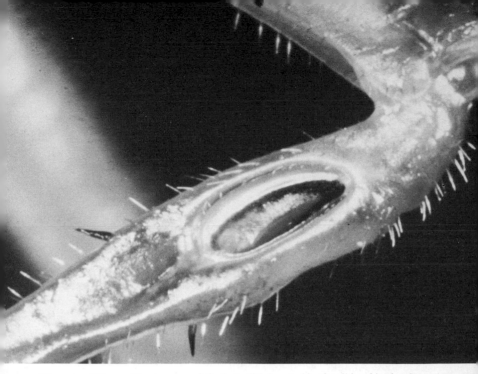

Close-up of the auditory organ of the katydid, located in the tibia of its foreleg.

In preparation for singing, or stridulation, the male katydid raises its forewings and then begins moving them rapidly back and forth across each other like the blades of a pair of scissors. Near the base of one wing —usually the right—there is a bladelike *scraper* and, on the opposite wing, a row of teeth which constitute the *file*. The scraper is on the under side of the uppermost wing and the file is on the upper side of the other wing. Thus, the scraper saws across the file when the wings are moved back and forth. This is done very rapidly, causing the wings to vibrate. This operation may be compared to drawing an ordinary file across the edge of a piece of tin. Adjacent to the file and scraper on each wing there are clear areas sometimes called "mirrors" that resemble somewhat the heads of drums. These are the resonance areas, and it is here that the vibrations of the wings are transferred or communicated to the surrounding air. The speed with which the wings are moved, or the rate at which the file and scraper are moved against each other, determines the pitch of the sound. The sound is also affected by the vibrations of the wings themselves.

The rate of movement of the wings can easily be determined in the laboratory by means of a stroboscope, an instrument which emits a series of flashes. The rate of flashing can be speeded up or slowed down. If a stroboscope is focused on a rapidly moving object such as the revolving blades of an electric fan, the rate of its flash can be adjusted to match that of the fan blades. When this is done the fan appears to stop. The speed of the fan can then be read on the dial of the stroboscope. A similar procedure can be used to determine the rate at which a katydid vibrates its wings. Insect songs can also be recorded and analyzed by means of various electronic devices of special design. By using such instruments and equipment, the songs of many katydids have been studied and analyzed with rather interesting results.

The cone-headed katydid (*Neoconocephalus ensiger*) is common in many places. The front of its head is shaped like a cone and extends forward beyond the bases of the antennae. The wings are very long, and the female has a slender, swordlike ovipositor at the tip of her abdomen. There are 108 teeth on the file of the male's wing, and when he is singing vibrations are emitted at the rate of 13,700 per second, but these are not continuous. About 500 to 800 teeth are struck per second, but the high vibration rate is due to wing resonance. The song consists of a string of twenty pulses, each about three-hundredths of a second in duration. Between each pulse, or burst of vibrations, there is a rest period of one-twentieth of a second. To the human ear, however, this sounds like a continuous buzz. Another cone-head (*Neoconocephalus robustus*) has only 50 teeth in its file but its wings emit about 7,000 vibrations per second as a continuous buzz.

Another, smaller, katydid (*Conocephalus*) has but 35 teeth in its file but the vibratory rate of its song is between 16,000 and 40,000. These are given in pulses several seconds long, between which there is a series of clicks. To the human ear, the song of this insect sounds something like *tse tse tse tse-e-e-e*. It sounds somewhat different to different people.

The meadow grasshopper (*Orchelimum*) closely related to the katydids, has but six teeth in its file, and it, too, emits its song as a series of pulses separated by intervals of several seconds, during which there are no clicks. Some members of the katydid tribe have very high-pitched songs, some of which have been determined as reaching 100,000 cycles per second.

These examples of the characteristics of katydids' songs are sufficient to show that each species has its own special sound-making technique.

This, of course, enables individuals in the various species to recognize each other. Just as the songs of birds are different, so are the songs or calls of katydids. We might also compare insect songs or calls to the diverse languages spoken by different human communities.

It is quite remarkable that with such simple instruments the various species of these insects can emit calls having precise, recognizable qualities. These differences are due to four factors: rate of vibration, intensity, wave form and phase. These sound qualities, as we have said, are more or less peculiar to each species. (Stridulation calls are also affected by temperature; there is a direct relationship between chirp rate and temperature.) Generally speaking, katydids' calls have high intensities or degrees of loudness and these insects usually mount high objects to sing. This seems to be related to the fact that katydids are never very abundant and their calls, to reach the ears of prospective mates, must be heard for some distance.

The crickets, in many cases, resemble katydids to which they are closely related. They have long antennae and many kinds are green, though black is the more common coloration. There are anatomical details, however, which set them apart. For example, the katydids have flattened, swordlike ovipositors whereas those of the crickets are spearlike. Most of them are enthusiastic songsters.

This strange little cricket (*Phyllocyrtus pulchellus*) sings from the safety of a curled-up leaf. It is brightly colored; its head and thorax are crimson-red.

There are many kinds of crickets, including the black field crickets, the pale-green tree crickets, the diminutive bush crickets and, last and least, the tiny ant-loving crickets found only in ant nests. In this clan we might also include the strange mole crickets which tunnel along just beneath the surface of the ground. Although mole crickets are not true crickets, they are closely related to them and are also instrumentalists. The field and tree crickets are chiefly responsible for the reputation of this tribe as sound-makers.

Black field crickets of the genus *Acheta* (*Gryllus*) are found almost everywhere and have been eulogized in prose and poetry, for example, in Charles Dickens' classic *The Cricket on the Hearth*. In rural England, the singing of crickets in the home was once considered to be a sign of good luck. To many people, the singing of crickets in the dusk denotes peace and contentment. They are so much a part of the normal night sounds that we are not even conscious of them. Henry David Thoreau describes the night songs of crickets as "slumberous breathing."

I once spent some months in a part of the world where there were no crickets or katydids. The nights were silent except for the rustling of leaves in the wind. I realized that something was missing and it gradually dawned on me that it was the songs of insects.

In many lands, especially China and Japan, crickets were once so esteemed for their singing that they were kept in cages and carefully cared for. Some of these cages were beautifully made and are now preserved in museums. One type was made of gourds which were allowed to grow inside bottles from the inside surfaces of which they took their shapes. Others were fashioned of porcelain or ivory. The lids were often of carved jade. Less expensive cages were made of bamboo or coconut shells. Caged crickets were always kept in the royal palace during the days of the ancient Chinese empire. Even now, crickets are sometimes kept in cages in Italy, Portugal, Spain and Japan.

Crickets have been kept not only for their songs. Since A.D. 960 they have been kept in China for their fighting abilities. Cricket fighting was once a national pastime, and the records of individual crickets were recorded just as we keep records of thoroughbred race horses. The fighting crickets were fed special diets consisting of rice, boiled chestnuts—and mosquitoes which had been fed on the trainers' arms. This was believed to enhance the little gladiator's abilities in the ring. Such combats ended with the death of the loser. Previous to entering the ring, the crickets were angered by being tickled with rat or hare whiskers set in bone handles.

Large sums were often bet on such matches just as in the case of American cock fights. In fact, there was once a famous fighting cricket in Canton, China, named Ghengis Khan that won $90,000 in one tournament! In these contests, the crickets were carefully weighed on small scales to assure that each one fought in its own weight class. These classes were designated as heavyweight, middleweight and lightweight.

The sound-making apparatus of the cricket clan is similar to that of the katydids, but, whereas the katydids have the file on one wing and the scraper on the other, the crickets have both a file and a scraper on each wing. Thus, they can swap wings in their singing.

The name "cricket" is an onomatopoetic word derived from the supposed sound of their songs. To many people these songs sound like *cree-ket, cree-ket*, but to others they sound like *treat-treat-treat, cree-cree-cree* or, even, *gru-gru-gru*. Their songs are influenced by temperature, which may account for some of the variation. Different species, of course, have their own distinctive songs.

The song of the common black field cricket (*Acheta assimilis*) sounds like a series of chirps to the human ear, but when the sound is analyzed by means of recording instruments, it is found that each chirp is made

The common black cricket (*Acheta*) is found almost everywhere. Its song sounds like *treat-treat-treat*.

up of three or more pulses. This series of three pulses is given in one-tenth of a second; after each series of three there is a pause of about one-fifth second. There is some variation among individual crickets; a few emit chirps consisting of four or even five pulses each. This pattern is the ordinary song which is often continued hour after hour in a monotonous fashion. Seemingly, it has little to do with courtship, except to proclaim ownership of breeding grounds. In the presence of the female, however, the male cricket dances about, at the same time giving high-pitched calls. These are given at the rate of about 17,000 vibrations per second, which is very near the upper limit of human hearing. It has been found that some of the songs of these insects are actually far beyond the range of human hearing. In this respect they are like "silent" dog whistles.

The snowy tree cricket (*Oecanthus*) is found in almost all sections of the United States. There are a number of different species, but they are all pale-green insects that lay their eggs in tree bark or stems.

The black-horned tree cricket has 46 teeth in its file and its call is given at the rate of 45 pulses per second. The song of the snowy tree cricket is made up of a series of chirps, each consisting of about eight pulses. To the human ear the call sounds like *churr-churr-churr*. Generally, these crickets do their singing from the concealment of short vegetation such as that found around gardens or in waste places. Each species has its own characteristic call as do the katydids. From an evolutionary standpoint, this has probably aided in maintaining the purity of the species.

In addition to his song, the male tree cricket uses another lure to attract the female. Once she has been enticed close to him by his song, she is further attracted by a glandular secretion just behind the bases of his wings. She is induced to feed upon this, and, shortly, the actual mating takes place.

Many years ago it was noticed that the chirp rates of tree crickets were directly related to prevailing temperatures and that formulas could be worked out by which temperatures could be determined from them. This, of course, is a very roundabout way of determining temperature, but it is an interesting scientific curiosity and the results are fairly accurate. As a matter of fact, the snowy tree cricket has been called the "temperature cricket" since its calls are so directly related to variations in air temperature. A number of formulae have been devised for telling temperature by listening to these insects. One of these is as follows: Count the number of chirps in 15 seconds and add 40. This gives the temperature in degrees Fahrenheit. Cricket calls can be used for temperature determination only between about 55° F. and 100° F.; beyond these extremes in either direction the insects do not sing.

Another formula, one devised by Professor A. E. Dolbear for the snowy tree cricket, is as follows:

$$\text{Temperature} = 50 + \frac{N - 92}{4.7}$$

$N =$ the number of chirps per minute.

Similar formulae have been worked out for other crickets and katydids. For the field cricket use the following:

$$\text{Temperature} = 50 + \frac{N - 50}{4}$$

For the katydid try this formula:

$$\text{Temperature} = 60 + \frac{N - 19}{3}$$

There is considerable variation in the formulae worked out by various students of the subject. Actually, stridulation rates are affected by humidity and there are also differences between individual insects. Usually, however, temperatures can be calculated within a few degrees or with an accuracy of about six percent.

The songs of crickets and katydids are quite complicated, and when we say that their notes are given at so many vibrations per second we have told only part of the story. If we delve deeper into the subject, we quickly find ourselves involved with complex harmonics. The note of the field cricket starts out at 4,600 vibrations per second and rises to about 4,725. It then drops to about 4,275 vibrations per second. This constitutes one chirp. The vibration rate determines its pitch. What the human ear hears as one chirp is actually made up of about three pulses of sound, each lasting about 0.023 seconds. Our ears are not sensitive enough to detect the short pauses between sound pulses; it is only when the songs are recorded and analyzed on electronic devices that their nature becomes evident.

Even though the songs of crickets and katydids are very complex and difficult to describe, it may be of interest to attempt to catalog some of them. These have been gleaned from various writers and may not sound the same to your ears.

Small meadow grasshopper or cone-headed katydids (*Conocephalus*) *s-s-s-s-s-s-s,* or *tse-tse-tse-tse-tse,* or *tse-e-e-e-e-e*

Large meadow grasshopper or cone-headed katydid (*Neoconocephalus*)
dzeet-dzeet-dzeet-dzeet
Pine tree katydid (*Orchelimum minor*)
s-s-s-s ———— *s-s-s-s*
Fork-tailed katydid (*Scudderia furcata*)
tzit-tzit-tzit-tzit
Angular-winged katydid (*Microcentrum rhombifolium*)
click-click-click-click
Texas bush katydid (*Phaneroptera*)
zeet-zeet-zeet-zeet
Oblong-winged katydid (*Amblycorypha oblongifolia*)
it-z-zic ———— *it-z-zic — it-z-zic*
Uhler's katydid (*Amblycorypha uhleri*)
itsip-itsip-itsip ———— *sh-sh-sh-sh-sh-sh*
True katydid (*Pterophylla camellifolia*)
katy-did—she-didn't—she-did (There are numerous interpretations.)
Meadow grasshopper (*Orchelimum*)
tsip-tsip-tsip-tsip, or *zrrrr-zrrrr* ———— *jip-jip-jip-jip*
Shield-back grasshopper (*Atlanticus*)
p-zee ———— *p-zee* ———— *p-zee*
Tree cricket (*Oecanthus*)
churr-churr-churr-churr, or *ch-ch-ch-ch-urr* ———— *ch-ch-ch-ch-urr*
Black field cricket (*Acheta assimilis*)
treat-treat-treat-treat, or *chee-chee-chee-chee,* or *cree-cree-cree-cree,*
or *gru-gru-gru-gru* (low temperature call)
Small ground cricket (*Nemobius*)
ti-ti-ti-ti, or *tiiii-tiiii-tiiii-tiiii*
Mole cricket (*Gryllotalpa hexadactyla*)
grrr ———— *grrr* ———— *grrr,* or *churp-churp-churp* (deep toned)
Tiny bush cricket (*Anaxipha exigua*)
ti-ti-ti-ti

At present I am seated beside a river in the deep forest, my favorite place to write. The hot August sun penetrates down through the dense foliage of oaks and hickories, casting patches of light on the forest floor. Filtering down from the sunlit world in the trees' upper story come the rasping sounds of the cicadas. Each songster begins its call in a rising crescendo that increases in tempo, then slowly fades away like an alarm clock running down. Soon the song begins again and is repeated over and over without change all during the daylight hours. The forest seems to vibrate with the combined songs of the cicada multitudes. Dusk is the time when most katydids and crickets begin their serenades, but the cicadas love the heat and the sunshine. This, perhaps, is not surprising when one considers that these strange insects have lived for many years in dark tunnels beneath the surface of the ground.

The "year of the cicadas" is the year when the thirteen-year brood is emerging. Thirteen years previously the parent insects sang in the sun and mated. After mating, the females alighted upon twigs and inserted their spearlike ovipositors, or egg-laying tubes. Clusters of eggs were deposited within the woody tissues, which often injured the twigs to such an extent that they died. Within a week or so the eggs hatched and the antlike young dropped to the ground and burrowed in. For the first year or two the young cicadas remained near the surface, feeding upon sap from trees' roots, and then they began moving deeper and deeper into the ground, always near the life-giving roots. Eventually, they were located five or six feet down, each one enclosed in a small cell. For these hidden insects, time seemed almost to stand still. During summer they sucked sap from the nearby roots, but when the sap flow stopped in winter they became inactive and waited, each one alone in its dark, silent cell. But there came a time during the thirteenth spring when some inner timing device told them that their hour was near. Each one tunneled upward to a point near the surface, excavated two connecting cells and waited. By this time they were slightly over an inch in length and brown in color. Their forelegs were shaped like a crab's claws, well suited to digging.

No one knows how the cicadas time their emergence from the ground, but all of them suddenly received the urge to return once again to the world of sunshine. During the night they crawled from the ground and slowly and awkwardly crawled up the sides of trees and bushes. Having selected a spot, they anchored their legs and settled down to await the processes of transformation. Soon a rent appeared down the back of each one; slowly this began to open and soon the adult, winged cicada crawled forth. At first it was pale and helpless, its wings mere fluid-filled sacs. Gradually these expanded into cellophane-like wings and the adult insects were then ready to fly away and sing, filling the forest with a cacophony of sound. For thirteen years they lived silent lives, but now the males seem overcome with the urge to make up for lost time. The females do not sing.

The above is the story of the 13-year cicada that occurs in southeastern United States. The 17-year cicada is merely a different geographical race of the same insect and occurs farther north. There is some overlapping

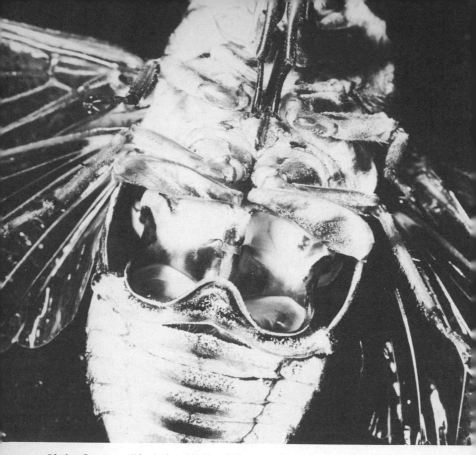

If the flaps are lifted the details of the sound-making organs of the cicada can be seen. The sound is produced by the timbal membrane located at the outer portions of the cavities on each side. In the forward portion of each cavity are located the folded membranes which serve as sounding boards. In the rear portion of each cavity are seen the "mirrors" which are actually the insect's auditory organs.

of the races, but their life histories are the same. There are many different broods, and periodical cicadas emerge somewhere each summer.

Besides the 13-year and 17-year cicadas, which should be called "periodical" cicadas, there are many other kinds. Some of these spend only two years in the ground in the nymphal stage. The males of all these cicadas are songsters of renown and occur in several parts of the world.

Cicadas are sometimes called locusts, but they are not even remotely related to those insects. The locust tribe contains the grasshoppers, crickets and katydids, while the cicadas are more closely related to the plant lice and the leafhoppers. In many ways, they are unique insects, not only in their life histories, but in their mode of sound making.

The cicadas' sound-making mechanism consists not of a stridulating organ, but of a pair of drumming organs located on the underside of the body on the first abdominal segment. These organs are quite elaborate and concealed beneath hard plates extending backward from the thorax. If one of these plates is lifted, the cavity containing the drumming mechanism can be seen. This consists of two structures, the *timbal* membrane and the *folded* membrane. The timbal membrane is located along the outer portion of the cavity and is caused to vibrate by muscles attached to its inner surface. The folded membrane located in the forward portion of the cavity acts as a resonator or sounding board, increasing the volume of sound. In the posterior portion of each cavity is a shiny, mica-like membrane called the *mirror*. Actually, this latter membrane is a sound-perceiving organ or "ear-drum" and plays no part in sound production. In operation, the "buckling muscle" attached to the inner surface of the timbal membrane contracts very rapidly, causing it to snap in and out at rates of from 184 to 360 times per second. This muscle is not under direct control of the central nervous system, the impulses arise in the muscle itself. Large air spaces within the insect's body increase the volume of sound, but the insect controls the volume by raising and lowering the plates covering the cavities. As a boy, I often imitated cicada calls by placing a tin aspirin box between my teeth and causing the lid to snap in and out. Actually, this is quite analogous to the cicadas' drumming organs. The loud buzzing song of the cicadas is difficult to describe. Perhaps the New Zealand Maori word for these insects, *kihikihi,* best describes it. Interestingly, there is a cicada in California that has taken up sound-making by stridulation, which is actually a more primitive method of sound production. This cicada strikes its wings together *beneath* its body, making a click-click-click sound. It has been called the "watch-winding" cicada.

In a way, the sounds or noises made by insects constitute their languages; they are the means by which they communicate moods of love, anger, fright or warning. Insects were the first creatures to raise their voices in a world that had known only the scream of the hurricane and the rumbling of ancient volcanoes.

chapter four

The Aerialists

IN the beginning the world's only plants were creeping forms like algae, mosses and liverworts, but as the ages passed taller plants evolved. During the millions of years when all plants were small, the insects were all crawling forms for there was little need for flight. Animals—or plants —that do not keep up-to-date in their habits and adaptations are soon eliminated from the struggle for existence. Thus, as taller plants gradually came into existence, the insects gradually developed adaptations to fit them for life above the surface of the ground. As time passed, certain crawling insects developed lateral extensions from the sides of their thoraxes, enabling them to sail from leaf to leaf or from tall plants down to the ground. This helped them to escape enemies or to get to other food plants more quickly, and those that had this ability were better fitted for the struggle and so were more apt to survive. In time these gliding vanes became larger and larger and more efficient, enabling the insects to sail for greater distances. In operation they resembled the "wings" of modern flying squirrels, which consist of furry membranes stretched between fore-legs and hind legs.

For several million years these insects were "content" to glide about on their thoracic vanes, but as they glided through the air the vanes tended to vibrate or flutter because of aerodynamic forces. Slowly, ever so slowly, muscles were developed to actively move the wings up and

The cockroaches and their ancestors have been flying for millions of years. From their ancestors were evolved all modern flying insects.

down against the air, enabling the insects to sail farther. This was an advantage and brought about further muscular development and, at long last, powered flight became a reality. One of the first of these flying "models" was *Stenodictya lobata,* a stonefly-like insect that is known from fossilized remains found in the Upper Carboniferous strata. This early flying insect had well-developed wings attached to the two hind segments of the thorax; in addition, it had short lobes extending out from the front segment. Thus, it is assumed that the earlier "models" had *three* thoracic extensions, but only those on the last two segments developed into true wings. The wings of insects developed from special organs and not from existing appendages as in the cases of all other flying animals. Birds and bats, for example, sacrificed one pair of legs in the development of wings.

All our knowledge of the early flying insects is derived from the fossils they left in ancient strata now hardened into stone. From such meager information we must piece together the story of the early flying insects. After the insects had developed functional wings they had the air to themselves for approximately 100 million years, until the rise of the reptile clan and the evolution of such flying reptiles as the pterosaurs or pterodactyls. The flying reptiles passed into the limbo of "discontinued models," but eventually the birds arose and flourished as highly successful flying machines.

The ability to fly is a great advantage to almost any creature and it would almost seem that flight is the ultimate aim of all animal groups. It makes it easier to evade enemies, enables predaceous species to capture prey, makes it possible for a plant-eating insect to get to its food plant, helps insects to obtain mates and facilitates moving to new areas where food may be more abundant or where climatic conditions may be more favorable. Flight has so many advantages that it is indeed remarkable that so many insects that once had this ability have abandoned it.

An insect that takes up a parasitic habitat or adapts itself to life underground has little use for wings. Queen ants are winged during the period of mating, but after this period the wings are severed for they would merely be in the way during the rest of their lives underground or in tunnels in wood. The same is true of termites. Almost every insect order has individual species whose wings have degenerated. Most flies are winged, yet the sheep tick (*Melophagus ovinus*) is actually a wingless fly as is also the deer parasite (*Lipoptena cervi*). In the case of the latter insect, however, wings are present until a host is found, after which the wings are cast off as it takes up a parasitic life. Another insect, the bee louse (*Braula coeca*), which is presumably a fly, is very tiny, measuring only about one-sixteenth inch, and clings to the bodies of bees, especially old queens. The bee louse has degenerated to the extent that it has lost its eyes as well as its wings. Many species of cockroaches, among the most ancient of flying insects, have dispensed with wings and seem to get along just as well.

Wings are found in almost all insect orders except the most primitive, such as the Thysanura (silverfish), Collembola (springtails), Mallophaga (bird lice) and Anoplura (sucking lice). It is of considerable interest also that all winged insects were derived from a common ancestor. Thus, we might say that nature only once evolved a successful flying machine and that all later models are merely modifications of the original. Evidence of this is found in the wings themselves, which all have the same basic pattern of venation.

While insect wings were apparently all derived from a common ancestor, the wings of the various present-day insects have become greatly modified. The wings of butterflies and moths are thin, expanded vanes covered with scales; those of bees and many other insects are cellophane-

The pale green wings of the luna moth are of unusual form. These moths are weak flyers.

like. Beetles have hard, hornlike fore wings, and membranous hind wings that are folded under them when at rest. In flight the beetles hold the fore wings up while the hind wings do the work of flying. A somewhat similar arrangement is found in the grasshoppers. In the case of the two-winged flies, or Diptera, the hind wings have disappeared. Some authorities believe that the *halteres* or so-called balancing organs of these insects were derived from the hind wings. In any event, the two-winged flies get along very well with only one pair of wings; in fact, they are among the best flyers of all insects.

Insect wings also vary in respect to size. The wings of the larger butterflies and moths have a great wing area and among them are found the insects with the largest wing expanse of any modern insect. Probably the greatest wing expanse of any insect was that of large dragonflies (*Meganeura*) that existed millions of years ago. The wings of these monsters measured more than two feet across! Probably the smallest of all flying insects are the fairy flies (*Allaptus*) that are just a little larger than a period in this book. These minutes flies, as you will read about in another chapter, swim down into the waters of ponds and lakes using their tiny wings like paddles. Here they deposit their microscopic eggs within the eggs of dragonflies. Fairy flies thus use their wings both in air and water, which is unusual since aquatic insects such as beetles and backswimmers fold their wings while submerged, using them for flight only when they take to the air.

When an adult winged insect emerges from its pupal case, its wings are fluid-filled sacs that gradually expand and harden into the typical wing form. These wings contain many hollow veins through which blood flows. The veins also serve as stiffening structures and along them, especially in the basal region, are found sensory organs. The veins in the front portions of the wings are heavier than those toward the rear margins so that as the wings beat up and down the rear portions of the wings flex, causing a forward thrust.

Flight, whether it be that of a man-made machine or an insect, is much more complicated than it might seem. The first human airplane designers, such as Leonardo da Vinci, knew nothing of the complex science of aerodynamics; they attempted to build flying machines that were patterned after birds. None of these contraptions ever got off the ground,

The cloudless sulphur butterfly migrates in late summer. Here a specimen comes in to a landing on a zinnia bloom.

which is not at all surprising. Even the first designers of planes that actually flew knew very little about the physical forces encountered by a vehicle that flies through the air. Insects, of course, know nothing about aerodynamics, yet by a slow process of trial and error they developed the ability to fly. The development of wings was, of course, a very slow process. The first wings were inefficient, but poor wings are better than no wings at all and so, by the slow process of evolution, modern wings came into being. Some insects fly at tremendous rates and carry very heavy loads considering their sizes. Antoine Magnan, a French zoologist, in 1934 made some very careful studies of bumblebee flight and came to the conclusion that bumblebees cannot fly at all! Fortunately, the bumblebees never heard this bit of news and so went on flying as usual.

The actual manner in which an insect's wings are caused to move up and down is very complicated and difficult to describe. Actually, it does not appear as if it would work at all—but it does! An insect's thorax is a boxlike structure having the wings attached to the upper corners. However, this box is not rigid; there are large muscles extending from the top to the bottom of the thoracic box and the contraction of these muscles pulls the top of the thorax downward causing the wings to rise because of the way in which the wings are attached. There are other muscles extending in a lengthwise direction and the contraction of these muscles causes the wings to beat downward. This is because the muscles running lengthwise cause the roof of the thoracic box to bend upward. The two sets of opposing muscles described above are called the *indirect* muscles because they are not attached to the bases of the wings but to the walls of the thoracic box. In addition to the indirect muscles, there are also *direct* muscles attached to the bases of the wings. In flight, the indirect muscles cause the wings to beat up and down while the direct muscles bring about other movements. Thus the movements of an insect's wing in flight are not merely up and down. On the downstroke the wing moves downward and forward and on the upstroke it moves upward and backward. As the wings move up and down, however, they also rotate on their axes. When an insect wing rises, its hind portion is deflected downward and when it beats downward the hind portion is deflected upward. These deflections tend to drive the insect forward like the rotating blades of a propeller. Laboratory study of a flying insect's wings discloses that the tips describe a figure eight and not simple up-and-down arcs. Moreover, the form of this figure-eight movement is not vertical but downward and forward, as we have already seen. This may seem strange since it would appear that the wing movement would be downward and backward. Such a motion is sometimes found when the insects are hovering, as in the case of syrphid flies, hummingbird moths or bees hovering before flowers.

The movement of an insect's wings through the air creates considerable turbulence which interferes with the efficiency of the hind wings. It is probably for this reason that many four-winged insects, such as the bees, butterflies and moths, have evolved contrivances for hooking the two pairs of wings together so that they function as a unit. The two-winged flies have solved the problem by the elimination of the hind wings. The dragonflies, which are the best flyers of all, have evolved another solution. In these insects the two pairs of wings beat alternately, that is, the

The best of all insect flyers are the dragonflies. Unlike most other insects their wings do not move up and down in unison. While their hind wings are rising their fore wings beat downward, apparently increasing their aerodynamic efficiency. The globular eyes are fitted for vision in all directions.

front pair beat downward while the hind pair are rising. The movement of the wings is timed so that the hind wings meet the undisturbed column of air before it is made turbulent by the front wings. Thus, each of the two pairs of wings encounters smoothly streamlined air, making for very efficient flight.

Considering the complexity of movement of insects' wings, it is remarkable that they can beat as rapidly as they do. The rates at which insects' wings beat have been studied by many people down the years. The first estimates were based on the sounds the wings made as compared to musical instruments of known pitch. This is not a very accurate method since the flight sounds may be produced by other structures. Probably the most precise method is that of allowing the tip of the insect's wing to brush lightly against the smoked surface of a drum rotating at a known rate. Such an apparatus is called a *kymograph* and is commonly used in physiology laboratories for making various tests. Stroboscopic lights are also used, as well as electronic equipment.

When at rest the locust's hind wings are folded fanlike beneath the stiff fore wings. This locust (*Schistocerca*), like its cousin the African locust, can fly with great power. The African species can maintain flight for many hours.

Many factors affect wing-beat frequency or speed; these include age of the insect, sex, temperature, fatigue and so on. Temperature is of major importance since insects are cold-blooded, that is, their bodies remain about the same temperature as that of their surroundings and all their body functions vary in relation to it. Many of us have noticed how an insect is often unable to fly on a cold morning. Before such a cold insect can fly it often vibrates its wings for awhile. This is because it must first raise the temperature of its flight muscles. In some insects, on the other hand, the rate of wing beat remains constant over a rather wide temperature range. For instance, the desert locust (*Schistocerca*) maintains the same rate from about 70 to 95°F. With respect to age, many insects' wings beat faster as they grow older—up to a certain point—then they slow down as old age sets in.

The flight speeds and wing-beat rates of various insects are given in the following list.

	Wing-beat rate	Miles per hour
Beetle (*Coccinella*)	75-91	—
Butterflies		
Papilio	5-9	—
Pieris	12	5.7
Monarch	—	6.2
Bumblebee	250	6.4
Dragonfly		
Aeschna	38	15.6
Austrophlebia	—	36
Meganeura (prehistoric)	—	43
Honeybee	250	5.6-13.9
Hornet	100	—
Horsefly	96	6-14
Housefly	190	4.4
Hover-fly (*Eristalis*)	190	7.8
Hummingbird moth	85	11.1
Midge fly (*Forcipomyia*)	988-1047	—
Mosquito		
Aedes	587	2.5-5.5
Culex	278-307	—
Noctuid moth	30-50	—
Hummingbird (for comparison)	30-50	—

As a general rule, large insects can fly faster than small insects. It has been claimed that some dragonflies can fly up to 90 miles per hour. Although this is doubtful, it is possible that some dragonflies can fly up to 40 or 50 miles per hour for short distances. The prehistoric dragonfly (*Meganeura*) listed in the table above had a wing span of 29 inches and its flight speed of 43 miles per hour is, of course, an estimate or "educated guess." The speed of an insect's flight often seems faster than it actually is because of its small size. I have often clocked small birds flying alongside my automobile and found that they were usually making about 30 miles an hour. Such birds appear to be flying faster to an observer standing still. To illustrate how confusion may arise as to insects' flight speed, we might recount the celebrated case of the deer bot fly (*Cephenemyia*) that *didn't* fly 820 miles per hour! In 1926 C. H. T. Townsend reported field observations indicating that this fly flew at that fantastic rate. Later studies of this insect proved that it could not possibly fly that fast and even if it did friction would cause it to burn up. It has also been calculated that the power required to drive the fly that fast would be somewhere in the vicinity of one-fourth horsepower. One of the unfortunate things about "facts" that are recorded in scientific journals is that once they have appeared in print it is difficult to eliminate them and they are quoted again and again for many years.

The measurement of the actual power output of insects in flight has attracted the attention of many scientists. Some of the techniques used are quite ingenious. In most cases the insects have been attached to wheels and allowed to fly. From this it has been possible to make rather precise calculations of power output. Dr. C. M. Williams designed a piece of equipment that has been used successfully on flies. This cleverly contrived, simple apparatus consists of two parallel blades or wires arranged in such a way that a fly attached to a balanced trapeze causes it to roll up an incline. From this the fly's power output can be calculated. Actually, the power output is a very complicated matter since a number of factors are involved. These include the energy needed to lift the insect, to drive it forward and to overcome air resistance.

Although theoretically, the larger an insect is the faster it should be able to fly, there is a limit to the weight. On the other hand, it is much easier for a tiny insect to stay aloft than a large one. If an insect is small enough, it will almost float without effort just as pollen grains float, but a small insect cannot fly very fast because its power output is small.

In the matter of food or fuel consumption, it has been found that the monarch butterfly, which is famous for its long-distance flights, can travel about 650 miles on the energy contained in the fat stored in its body. Fats constitute a very efficient source of power, being about three times as efficient as nectar. The flight ranges of some other insects are as follows: horseflies, 43 to 61 miles; mosquitoes, 14 to 33 miles; honeybees, 29 miles; desert locusts, 217 miles. It is estimated that about one-third of the energy expended by an insect in flight is negative or lost in various ways such as in the slowing down of the wings at the ends of their strokes. For example, it has been determined that the mechanical power generated by the desert locust is 13.7 calories per gram of body weight per hour. Of the 13.7 calories generated, 8.9 calories are expended in positive work and 4.8 calories are lost in negative work. Flight requires great energy consumption since the flapping movement of insect wings in flight is extremely complicated, involving elevation, depression, fore and aft movements and other manipulations of the wings. It is estimated that about as much power is needed to lift an insect in flight as is needed to drive it forward.

In all complex movements of the wings needed for stable flight there must be very precise nervous control. This comes from a variety of sensory organs located on both body and wings. The sensilla on the wings apparently convey information regarding air flow and pressure. In addition to these, there are organs on the head and antennae that are sensitive to moving air and which probably aid the insects in flight. Thus, just as an airplane must have many sensitive instruments to fly properly so must an insect have precise information regarding a variety of factors about the air through which it is passing. During flight the insect must be continually adjusting and compensating for variations in air currents. Flight is infinitely more complex than crawling over the ground, and it is remarkable that insects have mastered it.

Probably the most interesting of the sensory organs of flying insects are the *halteres*, or "balancing organs" that are found in two-winged flies. These organs were probably derived from the hind wings, but there is also evidence that they arose as special sensory organs. The halteres consist of a pair of shafts with knobs at their tips and are located just behind and below the wings. Although it has been known for a long time that these organs were related to flight, it has only recently been discovered that they vibrate very rapidly while the insect is in flight and that they move

This crane fly was photographed to show its *halteres* or navigational organs (arrow). During flight these organs vibrate very rapidly and function as gyroscopes.

at the same rate as the wings but in the opposite phase. It is therefore believed that the halteres are controlled by the same muscles that control wing beat. If the halteres are removed from a horsefly, for example, and the fly is then tossed into the air, it usually tumbles to the ground unable to fly. Usually a fly will not attempt to fly if its halteres have been amputated. Evidently, the halteres have more or less the same function as a spinning gyroscope and aid in the control of flight by their gyroscopic torques which are transmitted to the nervous system.

Such precise navigational control enables insects to execute complicated maneuvers in the air. For example, the question of how a fly lands on the ceiling has long been pondered. Some believed that the fly executed a half-roll and landed on its feet, and others believed that it flipped over. Recently, high-speed motion pictures have revealed that the fly brings its front end upward so that its fore feet can come in contact with the overhead surface, after which the other feet are attached. Gradually modern techniques and equipment are solving the mysteries of insect flight. Long ago these small creatures mastered the aerial realm, a realm that man himself is just now beginning to conquer. Man will, of course, far outdo the insects and, because of his intellect, will eventually journey to the stars. Of all flying animals, insects are the most expert—they can fly at relatively great speeds, hover in mid-air and maneuver with remarkable dexterity. Some can even use their wings in both air and water, and butterflies are known to fly at altitudes up to 20,000 feet.

chapter five

Insect Migration

LIKE birds, many insects migrate. Why this occurs with insects, however, is not obvious, since they usually do not survive to return to their places of origin. The migratory movements of birds are often adaptations to escape the cold of winter, when their foods are scarce. Insectivorous birds leave cold climates each autumn and fly to warm lands where insects are abundant all year. On the other hand, ducks and geese migrate northward to breed in the vast hinterlands of North America where aquatic life upon which they feed is abundant and where days are long. However, the basic purpose behind bird migrations is still under investigation by scientists. These migrations, in some cases, seem merely to be yearly returns to ancestral breeding or wintering areas. Some ducks, such as the redheads, move east or west across the United States at the same time that other ducks are flying north or south. How these and other birds navigate is an intriguing subject and one that is still being studied. Some birds, it has been found, navigate by the stars just as do human navigators. Other birds seem to have built-in compasses that guide them through fogs and cloudy nights when no heavenly bodies or other fixed reference points are visible.

Certain insects, too, seem endowed with the ability to navigate across the earth. In America, at least, the best known of these migratory insects

In the southern portions of their range monarch butterflies often congregate in large numbers and form nightly clusters.

are the monarch butterflies (*Danaus plexippus*), whose larvae feed upon milkweed. This butterfly is a native of North America, but perhaps because of its migratory habits it has spread to the Cape Verde and Madeira Islands in the Atlantic and to New Zealand, Australia, England and France. A slightly different color variety occurs in the West Indies where it has been isolated long enough for change to occur. Those individuals that appear in Europe are almost all of the typical North American variety; only one of the West Indian monarchs has ever been captured there. Monarchs are also common on many of the tropical Pacific Islands. I saw them flitting about in Pali Pass on the island of Oahu and on Guam. It was almost like seeing familiar faces from home even though they looked out of place among the lush tropical vegetation.

These common rust-colored butterflies overwinter in the southern portions of the United States and, probably, northern Mexico. With the coming of spring some instinct drives them northward as milkweed begins growing. The gravid females lay their eggs on the milkweed and fly on, following the advance of spring. Like the birds, they are in tune with the cosmic forces that govern the slow advance of the season. When the monarch eggs hatch and the larvae mature into adult butterflies, these, too, fly northward, urged on by unreasoning instinct. In this way they eventually cross the border into Canada, halting their northward push only when they have passed the limit of milkweed growth. They have been seen as far north as Alaska. While most of the monarchs that arrive at the spring breeding grounds in Canada are not the same individuals which had migrated southward the previous autumn, there is some evidence that a few actually do make the round trip. The southern flights in autumn are apparently triggered by the shortening of the daylight hours. Usually they fly as individuals, but on occasion in flocks. Their southbound flights are faster, seemingly prodded on by the coming winter. Now they no longer dally along the way breeding on milkweed; time is running out and they must hurry to avoid the cold. They push on southward, often congregating at night, then flying on when the sun's rays warm their bodies. Often these resting sites are located along the northern edges of natural barriers such as the Great Lakes.

Great monarch flights have been observed in several places. For example, a great migration of these butterflies occurred near Dallas, Texas, on October 24, 1954. The flying monarchs were spread out over a 20-mile front. In a few instances they have been seen migrating by moonlight. In 1888 there was a monarch migration in Maryland in which the butterflies were described as moving in a great swarm as high as the eye could see. They were flying against a stiff breeze.

A number of interesting studies of these southward-flying butterflies have been made. This has often been done by tagging them in a way similar to that used in studying bird migration. In the case of birds, metal bands are placed on the legs, but in the case of butterflies either paper tags are cemented to the wings or rubber stamps are used. The big difficulty with tagging butterflies is that very few of them are ever recovered. Most butterflies are captured by birds or come to unknown ends in the forest or on the prairie. The chance of a person capturing a marked specimen is very remote, indeed. However, Dr. F. A. Urquhart of the Royal Ontario Museum of Zoology and Paleontology has cemented thin paper tags

Tags are attached to the wings of monarchs to obtain information as to their migratory travels. One monarch tagged in eastern Canada was recaptured in San Luis Potosí, Mexico, a minimum distance of 1,870 miles.

to a large number of monarchs he captured as they congregated along the northern edge of Lake Ontario. Such a study requires tremendous perseverance. In 1950 and 1951 Dr. Urquhart tagged 3,000 monarchs but had only one return, and this from a specimen captured only 40 miles away. In 1955, with the help of many volunteers, he tagged 10,000 specimens and had 30 returns, some from as far south as Virginia. In 1956, 20,000 monarchs were tagged with about 125 returns. These specimens had been captured as far south as Texas and the Gulf Coast. The distance record of these tagged butterfly travelers was set by one recaptured in the town of Catorce in San Luis Potosí, Mexico. This butterfly had flown at least 1,870 miles, an almost unbelievable distance for such a frail insect. Consider the hazards. This butterfly first crossed Lake Ontario, which was no small feat in itself, and then flitted on through forests and across fields where every bird was a potential enemy. Continuing on, it crossed open prairies and deserts all populated by insectivorous birds of many kinds. Not the least of the hazards were winds and gales and, possibly, torrential rains, any of which could have damaged its paper-thin wings and brought it to the earth, bedraggled and helpless. Yet, in spite of all these possible tragedies, this butterfly traveled nearly two thousand miles. It would be interesting to know what percentage of the monarchs that leave Canada on southbound migrations are able to fly this far. Their speed of flight is usually about 10 miles per hour, but they can often attain a speed up to 30 miles per hour. It has been found that a monarch can fly about 600 miles on one "tankful" of nectar.

Dr. Urquhart and his associates have obtained many returns from tagged monarchs. It may be of interest to list a few recoveries of monarchs that flew the greatest distances. Most of these were tagged near the north shore of Lake Ontario.

Locations and tagging dates	Recovery points and dates	Miles flown
Meaford, Ontario Sept. 3, 1956	Galveston, Texas Oct. 18, 1956	1320
Bay Village, Ohio Aug. 28, 1957	Paragould, Arkansas Oct. 2, 1957	570
Highland Creek, Ontario Sept. 7, 1956	Deering, Missouri Oct. 1, 1956	772
Highland Creek, Ontario Sept. 12, 1957	Liberty, Mississippi Oct. 9, 1957	1060
Highland Creek, Ontario Sept. 13, 1956	Brownwood, Texas Oct. 25, 1956	1345
Highland Creek, Ontario Sept. 18, 1957	Roxie, Mississippi Oct. 5, 1957	1060
Highland Creek, Ontario Sept. 18, 1957	Estacion Catorce, San Luis Potosí, Mexico Jan. 25, 1958	1870
Highland Creek, Ontario Sept. 18, 1956	Sequin, Texas Dec. 27, 1956	1400
Highland Creek, Ontario Sept. 30, 1956	Silsbee, Texas Nov. 7, 1956	1233
Liberty Borough, Pennsylvania Sept. 22, 1955	Port St. Joe, Florida Oct. 25, 1955	788

Male monarchs have scent pockets on their hind wings, and it is believed by some that these males lay "scent trails" through the sky which are followed by the females. On their southbound flights the males apparently forge ahead. The scent emitted by male monarchs could also account for the return year after year to the same places—trees and shrubs —where they form large winter congregations. Such winter clusters have been recorded in many places from Florida to California. The most famous of these monarch winter resorts is Pacific Grove, California, where the butterflies have been returning year after year in large numbers for at least a hundred years. During the month of October the monarchs flutter into the area, where they form nightly clusters on eucalyptus trees and are protected by City Ordinance No. 352, which states that it shall be illegal "to molest or interfere with in any way the peaceful occupancy of the Monarch Butterflies on their annual visit to the City. . . ." There is a possible penalty of a $5,000 fine or a six-month jail sentence. Because Pacific Grove is an annual winter gathering place for the butterflies it has become known as "Butterfly Town, U.S.A.," and each autumn the local school children celebrate the return of the monarchs with a parade. Monarch roosting trees have been found in other places, also; these are along the Gulf Coast, in Florida and in other places.

Second only to the monarch in its migratory flights is the painted lady butterfly (*Vanessa cardui*), whose larvae feed upon thistles. This is a cosmopolitan species, perhaps because its food plants are also cosmopolitan. Migratory flights of these butterflies occur in both North America and Europe. Migratory movements have also been seen in Pakistan, South Africa and Australia.

The painted lady butterfly overwinters in western Mexico and flies northward in spring. The larvae feed upon thistle. Probably because of its migratory habits the painted lady is the most widely distributed butterfly in the world.

Painted ladies overwinter south of the Mexican border and, with the arrival of spring, fly northward in a broad front that fans out over the United States. Sometimes there are massed flights consisting of millions of individuals. One such flight was over 40 miles wide and was seen passing one point for three days. The butterflies were flying at about six miles per hour. As the season advances, the painted ladies gradually push on northward, but in North America there seems to be no evidence of southbound flights, so characteristic of the monarchs. Painted ladies are great travelers and they have been seen at sea a thousand miles from land and even beyond the Arctic Circle. While they occur in Florida, they seem content to remain there, and there appear to be no northward flights from there in spring.

On June 21, 1965, while driving eastward across southwestern Wyoming, I encountered a mass movement of painted lady butterflies along a 100-mile front. They were all flying southward against a three-mile wind, and as an indication of the number, it was noted that at least six individuals could be seen crossing the highway ahead of the automobile at any given time. Why they were migrating southward is strange since they should have been flying northward at that time of year.

In Europe and Africa the habits of these butterflies have been carefully studied and the story of their migrations has been recorded in considerable detail by Dr. C. B. Williams of England, the world's foremost authority on insect migration. The painted ladies spend the winter breeding in North Africa around the edges of the desert area. In early spring the butterflies emerging from their chrysalids begin flying northward across the Mediterranean to Europe. Sometimes they reach Iceland and Finland. They arrive in England in June, or sometimes earlier. South of the Sahara these butterflies move southward in September, which corresponds more or less to spring in the Northern Hemisphere. Dr. Williams believes that these African flights result from migrants that moved south from Europe. While southward migrations in autumn are, so far, unknown in America, they have been recorded in other places in the Northern Hemisphere. In Pakistan a flight was seen moving southeast at 17,000 feet in August. This is probably the greatest elevation at which migrating butterflies have been observed.

Like many migrating insects, it is the newly emerged adults that take to their wings in definite migratory flights. However, this statement is based on but one authenticated observation. Mr. S. B. J. Skertchly was traveling by camel in the desert near the Red Sea in March 1869 (some

In the Southeast, the most common migratory butterfly is the cloudless sulphur (*Catopsilia eubule*), often known as "the butterfly that flies toward the southeast." In late summer almost every individual flies in the general direction of Florida. In the Carolinas and Georgia its flight is southward; farther west it is toward the Southeast. Northward spring flights have been observed in Alabama.

records give the year as 1880). The butterflies were emerging in enormous numbers and as soon as their wings were dry—within a half hour—they flew off in an easterly direction toward the sea.

In eastern United States the butterfly that attracts the most interest because of its migratory flights is the cloudless sulphur [*Catopsilia (Phoebis) eubule*], whose larvae feed on cassia. They are larger than most of our other sulphur butterflies and their wings are bright canary-yellow and devoid of dark markings. In summer these conspicuous butterflies are seen flitting hither and yon sipping nectar from flowers, but with the arrival of autumn their flights take on a definite direction. Almost every one flies toward the South or Southeast, depending on the location. Seemingly, this is with reference to Florida. Their flight in the Carolinas and Georgia is orientated to the South, while farther west it is toward the Southeast. There is no mass movement; the individual butterflies merely fly along "as if going somewhere." They fly across fields and over trees, usually not deviating much from their paths of flight. Now and then they alight upon flowers but pause only long enough for a quick drink of nectar, then they are off again, hurrying along as if to keep an appointment at some destined place. In the states where these attractive butterflies are common they are usually known as "traveling butterflies" and everyone seems to be aware that they are migrating. Mr. P. H. Smythe, a meteorologist at Montgomery, Alabama, has kept careful records on the seasonal flights of these butterflies for nearly twenty years. He has noted the southeasterly migration each year from the end of July to late November. In addition, he has also noted smaller flights to the Northwest during March and April. This same butterfly also occurs in tropical America, where it exhibits seasonal flights. A closely related species (*Catopsilia florella*) is found in South Africa where it flies toward the Southwest in December and January and, to a lesser extent, in the opposite direction from February to April.

One of the most common of the sulphur butterflies in the eastern United States is *Terias* (*Eurema*) *lisa,* which is yellow with dark wing margins. It is a small species, measuring only about an inch in expanse. On several occasions large flights of the little butterflies have crossed the sea from the United States to Bermuda, a distance of at least 600 miles. In October, 1874, for example, swarms of them fell on a ship at sea. They were coming from the Northwest. Many other members of the sulphur butterfly tribe exhibit migratory movements, both in America and other parts of the world. This habit is, however, not confined to any group of butterflies; it occurs in almost all families. For example, the gulf fritillary (*Dione vanillae*) flies northward in spring and southward in autumn. The autumn flights are the most marked. Flights of these butterflies have also been observed in the Galápagos Islands and Argentina.

Observations on the migration of butterflies is a most fascinating subject and one to which almost anyone can make contributions. Unusual flights should be recorded as to species, direction of travel and dates. There are about 250 kinds of butterflies that have shown migratory tendencies.

Although butterfly migrations are fairly well known, many people do not realize that some moths are also migratory. Perhaps the most interesting of these is the black witch (*Erebus odorata*), which breeds in tropical America and flies northward, often traveling as far as central Canada. It has been captured at Edmonton, Alberta, and one specimen was found fluttering about in the snow during a storm that occurred on July 4th at Leadville, Colorado, at an elevation of 10,200 feet. Specimens have often been captured at sea, long distances from land. One specimen was captured on the remote island of Tristan da Cunha, which lies in the South Atlantic, 2,000 miles east of South America. The black witch measures about four inches across and is thus one of the largest of the moths of the family *Noctuidae,* most of which do not measure more than an inch or so across.

Another noctuid (*Alabama argillacea*) is also famous for its northward flights. The larvae of this moth commonly feed on cotton and are known as cottonworms. These insects overwinter in the tropics—probably in Colombia—and begin moving northward, generation after generation. Most years they do not reach the heart of our cotton belt, but some years these moths arrive in late summer and their larvae defoliate the plants. But not all the moths that develop from these caterpillars are satisfied to remain in the vicinity of their food plants; some instinct urges most of them to fly northward hundreds of miles beyond the last cotton plant. Some years they appear in Canada in large numbers. As far as is known, however, there is no southward migration and the moths die without reproducing. Thus, these northbound flights are "suicide missions," and the instinct that drives them north is a lethal trap. Once the urge to fly north begins to function, there seems to be no turning back, so they push onward until their legions are destroyed by the cold. Meanwhile, another exodus is in the making in northern South America and the cycle starts again.

It is probable that the migratory insect which has attracted attention for the longest time is the desert locust (*Schistocerca gregaria*) of Africa and nearby areas. In the Book of Exodus, which was written about 1500 B.C., there is reference to the depredations of these migratory in-

This is the lesser migratory locust (*Melanoplus mexicanus*), a native to the Great Plains and the Rocky Mountain area. In former years a migratory form of this grasshopper, *M. spretus,* caused great crop and range damage in the Mid-West. Before the turn of the century it was America's most destructive insect.

sects. It says "the Lord brought an east wind upon the land all that day and all the night, and when it was morning the east wind brought the locusts. And the locusts went up all over the land of Egypt . . . and there remained not any green thing, either tree or herb of the field, through all the land of Egypt. . . . The Lord turned an exceeding strong west wind which took up the locusts and drove them into the Red Sea." Actually, there are at least two species of locusts involved; in addition to the desert locust, there is the migratory locust (*Locusta migratoria*), which ranges over a wide area including Africa, India, China and Australia. Both kinds migrate.

For thousands of years these voracious locusts have been the scourge of the arid regions to the south and east of the Mediterranean, where they often destroy every sprig of vegetation. As a matter of fact, the Latin equivalent of "locust" means "a burned place."

African migratory locusts fly in dense clouds, sometimes near the ground, at other times high in the air. Their direction of flight often changes. In strong convection currents the locusts may be carried to great heights, the swarms reaching thousands of feet. In some instances, swarms near the ground may be traveling in one direction while another swarm, higher up, is traveling in another direction. Studies of these locusts on the central Niger River Delta in West Africa showed that there are three generations a year. Two generations are produced on the flood plains and the others develop on higher ground during the rainy monsoon season. The desert locust has two color phases or forms; there is a yellow, non-migratory form and a pinkish, migratory form. Both forms have dark markings. The migratory form is apparently induced by high temperature, low humidity and crowded population. The migratory movements of these locusts are apparently in the direction of the prevailing winds. It is interesting to note that modern research has merely proven the correctness of the quotation from the Book of Exodus with respect to the wind blowing the swarm into the sea. Actually, these locusts fly long distances over water, having been found 1,200 miles at sea.

The migratory movements of the locusts have little or no relation to food supplies. During the morning they climb up on vegetation and feed, but, later in the day, they descend to the ground and move about. When a swarm is on the move, it does not necessarily stop when abundant food is reached; the insects may actually fly on over the desert and away from food. Temperature and other weather conditions are the factors that seem to govern their movements. There appears to be a direct relationship between migratory flights and body coloration. Those forms that congregate in swarms are of darker coloration, which results in more absorption of the sun's heat. This has been called "swarming coloration."

Here in the United States, before agricultural activities destroyed the natural balance, there were great migrations of Rocky Mountain locusts (*Melanoplus spretus*). Great migrating hordes of these insects once darkened the skies on the plains east of the Rockies where crops were often destroyed; the worst years were those from 1874 to 1877. One of these migrating swarms was estimated to contain 124 billion locusts. During another migration in Nebraska it was estimated that the swarm of locusts averaged half a mile high and was 100 miles wide and 300 miles long. Surveying instruments were used to study the swarm, and it was determined that, in places, it was nearly a mile high. The swarm was flying about five miles per hour. It is said that such a swarm, with the locusts' wings beating against the breeze, sounds like the roar of a distant waterfall. Generally, these swarms take off from the ground against the wind, but, once airborne, they turn and fly with it. Warm convection currents help to lift them, often to great heights. During the great locust plagues the situation in Nebraska became so serious that the original State Constitution had to be rewritten to take care of the economic problems. The new document was known as "The Grasshopper Constitution." It is now believed that these locusts were a migratory form or phase of the lesser migratory locust (*Melanoplus mexicanus mexicanus*) which is still common there. In this respect, the American migratory locusts resemble their African relatives. In both regions the migratory forms arise as a result of crowding and climatic factors. The development of the migratory forms are apparently natural adaptations which bring about dispersal when locust populations become too crowded. Fortunately for our farmers, the migratory form—the so-called *spretus* species—no longer seems to occur regularly, although there was a serious outbreak as late as 1938 in midwestern United States and Canada. It has been fairly well established that *Melanoplus spretus,* the migratory form, arises as a result of crowded conditions. As a matter of fact, Dr. J. R. Parker was able to produce such individuals in captivity by feeding the young on a high protein diet consisting of other grasshoppers. Actually, there is no reason why the destructive migratory form might not again appear if conditions should become favorable.

There is mute evidence of an ancient locust migration in the Beartooth Mountain Range in Montana, near the northeast corner of Yellowstone

National Park. On these high mountains, at an elevation of 11,000 feet, there is a glacier known as Grasshopper Glacier, for it contains the frozen remains of an enormous number of grasshoppers or locusts that were apparently trapped by the cold during migration. Specimens of these grasshoppers have been identified as *Melanoplus spretus,* the migratory form and as *Melanoplus mexicanus.* Dr. J. R. Parker, who has made several trips to the almost inaccessible glacier, has seen piles of the dead grasshoppers two feet high in front of the melting face of the glacier. Birds and fish fed on the preserved insects. How long these insects have been frozen in the glacial ice is an open question since it has not been possible to establish their age by carbon[14] methods. Recent observations of locust flights may, perhaps, explain the presence of the insects in the glacier. It has been noticed that the swarms settle to the earth when storm clouds appear or when there are sudden drops in temperature. It is probable that such climatic factors over these mountains caused the high-flying swarms of locusts to settle on the glacier where they were numbed by the cold and later covered by snows which gradually solidified into ice.

Grasshoppers have been found in glacial ice in other places, such as the Crazy Mountains in Central Montana and the Teton Mountains in Wyoming. African migratory locusts have been found frozen on Mount Kilimanjaro, as well as on Mount Kenya at an elevation of 16,000 feet.

Besides the insects mentioned previously, there are many other insects that exhibit migratory tendencies. Large numbers of dragonflies have been seen, apparently in migration, in various parts of the world. Such migrations have frequently been seen along the coast of New England. These dragonflies were accompanied by monarch butterflies. Dr. C. B. Williams calls attention to the fact that certain liver flukes that are parasitic in chickens and turkeys are carried, in their immature stage, by dragonflies. Outbreaks of this disease seem to coincide with mass migrations of the insects. In Poland the inhabitants are aware of this and pen up their poultry during dragonfly migrations.

So far we have considered only the winged insects as migrants, but there are certain wingless ants that spend their lives in migratory or nomadic travel. These are the army ants of the American tropics (*Eciton*) and the driver ants (*Dorylus*) of Africa, both of which have similar habits. Some species of *Eciton* range as far north as the southern half of the United States. In the Southeast I have watched with considerable interest migrating columns of these ants moving, hour after hour, past one

The blind army ants (*Eciton*) of the American tropics spend their lives in migratory movements through the jungles. They are hunters, their colonies consisting of thousands of individuals.

point. The most spectacular species, however, is the army ant (*Eciton hamatum*) found in the tropical areas of Central and South America. These ants move like ancient Mongol hordes; they are predatory and live by hunting other insects or small animals. Their colonies are very large, consisting probably of several hundred thousand individuals. The entire colony is nomadic for seventeen days, at the end of which time they settle down in a hollow tree or a similar location for about twenty days before recommencing their wanderings. The nomadic period of the colony's cycle begins as a result of secretions or odors given off by the newly emerged or *callow* workers. These callow workers are lighter in color than the older ones and do not go out on hunting raids until they are about five days old. During the nomadic or migratory period the ants move to new bivouacs almost every night, but, during the day, long raids are carried out in the vicinity to obtain food. They move to new "campsites" each night, usually between the hours of 3:00 P.M. and 9:00 P.M. Not all the ants engage in the daily raids; those that remain at the campsite form a living, protective wall about the queen and brood. That night when the colony moves again the weary hunters tag along behind while the rested ants take the lead, carrying the brood. These daily moves range from a few yards to hundreds of yards.

In the meantime, the larvae gradually develop until they are at last ready to spin their cocoons. When this occurs the ants are no longer stimulated to travel and so settle down for about twenty days of sedentary life. During this period the daily raids are shorter since less food is needed by the colony.

The periods of nomadic wandering that alternate with periods of fixed bivouacs coincide with the reproductive cycle of the queen. During the period when the colony is on the move, the queen is slender and her body is not filled with eggs. When she becomes swollen with eggs and unable to travel, and when the larvae from her previous period of egg laying are ready to pupate, the colony becomes stationary. Within seven days after the colony goes into this stationary period, the queen begins laying eggs, and during the ensuing few days almost 50,000 may be laid. In the laboratory, army ant queens have been found to lay 178 eggs per hour.

When the eggs hatch, the larvae are fed and cared for. Short hunting expeditions are made to obtain food. Meanwhile, the callow ants have emerged from their cocoons and the new eggs have hatched into larvae; the queen has regained her girlish figure and is again able to travel. The colony now takes to the road for another period of nomadic wandering during which the larvae gradually develop. These are carried along underneath the bodies of the long-legged workers. A nomadic life is now necessary since much food is needed to feed the growing young and the game in one area would soon be depleted if the colony remained stationary. Although most of the stationary periods are devoted to rearing more workers, during the dry season one of these periods is devoted to producing males and a few queens. These queens mate and leave the parent colony, taking with them small groups of workers in order to establish new colonies. Unlike most queen ants, these queens are wingless. Only the males are winged and have eyes. These males are often attracted to lights. This blind condition of the army ant workers is more remarkable when one considers that they hunt during the daylight hours. It would certainly seem that acute vision would be a necessity to an insect that spends its life on the hunt, but apparently other senses serve as well. With the coming of dawn, the colony begins to stir and foraging parties begin leaving. Their columns are a few inches wide, the individuals lined up in more or less parallel fashion. The columns often break up, following and capturing game, and then joining up again. When game is found it is surrounded, torn to bits and carried off. These ants will attack almost any living thing, whether it be insect, mouse or lizard. Larger creatures may be killed if unable to escape. During the nomadic period of their cycle the colony hunts over an area about two hundred yards in diameter. The next day, of course, the colony will probably have moved on to another site and be foraging over another area.

In considering the daily activities of these remarkable ants, it is interesting to compare their nomadic behavior to the tribes of American plains Indians that once lived by following the great herds of buffalo upon which they subsisted. In a way, their economy was similar to that of the army ants that also live by the hunt.

The migratory movement of flying insects such as butterflies, moths and dragonflies have been observed for a long while but what causes them and how the insects find their ways are still largely unsolved mysteries. It is known that dragonflies tend to fly upwind and migratory locusts downwind. Butterflies and the larger moths, on the other hand, are not much influenced by wind direction in their travels; their flights are truly migratory and, in many cases, resemble those of birds. Unlike birds, however, butterflies breed at both ends of their yearly journeys. This is, of course, necessary since insects are short lived and usually cannot survive to complete the round trips. The monarchs travel northward in spring, generation by generation, until late summer when they migrate southward in massed flights. What is so amazing about the southward flights of the monarchs is their accuracy of navigation, for they return again and again to the same roosting spots at the southern end of their long flights. Remember that none of these individuals has ever been there before. Migrating bands of monarchs follow the same paths through the sky each autumn. Such a migrating column of these butterflies was observed as it crossed Lake Ontario. At one point over the lake the butterflies all turned east for awhile and then continued on south. Succeeding swarms went through this same maneuver as if following a map. Why? We do not know.

We may speculate that migrating butterflies follow a sun compass as do the honeybees, but this has not been proven. Perhaps they have built-in compasses and are sensitive to the earth's magnetic field. Such a thing is possible since it has been found that certain snails orientate themselves in response to this force. Snails, it was found, in a magnetic field turned in a clockwise direction a day or two before the new and full moons and counterclockwise just before the first and third quarter. There seems to be a relationship between the moon and the magnetic field, and the responses of the snails are reversed in a semimonthly rhythm. Here perhaps is a clue to the navigational ability of certain animals, possibly even that of butterflies and other migratory insects. In any event, there is no question but that certain insects such as butterflies do engage in migratory flights in definite directions. Dr. C. B. Williams has noticed that certain migrating insects position their bodies in crosswinds in such a way as to keep on course. Here is evidence that they are not at the mercy of winds but are following a true compass course.

On any summer day there are always large numbers of insects in the air, sometimes even at great heights. Some of these are active flyers whereas others ride the rising columns of heated air. The study of aerial plankton has been facilitated by trapping from airplanes. The winds are great travelers over the face of the earth, and with them are carried all manner of animal and plant life. It is thus that many insects—accidentally or otherwise—are carried to new areas. It is the regular means of dispersal of many aphids, moths, gnats and numerous other insects. Even wingless spiders have been trapped at great heights. Some insects such as the milkweed bugs cling to milkweed seeds to be airlifted great distances. We have already seen how certain ants as well as honeybees navigate by sun compass and also use polarized light. The navigation of insects is a fascinating subject and one that is open to further research.

chapter six

The Water Realm

IT was once my good fortune to live for a time beside a tropical coral reef. Each day I explored the deep pools in the reef where aquatic life in amazing form and color swam through the crystalline depths. Sometimes I floated face-down and watched the play of life through diving goggles; at other times I dived downward into the depths where the sunlight, broken into shifting patterns, rippled over the coral sand. Sometimes I explored the tide pools at night when the full moon illuminated the water with amazing clarity. But the days were the best. Always, of course, I was merely a temporary intruder from the world above—at best, a spectator.

Within those deep pools were dark caves extending beneath the reef, but there was no way of telling how far or where they went. Within them lived dangerous moray eels and octopi, and I dared not explore their recesses. It was the sunlit tide pools, however, that fascinated me most. Here colorful sea anemones spread their flowerlike rings of tentacles, and colorful, branching corals grew everywhere. At my approach the anemones withdrew their tentacles and became fleshy balls, but the corals were stationary and solid with calcareous skeletons capable of tearing the flesh of a careless swimmer. Among their branches lived small clownfish decorated in colorful, improbable patterns. Everywhere, beautifully colored fishes of rainbow hues darted about in the shifting sunlight. There were butterflyfish of many kinds and graceful Moorish idols. On the bottom, resting quietly, lay lionfish, attractively colored but protected by deadly spines. Here and there among the corals were pincushionlike sea urchins. These, too, were armed with poison spines. Each creature played its part in the underwater drama. Sometimes I captured the brilliant little reef fishes and took them to the surface, but their colors quickly faded—erased by death.

While exploring the depths of these tide pools it gradually dawned on me that something was missing. Living things in great variety were present, but I could not find insects of any kind. In any fresh-water pool at home the principal aquatic animals are insects, but the sea, even though it covers most of the globe, is deficient in insect life. I sometimes saw waterstriders (genus *Halobates*) skipping about over the surfaces of quiet estuaries along the tropical seashore, but, except for these semiaquatic insects, only a few others have been able to return successfully to the ancient cradle of life. The waterstriders are often found hundreds of miles from land, especially in areas covered with seaweed, but they are not truly aquatic—they live *upon* the sea, not in it. There are a number of insects that inhabit the tidal zone between the land and the sea. Here, where the sea meets the land, is a special habitat where organic debris is tossed up by tides and waves. Here also is where sea animals meet and compete with those from the land. Many insects live in this tension zone; there are a few beetles—tiger beetles, for example—and the common seashore springtails, *Anurida maritima,* that feed on dead organic matter. The beetles advance and retreat with the tides, but the springtails burrow into the sand when the waves advance. The larvae of the shore-flies (family Ephydridae) are true marine insects that live in sea water or in brackish pools in some parts of the world. The adult flies are often very abundant about tide pools, where they walk over the surface of the water. Some ephydrids also breed in salt lakes of the West where they are called "brine" flies." Here they often occur in great numbers, and the adults literally form clouds over the lakes. The species found in the Great Salt Lake is *Ephydra riparia,* but the species occurring in California's salt lakes is *Ephydra hians.* This latter species was known as the koo-tsabe fly to the Indians, who collected the pupae in large numbers and used them as food.

Even more remarkable are the petroleum flies, belonging to the same family. These flies (*Psilopa petrolei*) have been able to adapt themselves, during the larval stage, to life in natural pools of crude petroleum. This is strange indeed when one considers that petroleum and its products are often used as insecticides. These extraordinary fly larvae are found in California and in the Trinidad oil fields. So well are they adapted to life in thick crude oil that they can exist nowhere else. Here they swim about searching for food, and, as might be expected, take considerable oil into their digestive systems, but because this is not absorbed through the walls of the gut it does them no harm. The adult flies, too, are more or less adapted to this curious habitat, and they walk about over the oily surface with impunity.

A number of midge flies (family Chironomidae) have also invaded salt water, where their larvae sometimes occur in large numbers. In Australia and New Zealand, there is a caddisfly larva (order Trichoptera) that has adapted itself to life in tide pools where it feeds on seaweed. Its name is *Philanisus plebejus.* Other species of these interesting insects, whose aquatic larvae construct pebble cases, are very common in freshwater streams.

Thus, we find that some insects have successfully invaded not only the sea but the inhospitable environments of petroleum pools and mineral springs. It seems odd that more insects have been unable to do so. This is another biological mystery that has never been explained. There are, of course, some theories.

Any creature that dwells in the sea survives only in the face of the world's keenest competition, and it was to escape this competition that the ancestors of the insects left the sea in the first place. In order to leave the sea, they had, of course, to become air-breathers. In time their bodies became so perfectly adapted to this new way of life that they could not easily change back. The sea is a restless world. It is always in motion: winds cause waves to beat continually upon the shore and the gravitational pull of the sun and the moon causes tides to sweep across its surface. Life for an air-breathing insect in such an unstable medium would, to say the least, be complicated. More important, perhaps, is the nature of sea water itself. Sea water contains high concentrations of various salts which result in a high osmotic pressure. Thus, from a purely physiological point of view, life for an insect in sea water would require some basic body changes. Very few have made the necessary adaptations.

One of the most unique habitats occupied by any insect is that in hot springs which, in addition to being quite hot, are often highly mineralized. During the years from 1923 to 1932 Dr. Charles T. Brues of Harvard University carried on extensive research on the insect fauna of hot springs and made several expeditions to various parts of the West to collect and study them. He found that insect life apparently could not live in water above 122°F. Only the thermal mite (*Thermacarus*)—not an insect—was found living a degree or two beyond that point. This was also the hottest water in which he found higher plants growing. In Yellowstone Park, blue-green algae, however, have been found living at temperatures of about 193°F., which is very hot, indeed. Dr. Brues found that as water temperatures climbed, the number of insect species decreased. He recorded 60 different species of water beetles at 86°F., but found only two species living in water at 115°F. Soldier-fly larvae were also found in water at the latter temperature. Actually, insects are never very abundant in warm springs, even those of lower temperatures. One might wonder why more insect life is not found in such situations since these would seem to be ideal habitats, free of extreme temperature fluctuations. The answer probably lies in the life cycles of the insects which must, in most cases, leave the water to mate. Since the temperatures of warm springs are constant, insects cannot adjust their cycles to coincide with the seasons. A dragonfly larva, for example, that emerged from the warm water and transformed to the adult, winged stage in winter would have little chance of survival.

Many millions of years ago when the remote ancestors of the insects left the water and became air-breathers, they evolved in infinite variety and abundance and spread to every habitable land. But the water, especially the fresh water of lakes and streams, was still there. Here was a habitat that offered refuge from the land where life was becoming more and more crowded. As a result, many insects returned, step by step, to the realm below the water's surface. Evolution had changed its mind, so to speak. In the water the insects encountered keen competition, of course. There they were met by the fishes and crustaceans that had never left the water, but they survived in spite of this. It is probably safe to say that no insect is completely aquatic; beneath the water's surface they live on borrowed time, and most of them must return to the air to mate and lay eggs. Generally speaking, it is only during their immature stages that they are ever completely adapted to life without air. When adult forms dwell below the surface, some provision must be made for them to obtain air from the surface just as a skin-diver must take a supply of air with him. Water, itself, is composed of oxygen and hydrogen, but no animal has ever solved the problem of separating the atoms of oxygen from those of hydrogen. Only green plants have this ability. Many insects, of course, do use the oxygen that is dissolved in water.

The larvae of mayflies (order Ephemerida) live in ponds and streams. The adults often emerge in large numbers but their adult lives are very short.

We can divide the aquatic insects into three categories. First, there are those that merely live in the vicinity of water, or on its surface. Examples are waterstriders and toad bugs. The bodies of these insects are usually not greatly modified. In the second category are those that live beneath the surface but often take to the air and fly. Here are included the diving beetles and water bugs. Last are the so-called true aquatic insects that live beneath the surface film and will die if exposed to air. Examples are dragonfly young and the immature stages of flies. Yet, even in these insects it is only the immature forms that are aquatic—when they become adults they must return to the air.

As we have seen, the deficiency of oxygen in water is the factor that complicates it as an environment for active creatures such as insects. Dissolved oxygen, in varying concentrations, is always present in all

The voracious larvae of dobsonflies (*Corydalus cornutus*) live in water where they feed on other aquatic insects. After about three years they leave the water and transform into the adult winged stage. The larvae are often called hellgrammites.

bodies of water, but it varies with the depth and the season. Oxygen is always being absorbed into lakes, especially at their surfaces. During the warm days of summer the surfaces of deep lakes are heated and the surface water becomes lighter in weight. The water in the depths remains cool and heavy. Thus the light surface water does not mix with the deeper, heavier water; the two remain sharply separated. The deep water becomes stagnant and more or less devoid of life because there is little oxygen there. Here live only a few especially adapted insects such as bloodworms or the young stages of *Chironomus* midges. In winter the lower water levels are better supplied with oxygen and many aquatic animals then move down. A number of aquatic animals, such as copepods, shift up and down in a daily rhythm in many lakes and ponds. These are fed upon by phantom midge fly larvae (*Chaoborus*) that rise to the surface at night and descend into deep water during the day as do their prey. These transparent larvae are equipped with two pairs of gas bubbles that enable them to rise and sink quite rapidly. This is accomplished by compressing the gas bubbles or allowing them to expand to control their buoyancy. A similar mechanism is found in mosquito larvae of the genus *Corethra*.

The aquatic realm is a unique habitat. Most substances become heavier and denser as their temperatures are lowered. Water, on the other hand, reaches its greatest density at 39°F., then begins to expand and become lighter again below that temperature. Thus, ice is lighter than water and floats. This one fact makes aquatic life possible in northern climates. Ice forms on the surfaces of ponds and lakes, leaving the bottom free of ice and available to aquatic insects, fish and other animals. Of course, if a body of water froze solid it would be unsuitable as a habitat to most aquatic creatures.

In order for an insect to thrive in the water it must first solve the problem of obtaining an adequate supply of oxygen. In this respect we can divide the aquatic insects into two groups. First, there are those insects that utilize, in one way or another, oxygen obtained directly from the air. This is done in several ways. The water beetles and some other insects make periodic trips to the surface to trap air bubbles, and when the oxygen in these bubbles is exhausted they return for new bubbles. These bubbles not only serve as underwater supplies of air, but also function

The larvae or nymphs of stoneflies live in streams where water is well aerated. They probably feed mostly on vegetable material and are an important item of fish food in many places. The adults are winged and do not feed.

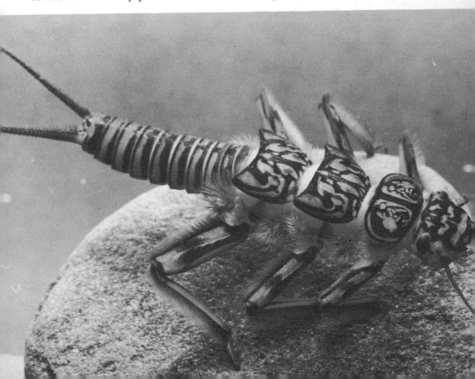

Ranatra, the water scorpion, has raptorial front legs for capturing prey. It breathes by pushing its snorklelike tail up through the surface film.

as hydrostatic organs which enable the insect to maintain its depth in the water as in the case of *Chaoborus*. These hydrostatic organs resemble the swim bladders of fishes or the ballast tanks of submarines. Other insects, such as the water scorpion (*Ranatra*) and giant water bug (*Belostoma*), have snorkle arrangements or breathing tubes which are pushed up through the surface film to obtain air. Mosquito larvae, or wrigglers, have a similar arrangement. It has been found that a *Culex* mosquito larva can normally obtain enough oxygen to last about ten minutes.

To large creatures like ourselves, the surface film of water does not appear very strong, yet if we gently lay a greasy needle upon it, the needle will float. This is because the surface film acts like a thin, stretched membrane. This surface film pulls in all directions; it has *surface tension*. This tension has considerable force.* To a small creature the surface

* The tension value for water at ordinary temperatures is about 75 dynes per centimeter. A dyne is the force needed to give a mass of one gram an acceleration of one centimeter per second squared.

film of water constitutes a definite barrier through which it must break to obtain air. It is also a surface over which such insects as waterstriders can easily walk. As a matter of fact, even water shrews, which are mammals the size of small mice, often run over the surface of woodland pools. If a small nonaquatic insect is so unfortunate as to be trapped beneath the surface film, it will drown just as if the water's surface were covered with ice. When a mosquito wriggler rises to the surface its breathing tube penetrates the surface film and a ring of greasy hairs expands, locking it, so to speak, to the surface. In this position the breathing tube is open to the air. These hairs are called *hydrophobe* hairs (a term meaning "water hating") since they repel water. That is the reason they can readily penetrate the surface film and automatically spread out. In most such aquatic insects there are small oil-secreting glands that keep the hydrophobe hairs oiled. These hairs are also used for aquatic respiration in another way. The bodies of some aquatic beetles are entirely covered with water-repelling hairs so that a thin film of air encases the insect. Such insects, when submerged, look as if they had been coated with silver. Dytiscid beetles carry quantities of air beneath their elytra, or wing covers. The silvery coating of air on the bodies of insects such as backswimmers (family Notonectidae) and water boatmen (family Corixidae) serves a dual purpose. It not only serves as an immediate supply of air while the insect is submerged but also absorbs oxygen from the surrounding water. When the oxygen content of the air film surrounding the insects becomes low, more oxygen is absorbed into it. Thus, this air film serves as a sort of external lung. Water beetles, too, obtain oxygen by absorbing it into their trapped air bubbles and, as a result, can remain submerged for as long as 36 hours. When actively swimming, however, most of these insects cannot usually obtain enough oxygen by this process and must go to the surface at intervals for new supplies. This is especially true during warm weather when the oxygen content of water is low.

Best adapted, probably, to an aquatic life are those insects that are equipped with gills during their immature stages, as, for example, the dragonflies, damselflies, mayflies and caddisflies. Such insects have closed tracheal systems; they do not come to the surface to renew their oxygen supply, but absorb it through gills which usually contain numerous branches of the tracheal system. Actually, these gills are merely extensions of the insect's body wall which allow more surface contact with the water, from which oxygen can be absorbed and carbon dioxide diffused

Dytiscid water beetles dwell beneath the surface but often leave the water and fly. Now and then they swim to the surface for bubbles of air which are trapped beneath their wing covers. Their larvae are elongate and are called water tigers since they capture and devour small water animals including small fish and tadpoles.

out. Gills may be located almost anywhere on the body. Damselfly and mayfly nymphs have three gills located at the tip of the abdomen. Aquatic moth larvae of the genus *Nymphula,* have 400 gill filaments. Caddisfly larvae also have many gill filaments. The skin of black fly larvae (*Simulium*) is supplied with a network of fine capillaries for respiratory purposes. These larvae live in swiftly flowing streams where oxygen is relatively abundant. A similar arrangement is found in midge larvae (*Chironomus*) and some other insects.

Probably the most interesting respiratory gills are those of the Odonata, the dragonflies and damselflies. Damselfly nymphs, as we have said, are equipped with three caudal gills, but dragonfly nymphs have their gills within the rectal cavity. The water which is sucked in and out of this cavity is used in respiration and, as well, jet-propels the insect through the water.

Caddis nymphs, also, have rectal gills in addition to gill filaments on their body surfaces. If the gills of these nymphs are amputated the nymphs appear to live normally, indicating that these gills may merely be safety devices, needed during periods when the water becomes deficient in dissolved oxygen. When the water warms up, as in mid-summer, its dissolved oxygen content drops. Cold water usually contains more oxygen than warm water, which is the reason that aquatic life is usually more abundant in cold mountain streams and lakes than in warm southern waters. The same situation also occurs in the ocean.

Another, and rather unique, means by which some aquatic insects obtain air, is by piercing the air-filled stems of submerged plants. The riffle beetles (*Elmis*) and caterpillars of the genus *Hydrocampa* bite into the tissues of plants to obtain air. The larvae of certain leaf beetles (*Donacia*) feed on the roots of aquatic plants and pierce with their hollow spines the same plants' air reservoirs for oxygen. This air trapped by plants often contains as much as ten percent oxygen. Of interest, too, is the method of obtaining air used by *Mansonia* mosquitoes, both larvae and pupae. These mosquito young live in ponds and pools, usually with muddy bottoms, where aquatic plants are abundant. The larvae, or wrigglers, attach themselves to submerged plants or their roots by penetrating them with their siphons or air tubes. The larva approaches the plant, tail end first, and the strong bristles are inserted into it. Three pairs of minute hooks then emerge from the siphon and anchor it firmly. The pupae, too, obtain air by piercing plants with their sharp breathing tubes, or "trumpets." The pupae of some species of *Mansonia* mosquitoes attach themselves permanently to plants, but in others the attachment is temporary and they can move from one plant to another. These mosquitoes are commonly associated with such plants as water lettuce, *Pistia;* cattail, *Typha;* water lily, *Nymphea;* and arrow-head, *Sagittaria.* Most other kinds of mosquito larvae and pupae move freely about in the water, usually resting just below the surface with their breathing tubes penetrating the surface film for air. When disturbed they descend by wriggling motions until all is quiet and then return to the surface. In Africa there is a mosquito, *Aedomyia,* which obtains air by inserting its siphon or breathing tube into air bubbles trapped on the undersides of aquatic plant leaves.

Insects that live in water have developed methods of locomotion that are considerably different from those used on land. A few kinds, such as caddis larvae, merely crawl about on the bottom or among aquatic plants. These require no special adaptations to the fluid habitat. In most cases, however, water locomotion requires considerable specialization and some of the ways in which aquatic insects have solved the problems are quite interesting. The water film, as we have already seen, is like a stretched membrane to small creatures, on which they can run or walk about. The water striders (family Gerridae) have greatly elongated legs on which they are able to walk easily over the water surface. Their tarsi, or foot segments, contain oil glands that keep them water-resistant. If one of these insects is examined closely as it rests on the water, it can be seen that its feet make tiny depressions in the elastic surface film. This film is so strong that this lightweight insect probably could not break through even if it attempted to do so.

Actually, considerable water area is required to support a full-grown water strider, which accounts for the long, widely spread legs which distribute its weight. It is especially the two hind pairs of legs that are used for walking over the water; the front pair are used for capturing small insects upon which they feed.

While most water striders spend their lives above the surface, the marine waterstriders, mentioned previously, often crawl beneath the surface during calm weather. How they survive severe storms is still a mystery, but they seem to be completely at home on the sea, where they lay their eggs on seaweed, often long distances from land.

Other insects besides the water striders can walk upon the surface film. One of these is the water measurer (family Hydrometridae) that lives among submerged vegetation and is often seen walking slowly over the surface. They are shaped somewhat like miniature walkingstick insects. Flies of various kinds can also walk in safety over water. Some of these midges and gnats have long legs and thus seem especially adapted to life there. Some of these flies are quite large. Crane flies (family Tipulidae) often alight on water.

The smaller the insect, the easier it can walk or jump over the surface. Very tiny insects do not need widely spread feet to support their weights. Perhaps the best example of these featherweight insects is the water spring-

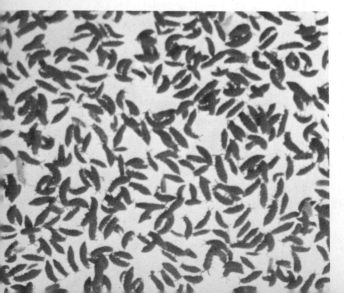

To such tiny insects as springtails, the water's surface film is a relatively solid surface and they have no difficulty in hopping about over it.

tail (*Podura aquatica*); this minute insect can hop about over the water surface as if it were as solid as concrete. Its adaptation for life on water film is rather unique. Like all members of the collembola family, these insects have a ventral tube, or *collophore,* extending downward from the first abdominal segment. A pair of adhesive sacs are present at the end of the collophore and these can be everted and used to anchor the insect to any smooth surface. In the case of the water springtail, the collophore is "water-loving" or *hydrophilic* and penetrates the surface film, anchoring the insect in place. Like all springtails, too, the water springtail has a jumping organ or spring attached to the tip of its abdomen. When the insect is at rest this spring is bent forward under the body, and locked in place by a catch. When the insect finds it necessary to jump, this spring is released and strikes against the surface, propelling the insect through the air. The aquatic springtail's short legs are waxy and rest upon the surface film.

Insects that propel themselves through the depths of the water have even more specialized equipment than those that live on the surface. Propulsion through water is like flying in many respects, the chief difference being the density of the medium. Because of its greater density water tends to support the insect, so it is not faced with the need for expanded wings as are insects that fly in the air. The propelling organs usually consist of legs modified into oars. The water boatmen, backswimmers and diving beetles have their hind legs elongated and covered with stiff hairs to fit them for propulsion. In swimming, these legs are usually moved in unison like oars. Water-scavenger beetles, however, move the swimming legs alternately just as beetles do when walking on dry land; this causes them to swim with a wobbling motion. Since most water insects swim by using their legs like oars, their movement through the water usually consists of a series of darting motions.

The use of wings in underwater propulsion is quite rare, but this is the method employed by the fairy fly. This is actually a minute wasp (family Mymaridae) that uses its paddlelike wings to swim down into the water in search of dragonfly eggs in which it deposits its own eggs. Within the dragonfly eggs the fairy fly larvae develop as parasites. These minute wasps are among the smallest insects known, some of them having bodies as small as 0.21 millimeter (about a hundredth of an inch). Since some dragonfly eggs are inserted in aquatic plants, the fairy flies must penetrate the plants as well as the walls of the dragonfly eggs to lay their own microscopic eggs.

Of all the methods of swimming used by aquatic insects, however, that employed by dragonfly larvae or nymphs is by far the most interesting. When not alarmed or when stalking prey these insects use their legs to crawl about, but if alarmed they use jet propulsion. Water is drawn into the rectum and forcibly expelled. This is done very rapidly, causing the larva to be propelled through the water in a series of spurts. During escape the legs are also employed as oars. Jet propulsion is not used by all dragonfly larvae, but it is certainly an interesting innovation and one also used by marine squids and octopi. Which animals can claim priority for the "invention" of this swimming technique is open to question.

There are a number of different families of beetles whose members dwell in water, but the main ones are diving beetles belonging to the families Dytiscidae and Hydrophilidae. These beetles are quite similar in general appearance, and differ from each other only in anatomical details and in feeding habits. Another family of water beetles, the Gyrinidae, is quite common in most places. They are called whirligig beetles because they swim rapidly about in circles over the water's surface.

The diving beetles are rather large, hard-bodied insects that swim rapidly with their oarlike legs. Sometimes they take to the air and fly, and are frequently attracted in large numbers to bright lights. They fly from pond to pond, thus populating new bodies of water. They are predaceous in both adult and larval stages, although some hydrophilids are supposed to feed largely as scavengers. Water beetles are voracious predators, often capturing and devouring aquatic insects, snails, worms, leeches, tadpoles, small fish and frogs. The female beetles usually insert their eggs in water plants, but the female of the great silver water beetle of England clings upside-down to some water plant or floating leaf and spins a silken cocoon complete with a periscopelike air tube projecting above the water surface. Within this container she lays her eggs. Water beetle larvae are known as water tigers; these elongate larvae are equipped with long legs and sharp, sicklelike jaws for the capture of prey. In feeding, the prey is not chewed up and swallowed as in the case with most beetles. After capture, an enzymelike material is injected into the prey and its fluids are then sucked into the water tiger's stomach through grooves on the inner sides of the mandibles. It is interesting that although the diving beetle larvae are truly aquatic, they always leave the water to pupate.

Whereas the diving beetles inhabit the depths of the water, the gyrinids or whirligig beetles dwell mostly upon the surface, half above and half below the surface film. These common beetles are quite gregarious, often being seen swimming about on the quiet surfaces of ponds in large numbers. In spite of the fact that they swim at high speed, they never appear to bump into each other or other objects. It is believed that a sensory organ called Johnston's organ, located on the second segment of the antennae, enables them to detect the presence of nearby objects or the shoreline. It is possible that this is a sort of radar sense that detects compression waves in the surface film through which they swim. Since their bodies are half submerged, their eyes are divided so that one portion of each eye is above the water and the other portion below the surface. This enables them to detect enemies or prey both above and below the surface film giving them the appearance of having four eyes. They are predaceous, feeding upon small insects during both adult and larval stages. The larvae, which live at the bottoms of ponds, are elongated and bear tracheal gills along the sides of their bodies.

Gyrinids swim by means of their middle and hind legs, which have the form of short paddles. The forelegs are adapted for grasping prey. Most of our native gyrinids are black, but some of those found in other parts of the world are of bright metallic colors. Some have glands that emit a musky odor, and these are often called "mellow-bugs."

The water world seems to have attracted quite a collection of members of the bug clan or Hemiptera. These range in size from minute kinds to giant water bugs up to three or four inches long. The largest kinds are found in the tropics. As in land-inhabiting forms they are equipped with piercing and sucking mouthparts and almost all are predaceous.

Probably the most common of the aquatic bugs are the water boatmen (family Corixidae) and backswimmers (family Notonectidae). Both resemble miniature submarines, but they swim with oarlike legs. As their name implies, the backswimmers swim on their backs. Just why nature saw fit to evolve these insects in an upside-down position is a mystery. Perhaps it is an adaptation for capturing prey, for they approach their game by drifting up under it. If handled carelessly, backswimmers can bite severely. Their cousins, the water boatmen, are quite similar except that they do not swim on their backs. Both kinds obtain air by trapping it in or on their bodies, where it shines like a silver envelope. They often leave the water and fly. It is said that in Mexico the eggs of water boatmen are so abundant that they are often collected and used as food. Usually water boatmen and backswimmers attach their eggs to aquatic plants, but there is one kind of water boatman that glues its eggs to crayfish.

There are many other aquatic bugs. The voracious giant water bugs (family Belostomatidae) are discussed in a later chapter on hunting insects. Classified also among the bug clan are the water striders (family Gerridae) and toad bugs (family Gelastocoridae). The toad bugs hop about on the damp margins of streams and lakes capturing minute insects. They resemble small toads, even to their protruding eyes.

No consideration of aquatic insects would be complete without mention of the remarkable caddisflies (order Trichoptera) which, during their larval stages, construct portable stone or stick cases in which they live safe from most enemies. Because of their special interest as insect craftsmen they have been discussed at length elsewhere.

Probably the commonest as well as the most interesting of the insects that inhabit the water realm are the dragonflies and their near-relatives, the damselflies. They belong to an ancient insect tribe (order Odonata) whose ancestry extends far back in time. Like most aquatic insects, it is only during their immature stages that they dwell beneath the surface film. The order Odonata is divided into the Zygoptera, or damselflies, and the Anisoptera, or true dragonflies. Damselflies are usually smaller than dragonflies and rest with their wings folded over their backs. Damselfly nymphs or larvae have three expanded gills attached to the posterior ends of their abdomens. Dragonflies are usually much larger; they are stronger flyers and always rest on perches with their wings held at right angles to their bodies. In wing expanse these insects vary from less than an inch to seven and a half inches in the case of *Megaloprepus caerulatus,* a tropical American dragonfly. They are all highly predaceous, capturing small insects on the wing, which are devoured in flight or at rest. As an indication of their wide distribution, the Odonata are known by many common names, including snake doctor and devil's darning needle. The adults are among the most graceful and swiftest of all flying insects. Some are quite colorful; the wings of many are marked with red and other bright colors. The green darner has a bright green thorax and its abdomen is sky-blue with black markings. Few butterflies are more attractively dressed.

From the standpoint of aerodynamics, the wings of dragonflies are well designed. Their leading edges are thickened so that as they vibrate up

and down, the hind portions of the wings flex causing a forward thrust.
Unlike most other four-winged insects, their fore wings and hind wings
do not move in unison, but as the fore wings rise the hind wings beat
downward.

During the first part of their adult lives dragonflies spend their time
flying about over the countryside hunting prey, but as the time for mating approaches they tend to congregate about pools or other damp locations, depending on the habitat preferred by that particular species. The
males usually establish territories as do birds and patrol and defend these
against other males. The size of the territory tends to be about the same
for the members of a species, and it varies with the size of the dragonfly
—large species having larger territories than the smaller species. These
territories vary in width from a foot or two to eight or ten feet, and the

The dragonfly is a hunter without peer in the insect world. It hunts on the
wing. The young or larvae dwell beneath the surface and are also predaceous.

length is, in general, about as far as the insect can detect motion, which is up to approximately thirty feet. Any other male dragonfly that flies into this zone is attacked with vigor and a noisy clash of wings can often be heard. Some males do not physically attack each other, being satisfied merely to engage in aggressive displays. Within this zone the male does his courting and, if he is successful, mating occurs and eggs are laid.

Dragonflies have most unusual mating habits. The copulatory organs of the male are located at the front end of the abdomen on its lower surface. Before mating, the male bends the tip of his abdomen forward and transfers sperm into the copulatory organ. During the act of mating, the male, using clasping organs at the tip of his abdomen, grasps the female by her neck or prothorax. She then bends her abdomen forward and receives sperm from the male's copulatory organ. In the vicinity of ponds it is a common sight to see mating dragonflies flying in tandem, since they remain attached for some time. In some species the female lays her eggs while still clasped by the male. This even occurs in species in which the female crawls down beneath the surface of the water to lay her eggs on aquatic plants. In some species the male picks out what he considers to be a suitable site for egg-laying before the arrival of the female. However, the female may or may not choose to lay her eggs in that location. There is another remarkable feature of mating of these insects. In many species the clasping organ of the male is shaped so that it fits the part of the female clasped during copulation. Seemingly, the male organs will not fit females of other species. They are thus like keys and apparently prevent mating with other species.

The selecting of egg-laying sites is largely done as a result of visual stimulus. Dragonflies can often be seen flying low over the surface of the water and dipping the tips of their abdomens. It is believed that this is a testing act to make sure that it is a water surface. However, these otherwise alert insects are often deceived since they have been seen laying eggs on the shiny tops of automobiles or on shiny cement floors. Dragonflies have also been seen flying along paved roads, acting as though they were following water courses. Usually, however, they are quite particular about the locations in which they lay eggs. Some kinds prefer bogs while others are partial to open lakes or streams and will oviposit only in those locations to which their young are, presumably, best adapted. Some kinds even specialize in certain types of streams—some prefer streams with irregular margins, while others are partial to those having straight shorelines. Still others favor rapids where they are apparently attracted by the bright reflections from the tumbling water.

The eggs of many stream-dwelling dragonflies are covered with a gelatinous material that expands and becomes adhesive on contact with water. This causes the eggs to adhere to aquatic plants and prevents them from floating downstream. A most unusual adaptation has recently been found in a small African dragonfly which lays its eggs in rapidly flowing streams. The eggs of this species have an attached filament that uncoils after the egg is laid in the water and anchors it to plants. There is considerable variation in egg-laying habits among the various species of dragonflies. Some merely drop their eggs on the surface, while others actually crawl down and cement their eggs to aquatic plants or insert them into plants. In still other cases the eggs are attached to plants or twigs above the water. Some kinds that crawl beneath the surface do so with their wings closed in such a position that a bubble of air is trapped between them. It is believed that this air serves for respiration while they are submerged.

Although we ordinarily think of dragonflies and damselflies as inhabitants of streams and pools, there are some off-beat species that lay their eggs in unusual circumstances, to which their larvae or nymphs seem to be especially adapted. For example, a few dragonflies that inhabit dense tropical forests lay their eggs among the dead leaves on the forest floor, where their larvae develop. In many parts of the world, including North America, certain dragonfly larvae dwell in damp bogs where they construct burrows in the mud, from which they emerge at night to hunt for small nocturnal insects and spiders. The larvae of other Odonata have adapted themselves to life in the pools of water, or leaf-tanks, held in air plants or bromeliads which often grow high on trees in tropical areas. Some larvae also develop in the water that collects in the leaf axels of the tropical screwpine, or pandanus. In this same habitat dwell the larvae of the pandanus mosquito (*Aedes pandani*) one of the most vicious biters of the tropics. The larvae of dragonflies seem to have adapted themselves to a wide variety of situations. Seemingly, almost any damp location or pool of water can serve as a larval habitat. The length of time spent in the larval stage varies greatly among the various species. In some, larval development is completed within a month, but in others five or six years are required.

The larvae of nearly all the Odonata are predaceous, feeding upon small aquatic insects, especially the larval forms of chironomids and even

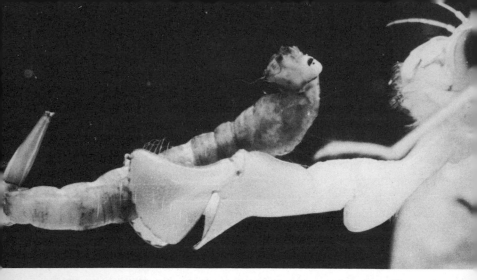

Dragonfly larvae have unique mouthparts that fit over their faces like masks. When any small insect approaches, the "mask" flips out and grasps it. Here a dragonfly larva has captured a mosquito wriggler.

When full grown, a dragonfly larva crawls up out of the water and the adult insect emerges. This transformation usually occurs at night.

mosquito wrigglers. It is their unique method of capturing prey, however, that is of special interest. The lower lip, or *labium,* is elongated and hinged near its base so that it can be extended like a human arm. At the tip of this organ are two jawlike structures which are used in capturing and holding prey. In feeding, the prey is slowly approached and the labium then flashes out and grasps it. Large dragonfly larvae can seize prey as far as an inch away. When not in use this labial organ is folded over the lower portion of the insect's "face" like a mask. No similar structure is found anywhere else in the insect world.

When growth is completed, the larva crawls toward the shore and eventually onto a plant; a split appears down its back and slowly the adult dragonfly or damselfly emerges. At first its wings are wet and crumpled, but these rapidly expand into cellophanelike vanes and the adult insect is ready for the air. It is quickly transformed from an ugly creeping creature dwelling beneath the water into the insect world's most agile and alert aerial acrobat.

Probably the world's most unique aquatic insect is a grasshopper (*Marellia*), found in Uruguay, Argentina, Peru, British Guiana and Surinam, that has its hind legs modified into oars for swimming. It lays its eggs underwater, where they are attached to the undersides of the leaves of aquatic plants. While these unusual grasshoppers are usually to be found on the upper surfaces of water lily leaves, they take to the water readily when alarmed.

Here in the United States is found another aquatic member of the grasshopper tribe. This is *Orchelimum bradleyi,* one of the long-horned meadow grasshoppers that has been recorded from Florida and from the Okefenokee Swamp. Its aquatic habits have been recorded by Francis Harper and by other observers. These insects live among the grasslike plants that grow out of the water of lakes and the watery stretches of the Okefenokee, but when alarmed they jump into the water and vanish. Here they cling to submerged plants until danger has disappeared. Apparently they can remain submerged for several minutes.

chapter seven

The Hunters

INSECTS are versatile creatures; among them are found many "trades" or ways of making a living. The similarities between certain insect and human professions are often quite amazing. Indeed, such professions were practiced by the insect legions millions of years before the time of modern mammals and man. During the long, slow evolution of insects these professions gradually came into being as specialized habits developed. The majority of insects are plant feeders, but from them were evolved the keen-eyed hunters, the seed gatherers, and the fungus growers, as well as the gangsters and chiselers which live by their wits. With the passing of time, each insect gradually perfected its own special means of competing for a living with other insects and other animals.

The first insects may have been scavengers like their remote ancestors, the trilobites, but at an early date they became plant feeders and many —probably the majority—still are. Eating plants is a simple and unspecialized means of gaining a livelihood, but during the Permian and Upper Carboniferous periods the hunting profession came into vogue. Thus, insects have been preying on each other for at least 200 million years. The gigantic dragonflies of the ancient Carboniferous forests practiced the original aerial warfare against flying insects of lesser size. Even in their nymphal stages these dragonflies probably had predatory habits.

Bull-dog ants (*Myrmecia*) of tropical countries are very vicious as might be guessed from their appearance. They are large and aggressive.

You may wonder why predatism developed at all in view of the abundance of plant foods. It is a fact, however, that among almost all animal groups the flesh-eating habit has become the established way of life for certain species. A carnivorous diet has the advantage of a high protein content; the food has already been converted from plant to animal tissue.

No one insect group has a monopoly on hunting, and the habit occurs in almost every order. Closely allied to the hunting trade are those of trapping and ambush; these are merely variations in hunting techniques. The great tarantula hawk wasp seeks out tarantulas and stings them with its poison dart; the green-camouflaged mantis rests quietly among the leaves and its raptorial front legs flash out and impale any insect so foolish as to stray too near. In the insect world there are really only two kinds —the hunters and the hunted. The hunters live by strength and skill and the hunted continue to exist through the effective use of camouflage, by hiding, or by sheer reproductive capacities. The methods of defense are as varied as the techniques of the hunters. It is safe to say that no method of capturing game used by man, up until the time of gunpowder, has not been used by some insect, and the insects' modes of evading capture are often similar to our own. The war between the insects goes on continually, and in each patch of field or forest there are unseen little dramas of life and death being enacted every hour of the day and night. The same is true of the watery world beneath the quiet surface of each pond. It is a ruthless kind of internecine warfare where no quarter is ever given and none is asked.

Insect hunters are usually well suited to their trade, for they are active, alert and keen of vision. Consider the contrast between the dim-witted caterpillar feeding on a leaf and the agile dragonfly with its wings flashing in the sun. Those insects that live by ambush or trapping are also different, for the techniques of obtaining game require different characteristics.

Almost any field or prairie can be compared to a miniature jungle. For their size, the beasts which inhabit these "jungles" are far more terrifying and deadly than any found in the deepest jungles of Africa. Probably the most spectacular of these miniature predators are the *Pepsis* wasps or tarantula hawks, the largest of all wasps. They are beautiful but formidable insects; some of them are an inch and a half in length and have wing spans of four inches. The *Pepsis* wasps are found only in the warmer parts of North and South America, where several hundred species occur. Fourteen species are found across the southern United States. The bodies of these great hunting wasps are metallic blue and they fly with a deep-toned hum accompanied by ticking sounds. Their wings are orange or fiery-red and their tails are armed with poison stings. When about to attack they give off a pungent odor. These huge wasps are alert hunters but do not appear to fear man; in fact, they are sometimes quite aggressive in defense of newly captured prey. To a human their stings are very painful.

The *Pepsis* wasps are hunters, but the game they hunt is not used as food for themselves but for their larvae. It is a strange paradox that their

The Mantispa adult has raptorial front legs which it uses to capture other insects. During their larval stage these strange insects are parasitic in the egg sacs of spiders.

own food consists of flower nectar. The *Pepsis* wasps prey upon taran-tulas, the huge, hairy spiders of the Southwest that often have leg spans of five inches. The tarantulas themselves are hunters of repute; they feed on a wide array of insects and other small creatures which are seized by the tarantulas' chelicerae, or fangs, and killed with venom. The luckless victims are then crushed and their bodies sucked dry of nutritious fluids. But just as the tarantulas live by the sword they often die by the sword (or perhaps we should say by the sting).

Only a few lucky observers have actually observed encounters between tarantulas and *Pepsis* wasps, but these are quite spectacular. Like all hunting wasps, the tarantula hawk is a specialist; she hunts only taran-tulas, and each species of wasp hunts only one species of tarantula. Also, like all hunting wasps, it is only the female that hunts game. The abode of the tarantula is usually barren and desertlike and this is the hunting ground of the wasp. She alights upon the sandy ground and pushes through the sparse vegetation in her search for tarantulas or tarantula burrows. Having at last located her prey, there is a battle to the death— the death of the tarantula. These encounters sometimes occur in the dark-ness of the tarantulas' underground tunnels, but in other cases the duels are in the sun. The great tarantula faces its adversary, instinctively real-izing that danger threatens. As the wasp approaches, it attempts to seize her, but its fangs slide harmlessly over her armored body. In the struggle the tarantula may roll over on its back, and at this point in the battle the wasp grasps one of the tarantula's legs and bends her abdomen forward, bringing the lethal sting into position to plunge it into the soft mem-brane between the basal joints. When this occurs the spider goes limp, and for all practical purposes the duel is over. The wasp occasionally administers a final sting into the underside of the tarantula's body or cephalothorax. Actually, the tarantula is not dead; it is merely paralyzed. A dead tarantula would be of no value to the wasp since it would quickly decompose and be useless as stored food.

The wasp now faces a major problem. She must excavate a tunnel and drag the huge tarantula into it. This is no small feat when the relative sizes of the two creatures are considered. Some *Pepsis* wasps dig new burrows, while others drag the paralyzed tarantulas back into their own burrows. In one case a *Pepsis* wasp was observed to drag her large game a hundred yards to an abandoned gopher hole.

In digging its own burrow, the wasp uses both mandibles and legs to loosen the sand and toss it out. If the soil is loose and sandy, the work goes rapidly and is completed in about three hours. The finished tunnel is sloping and has an enlarged chamber at its lower end. It is about a foot long. The wasp, now satisfied with her work, returns to the prostrate tarantula and inspects it. Perhaps she is estimating its dimensions. She then returns to the tunnel and makes a few adjustments in size. Her next problem is moving the tarantula into the burrow. It is a tribute to her strength that after considerable tugging and straining the wasp is at last able to drag the tarantula into the burrow. Here she straddles the tarantula and, using her forelegs, brushes and scrapes the fine hair off of an area of its abdomen. It is to this bare spot that she cements her egg. After the egg is laid she walks out of the burrow without a backward look, and begins sealing the burrow entrance with soil and sand. Having brought this episode to a successful conclusion, the *Pepsis* wasp goes hunting again or spends some time sipping flower nectar. In the course of her life she may kill and store many tarantulas. Old wasps often have frayed wings which testify to many battles.

In the darkness of the burrow the wasp embryo in the egg, so carefully laid on the tarantula, slowly develops and, after about three days, hatches into a legless grub. When it hatches it is already positioned so that its sharp jaws face the abdomen of the tarantula. Rapidly, it makes an opening through the body wall and begins sucking out fluids. As time passes, the grub gradually grows larger at the expense of the tarantula. It molts its skin four times to allow for increase in size. By this time the contents of the tarantula are all consumed and the wasp grub is two inches in length. It now spins a silken cocoon and transforms into the pupal, or resting, stage. Here it rests quietly while its organs are slowly rebuilt into those fitted for winged life above ground. Within a few weeks the adult wasp emerges from the pupal case and cuts its way out of the cocoon. It then digs its way up through the relatively loose sand that fills the tunnel and emerges into the light. If the tarantula was captured and buried in late summer, the adult will not emerge until the next season, or almost a year later. There is some variation in habits among the various species of *Pepsis* wasps, but, in general, the sequence of events recounted above is typical. It should, perhaps, be mentioned that some kinds of tarantulas make almost no effort to defend themselves against attack by *Pepsis* wasps. Why this is, no one knows.

Second in size only to the great *Pepsis* wasps in North America is the cicada killer (*Sphecius speciosus*). Sometimes this insect is also called the "king hornet." It is black in color and banded with yellow, and it often reaches a length of more than one inch. As with the *Pepsis* wasp it is only the female that hunts.

As in most insects, the cicada killer's actions are stereotyped and follow a definite sequence. Her first act is the digging of a burrow in the ground. This she seems to do with enthusiasm, vigorously tossing out sand as she works. When she has completed her tunnel it is nearly a foot long and angles downward to an enlarged chamber at its lower end. In general, it is quite similar to the burrow of the *Pepsis* wasp. Having finished this nest burrow to her satisfaction, she next makes exploratory flights about the vicinity to fix the landmarks in her brain so that she can find the place again. Then she goes hunting.

The prey of these wasps are the cicadas that sing so happily in the trees after dwelling for many years beneath the ground sucking sap from tree roots. As might be expected, the cicada killer locates her prey by sound rather than by sight. One second the cicada is singing high in a tree; the next second there is a discordant screech as the wasp suddenly strikes. Usually both wasp and cicada tumble to the ground, where a life and death struggle occurs. But the cicada has little chance against the poison dart of the wasp. The wasp soon locates a vital spot on the cicada's undersurface and plunges in her quarter-inch sting, quickly paralyzing it. The wasp is now faced with a problem. It is likely that she has located and paralyzed her game a considerable distance from the previously prepared nest. The cicada must be transported to it, but it weighs more than the wasp. An air-lift is the logical method of transportation, but the wasp cannot lift-off with such a weighty burden. Here an instinctive behavior that appears almost to be intelligence is exhibited by the wasp. She drags the inert cicada to the base of a tree or tall weed and hauls it up, usually several feet from the ground. Now she straddles the cicada and, grasping it with her feet, flies off like an eagle carrying a lamb. The cicada is carried upside-down. The high elevation gives her sufficient start, and once airborne she flies easily with her prey, her powerful wings carrying her over trees or other obstacles.

Having arrived at the burrow she previously excavated, she drops the cicada a foot or so from the entrance and reconnoiters the tunnel to make sure all is well. Satisfied with her inspection she then drags the cicada inside and places it in the enlarged cavity at the bottom. One last act must be performed; this is the laying of an egg on the cicada. The egg is deposited beneath the cicada's middle leg in such a position that the grub that hatches from the egg will have no difficulty in feeding upon the still-

The cicada killer wasp (*Sphecius speciosus*) captures and paralyzes cicadas and then flies with them to its burrow.

living cicada. It is interesting to consider what a remarkable adaptation this method of storing foods is. The paralyzing sting serves the same purpose as a deep-freeze. The stored food is kept in a fresh and edible condition long enough for the wasp's young to devour it. This may seem cruel to us, yet it is the wasps' way of meat preservation.

It is a strange fact that the cicada killer sometimes stocks her nest with *two* cicadas instead of one. Why? It is possible that the female larva, being larger, requires more food for development. This, of course, implies that the wasp knows which sex her next larva is going to be. Remember that the queen honeybee lays only male or drone eggs in drone cells and worker (female) eggs in worker cells.

As in the case of the *Pepsis* wasp, the cicada killer larva feeds upon the paralyzed prey, killing it at last. When it has consumed all the stored food, the larva spins a cocoon and goes into a resting stage or condition of *diapause*. By then it is winter and the ground is blanketed with snow. During the cold months the larva remains dormant, but with the coming of spring it transforms into the pupal stage. When the full warmth of summer arrives, the adult wasp emerges and digs its way up out of the ground. The cycle has been completed, and another generation of cicada killers begins its depredations on the happy cicada throng. The cicadas would soon die anyway; they normally live only a few short weeks. In nature's economy their destinies have been fulfilled, especially if they have already mated and laid their eggs. It is only the male cicadas that sing so they are the usual prey of the cicada killers that hunt by sound.

There are thousands of different kinds of hunting wasps, each of which specializes in the capture of certain insects—or spiders—for the stocking of its nest. The reason why these predaceous wasps tend to specialize is fairly obvious. All insects have fairly stereotyped instincts and cannot easily change their habits to fit new situations. Each kind of prey requires somewhat different treatment; thus, the hunting wasps are more successful if they specialize in one type of prey or, even, one species as do the *Pepsis* wasps.

Most of the hunting wasps have quite similar life histories; their habits vary only in respect to their prey and the location of their nests. The great majority nest in the ground since it is not only a safe location for hiding things, but forms an excellent insulation against both heat and cold. The digger wasps of the genera *Tachytes* and *Tachysphex* stock their

Many wasps and flies deposit their eggs on other insects and their larvae feed as parasites within the host insects. Shown here is a large *Thalessa* wasp drilling a hole in a tree. She will lay her egg in a wood-boring larva.

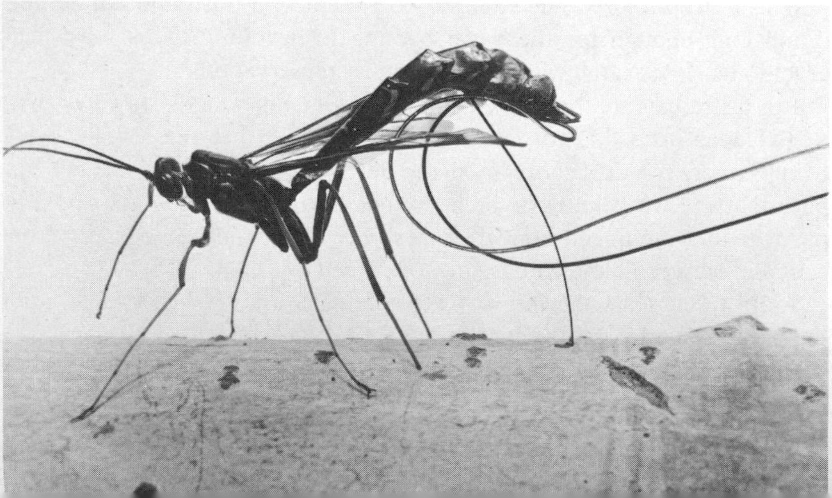

underground nests with grasshoppers, and others, such as those of the genus *Motes,* specialize in crickets. Wasps of the genus *Larra* capture mole crickets that burrow just beneath the surface of the ground.

The *Ammophila* wasps specialize in caterpillars as do the potter wasps of the genus *Eumenes.* These wasps, like the *Sceliphron* and *Trypoxylon* wasps, construct clay cells. They are often called mason wasps. Wasps of the two latter genera, however, stock their nests with spiders. As might be expected, there are also lazy wasps like the blue burglars (*Chalybion*) that break open the clay cells of the mason wasps and restock them with their own spiders, thus saving the time and labor of nest construction. Others, such as the graceful little tenant wasps (*Odynerus*) use abandoned mason wasp cells which they stock with small caterpillars. Some wasps nest in hollow stems or other cavities; a few even use the open tubelike leaves of pitcher plants while others take advantage of keyholes or the open ends of garden hoses. Another hunting wasp (*Aphilanthops laticinctus*) specializes in harvester ants, which it captures and places in its underground nest. This wasp has an interesting adaptation for preventing the escape or pilfering of its prey while its nest is being reopened. The captured ant is firmly held by the terminal segment of the wasp's abdomen which is recurved and used as a pincher.

The hunting wasps are not true predators for they do not actually devour their prey, but most other hunting insects consume whatever game they are able to capture. Bugs of the order of Hemiptera are all equipped with piercing and sucking mouthparts, so they are well fitted for siphoning out the body fluids of captured prey.

Probably the most common of all hunting bugs are the assassin bugs, some of which are active hunters while others use ambush techniques. Nature has fitted the assassin bugs well for the profession of hunter. Their legs are equipped with special adhesive pads that enable them to grasp and hold their prey while they insert their beaks. Like the wasps, many of the assassin bugs specialize in capturing certain insects; some specialize in bees while others capture ants or other insects.

One of the most interesting of these insects is an East Indian bug named *Ptilocerus ochraceus.* It apparently has no common name. Ants of the genus *Dolichoderus* are its specialty and it captures them by an underhanded trick. *Ptilocerus* takes up a position beside an ant trail and raises its forelegs to display a tuft of fiery red hairs on its abdomen. Concealed beneath this tuft is a gland which secretes a substance that is very attractive to the ants. When an ant is enticed to the bug and begins licking the secretion, it soon finds that, in addition to its attractive odor and taste, it also contains a narcotic that paralyzes the ant. The bug then grasps the ant between its forelegs and plunges its beak into the neck membrane. In a short time the ant's body is sucked dry and the bug awaits another foolish ant.

In North America there are many assassin bugs, all of which hunt other insects, but a few kinds, such as the so-called "kissing bug" (*Triatoma*), often bite people. This red and black assassin bug received its name from a case in Washington, D.C., many years ago in which a woman was bitten on the lip. Sometimes these insects bite severely. In South America there is a species of *Triatoma* that transmits Chagas' disease from one person to another.

Besides the kissing bug, we have the common wheel bug (*Arilus cristatus*) that is easily identified by the cogwheel-like crest on the top of its thorax. All these bugs have specialized hypodermic instruments to enable them to kill and feed upon their prey. Their beaks consist of slender stylets that fit together into a tube containing two hollow ducts. The bug's salivary glands secrete a powerful venom which is injected into prey through one of the hollow ducts. The venom is forced out by a pump arrangement in the bug's head. Thus it is equipped with a very efficient hypodermic needle. Large quantities of the venom are injected, and this has the power to digest and liquefy the inner tissues of the prey. The dissolved material is then pumped into the assassin's stomach through the second channel between the stylets. Thus, this predatory insect actually digests its food outside its own body. There is one question, however, that scientists have not been able to answer. How can the assassin-bug's venom, which is very powerful and will quickly dissolve almost any insect tissue, be stored by the assassin bug for future use?

There are many other hunting bugs that prey on insects. These include the thread-legged bugs that somewhat resemble walkingstick insects. The forelegs of these bugs are raptorial; that is, they are fitted for grasping prey, as are those of the praying mantis. Here also are included the toad bugs (Gelastocoridae) with their protruding eyes. These alert little bugs live along the wet margins of streams and ponds where they capture prey by leaping upon it. The water realm is a favored habitat for many of the hunting bugs. The water striders (Gerridae) skate over the water's surface, capturing and devouring small insects while the backswimmers (Notonectidae) and water scorpions (Nepidae) capture their

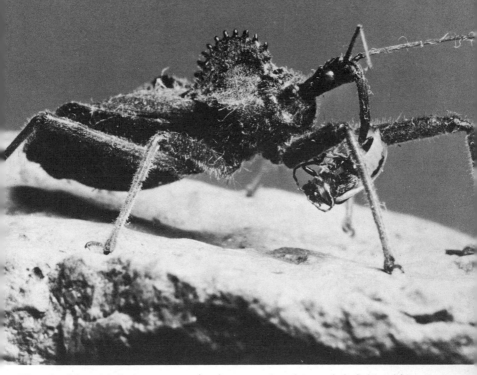

The wheel bug (*Arilus*) captures other insects and sucks out their fluids with its sharp beak.

game beneath the surface. The watery realm is also the habitat of the most powerful of all hunters, the giant water bugs (Belostomatidae). These insects vary in size from an inch to giants more than four inches long. Their bodies are flattened and streamlined and the two hind pairs of legs are oarlike and used for propelling the insects through the water. Their forelegs are fitted for grasping and holding prey. After prey is captured a venom is injected which quickly kills it; its body fluids are then siphoned out by the sharp beak. The venom enables the giant water bug to subdue relatively large animals, including small snakes, fish and, possibly, even birds. There is a case on record of a woodpecker being found in a tree with a giant water bug attached to it. The writer has seen and photographed these bugs in the act of killing both snakes and fish. Sometimes they are serious pests in fish hatcheries. Even though these fearsome insects are aquatic, they often leave the water and fly about, especially at night. As might be expected, they can inflict painful bites if handled carelessly.

Among the bugs best adapted for the profession of trapper are the ambush bugs (Phymatidae) that hide in flowers and catch insects that

come seeking nectar or pollen. They are rather small insects, usually less than a half inch in length, yet they are successful in capturing insects as large as bumblebees or even wasps. The bodies of these insects are irregular in shape and usually marked with concealing colors. They lie in wait and grab their prey with their raptorial front legs. One of their favorite trapping locations is the yellow flowering spike of goldenrod, where they can almost always be found in autumn. Here they compete for game with the camouflaged crab spiders which use similar trapping techniques.

No discussion of predatory insects would be complete without mention of the praying mantis (family Mantidae), which are close relatives of the grasshoppers, katydids and cockroaches. There are many different species and they are found in almost all parts of the world, especially in the warmer regions. They are particularly abundant in variety and form in the tropics. In the United States there are a number of species ranging from an inch or so to five inches in length. Their coloration is either bright green or brown, but they all have at least one thing in common: their forelegs are in the form of raptorial grasping organs armed with vicious spines. These legs are never used for walking but are normally held in the attitude of prayer, which is ironic since their use is far from that of supplication.

The movements of mantids are slow and deliberate, but if an unwary insect, such as a fly, approaches too closely the armed front legs flash out, seize it and bring it to the mandibles, which at once begin cutting into its body. It makes little difference which part of the prey reaches the mandibles first; if a leg is first the mantis devours this. They have voracious appetites and never seem satisfied. They are among the most alert of all hunting insects; their eyes are large and apparently they have keen vision. The small head is seemingly loosely attached to the end of the long prothorax and can be moved about as it watches anything going on in its vicinity. While their usual hunting technique is that of waiting for prey to approach, they will also slowly stalk their game. Usually, however, they follow the philosophy of "all things come to him who waits." Here

The giant water bug (*Belostoma*) captures relatively large animals, such as fish, frogs and snakes, and siphons out their fluids through its beak. The prey is killed by a poison which is injected into it.

again, patience is the basic requirement of the hunter that lives by stalking. While most mantids live by capturing relatively small insects, some of the larger, tropical species are able to capture small birds, lizards and frogs. So voracious are mantids—even our own species—that the female usually consumes her smaller mate, sometimes even during the mating act!

Mantids have attracted attention for thousands of years and various superstitions have grown up around them. The Greeks thought that they had supernatural power and Moslems believe that they turn their faces toward Mecca while holding their forelegs in prayerlike attitudes. Here in our own country they are called praying mantids or "rear-horses" and it is believed by some that if they spit in one's face blindness will result.

Probably the most common praying mantis in the eastern United States is *Stagmomantis carolina,* the female of which measures about four inches in length and is green in color. The male is brown and somewhat smaller. A European species (*Mantis religiosa*) has been introduced and now occurs in many places as does a large Oriental species, the Chinese mantis (*Paratenodera sinensis*). Both of these foreign species entered the country in the form of egg masses on nursery stock. Mantid eggs are laid in clusters on twigs and covered with a frothy substance that hardens and protects them. Other species of mantids occur in various parts of the country, most of which are of smaller size.

The mantids are among the most voracious hunters, capturing and devouring insects of many kinds. Shown here (left) is the introduced Chinese mantis (*Paratenodera sinensis*) feeding on a captured long-horned grasshopper and (right) the native Carolina mantis (*Stagmomantis carolina*). Other species of praying mantids occur in various parts of the United States.

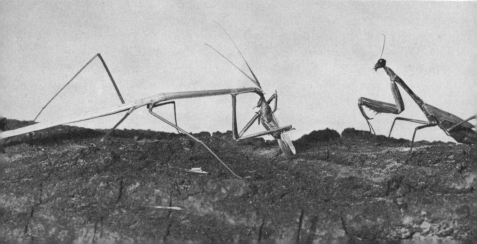

It is in the tropics that the mantis clan has reached its full development. There, mantids of fantastic form and coloration have evolved. In Panama there is a mantid with leaflike expansions extending out from the sides of its prothorax; in Africa there is a species known as the "devil's-flower" (*Idolum diabolicum*). This latter species has both thorax and legs decorated with the leaflike expansions, enabling it to hide in vegetation. Of special interest are those tropical kinds that simulate flowers. One of these is the rose-leaf mantis of India, which, in addition to having leaflike body expansions, is beautifully colored in hues of lavender and pink, making it resemble a flower. This mantid hangs downward among leaves and now and then it sways back and forth further simulating a flower swinging in the breeze. As might be expected, insects are attracted, but instead of finding nectar and pollen they encounter the deadly jaws of the mantis. Tropical mantids are camouflaged in various other ways. For example, there is one kind in South America that resembles bird droppings and another that resembles tufts of lichen. One of the most interesting South American species is one that resembles a phasmid or stick-insect. Apparently it joins groups of these dull-witted, leaf-eating insects and devours them.

While the mantids are all voracious predators that are continually on the prowl for insect game, there is at least one instance where the tables are turned. In Europe there is a small wasp (*Rielia manticida*) that parasitizes the eggs of *Mantis religiosa*. This wasp, which is only a tenth of an inch long, uses an interesting trick. The female wasp locates a mantid and alights upon it, usually at the base of its wings where it is safe from the mantid's jaws. The wasp then severs her wings and settles down to wait. Eventually the mantid lays her cluster of eggs and the wasp then crawls upon this cluster and deposits her own eggs. Her larvae then feed upon the mantid eggs. Here perhaps is a sort of retribution for the depredations of the mantid clan on other insects.

Patience is an important characteristic of the insect hunters, but it is absolutely necessary to those that make their living by trapping. For an insect that lies in wait for its game there are often long periods between meals. No insect better exemplifies the need for eternal patience than do the antlions (family Myrmeleontidae). These belong to the nerve-winged order (Neuroptera), comparatively obscure insects although some of them, like the antlions, have interesting habits.

Almost everyone is familiar with the small pits excavated in protected, sandy locations by the antlions, or "doodlebugs" as they are popularly called. The average person, however, knows but little about the strange little creatures that dwell at the bottoms of these pits. Only if you were as small as an ant or other crawling insect would these pits be of major concern to you, since they are actually pitfalls used to capture game. Pitfalls have been used by African natives for perhaps centuries, but the antlions have been doing it for millions of years. Thus, once again, a technique used by an insect far antedates a similar one used by man.

Antlions are found in many parts of the world, and their interesting habits have been observed by many biologists. If you carefully probe into the sand at the bottom of an antlion pit, you will find a strange-looking little creature with a robust body and slender neck. Its head bears a pair of sicklelike jaws. This is the antlion, and, while its method of trapping might appear to be ineffective, it evidently works or there would not be so many antlions. The insect you find at the bottom of the pit is actually the larval stage. It hides quietly beneath the sand and waits. An hour may pass, or perhaps a day, but eventually some unwary ant comes walking along and strays near the pit. Sometimes the ant may deliberately walk across the pit or be attracted to it by curiosity. In either case, when the ant approaches the pit the hidden antlion starts tossing sand into the air. This causes little landslides on the sloping walls of the pit and the luckless ant is apt to tumble to the bottom. If this occurs, it is grabbed by the antlion's jaws. If the ant—or other insect—is large, it may escape, but usually it has but little chance for the sicklelike jaws of the antlion are hollow hypodermic needles like the beak of the assassin bug. Once these sharp jaws have penetrated the victim's body, a powerful venom is injected and the battle is over. Again like the assassin bug, the antlion's venom has the ability to digest and dissolve the body contents of the prey so that it can be siphoned out through the hollow mandibles of the attacker. This, of course, takes time, but the antlion pulls its prey beneath the sand where it does not have to hurry. After the body of the prey is sucked dry, it is tossed out of the pit and the antlion secretes itself at the bottom of the pit and again waits patiently for passing prey.

Antlions can be kept in dishes of sand and their crater-building activities studied. They will also live happily in sugar or salt. In excavating their pits they employ an interesting technique; they crawl backward in a circle, at the same time tossing sand in the air with their mandibles. As they move 'round and 'round, the pit gradually becomes deeper until at

Antlions excavate small pitfalls in sand in which small insects such as ants are trapped and eaten. The larval antlions conceal themselves at the bottom of the pits.

last it may measure an inch or so across and an inch deep with steeply sloping sides.

Antlion pits are usually to be found in the sand or dust below overhanging rock ledges or under buildings. Almost any dry place that is protected from rain will do. In the southwestern United States there are certain fly larvae of the genus *Vermileo,* the so-called "wormlions," that construct pits and capture game in a manner very similar to that used by the antlions. These unusual fly larvae belong to the family Rhagionidae, the snipe flies, most of which are predaceous.

Because of the uncertainty and irregular nature of their food supply, the life histories of the antlions are unusually long, generally requiring from two to three years from egg to winged adult. The tiny antlion that hatches from the egg laid in the dust or sand at first specializes in very tiny game, but as it grows larger it constructs larger pits and catches larger insects. During its larval period an antlion excavates many pits and may even change trapping grounds, but in time it becomes full grown and ready to transform into the pupal stage. The cocoon within which this transformation takes place is constructed of grains of sand cemented together with silk to form a small sphere. That the creature is able to construct this cell beneath the sand without getting sand inside is a neat trick. When the cocoon is finished, the larva transforms into the pupal stage which lasts for about two months. When the time arrives for it to change into the adult stage, the pupa breaks through the wall of the sand cocoon and pushes itself up to the surface. As with a moth pupa, the skin splits down the back and the bedraggled adult crawls out. Soon its wings expand and harden and it flits away to mate and lay eggs. Adult antlions resemble dragonflies, but they are very weak fliers and do not feed at all. Sufficient food must be consumed during the larval, trapping stage to last the rest of their lives.

Closely related to the antlions are the trash-carriers or hemerobiids that capture their game by another trick. They do not have the patience of their cousin antlions but take the initiative and actively hunt their prey. You may have seen these strange little insects without realizing what they were, or even that they were insects. At a casual glance they appear to be small heaps of trash that, by some mysterious means, crawl about over the bark or limbs of trees. If one of these animated trash heaps is examined under a hand lens, it is found that a strange little insect is hiding underneath. The trash is held in place by projections of the insect's body that bear hooked spines or bristles. Projecting out from under one end of the trash is the insect's head bearing sicklelike mandibles with which it captures aphids, mealybugs or other small insects. When these have been sucked dry, their remains are attached to the creature's back, forming an excellent camouflage. In other words, these unique little beasts carry the remains of their past meals along with them. This trick not only enables them to creep up on unsuspecting game but, what is more important, protects them from birds or other enemies. The trash-carriers add debris and food remains to their packs by bending their heads over their backs and attaching the material with their mandibles. The adults are similar to antlion adults but smaller in size; sometimes they are called brown lacewings.

Another group of antlion relatives are the lacewings (family Chrysopidae), that feed during their larval stage on aphids and other small insects after the manner of the trash-carriers. These predaceous larvae are slender and alligator-shaped and equipped with sicklelike jaws. The adults are delicate, green-winged insects that flit about and are often attracted to lights. Most of our species are of medium size; generally they have a wing expanse of an inch or less. In South America there is a pretty lacewing (*Loyola crassus*) that measures nearly three inches across. The winged adults of these insects do not seem particularly interested in feeding, although they are predatory to small insects. It is their method of egg laying, however, that is of special interest. The eggs are laid on leaves or twigs, each one on a slender stalk which holds it above the flat surface.

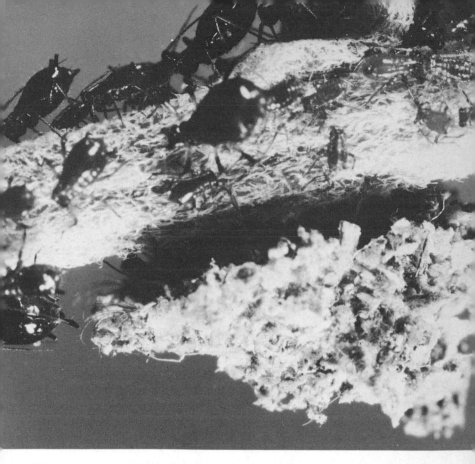

The trash carriers (*Hemerobius*) attach the remains of past meals to their backs as a means of camouflage. They capture and devour aphids and other small insects.

The larvae which hatch from these are so voracious that the first one out of an egg would immediately devour the other eggs in the group if they were not inaccessible.

The beetles are "double-threat" insects since the predaceous forms usually capture and eat insects and other small animals during both larval and adult stages. Generally speaking, if a beetle larva is flesh-eating, the adult will also be flesh-eating. Of course, as usual, there are exceptions. The larvae of blister beetles (family Meloidae) live underground where they devour grasshopper egg masses or ground-dwelling insects. Sometimes they prey upon ground-nesting bees. When the adult stage is reached, however, their food habits change and they become plant feeders. Some of them are serious agricultural pests.

The tiger beetles (family Cicindellidae) illustrate another interesting way in which insects' feeding habits change when they transform into the adult stage. Tiger beetle larvae live in holes in the earth, from which they emerge to capture passing insects. They are strange-looking creatures; when full grown they measure over an inch long and have sharp jaws. Only the head and forepart of the body is hard and chitinized; the remainder is white and unprotected. This part needs no protection because it is seldom exposed to harm. On the larva's back, on the fifth abdominal segment, there is a hump bearing two forward-directed hooks.

The small, vertical holes in which the tiger beetle larvae live are usually in places that are clear of vegetation, such as beaten paths. These holes are almost as large as a lead pencil and vary in depth from a few inches to a foot. Sometimes these insects—as the antlions—are called "doodlebugs," but in New Zealand they are called "penny doctors." If you watch one of them patiently from a distance, you may be rewarded by seeing enacted one of nature's dramas of life and death. If all is quiet, the head of the larva appears at the top of the hole with its mandibles widely spread like the jaws of a trap. In this position the larva patiently waits. Your own patience will probably run out long before that of the insect, but if you are lucky you may see an ant or other insect stray too close. If this occurs, the tiger beetle larva's head flashes out and its jaws impale it. If the captured prey is strong, it may attempt to escape, but it cannot jerk the larvae out of its den because the spines on its back anchor it firmly. Once subdued, the prey is dragged down to the bottom of the lair and consumed.

Adult tiger beetles are just as bloodthirsty as the larvae. They are commonly seen on open ground along the margins of lakes and ponds, but some kinds frequent ocean beaches. When alarmed they fly short distances and alight, always facing the intruder. They have keen vision. Most tiger beetles are about an inch long. Many of them are beautifully colored in hues of metallic green, blue, purple or bronze and their wings are marked with contrasting stripes or bars. Their legs are long and they can run rapidly. Like their larvae, they are equipped with sicklelike mandibles and are among the most vicious of all insect predators. They are called tiger beetles and they live up to their name.

Another family of bloodthirsty little beasts are the ladybird beetles (family Coccinellidae). Most people do not realize their true nature, which is anything but ladylike. Like the tiger beetles, these common insects are predators during both larval and adult stages. Ladybirds are specialists, usually preying upon aphids; however, some kinds also feed upon flower pollen and nectar. The Australian ladybird beetle—also called the vedalia beetle—is so enthusiastic over a diet of cottony-cushion scale of citrus that it was introduced into the United States in 1888 to control these pests. Many millions of these beetles are now reared artificially and liberated in citrus orchards each year as a means of scale control. This method of controlling an insect pest is an example of "biological" control as contrasted to control by insecticides.

Ladybird beetles are among our most common insects; they are small oval beetles, usually orange or red with contrasting spots on their elytra, or wing covers. As a matter of fact, their family name Coccinellidae comes from the Greek word meaning scarlet. Their larvae are small, alligator-shaped creatures that, like the adults, feed upon aphids. Usually the eggs are laid near aphid colonies on plants so an abundant source of food will be close at hand. Ladybirds and their larvae descend upon such an aphid colony like wolves on the fold. It is always interesting to watch such an attack on an aphid colony that is being protected by ants. Ants protect aphids in return for the sweet exudate or honeydew which they secrete. When danger from these traditional aphid enemies threatens, the ants become greatly excited and attempt to drive them away. Aphids are completely defenseless and are preyed upon by many insects.

Second in abundance among the hunting beetles are the ground beetles (family Carabidae), which are usually found crawling on the ground or under boards or stones. They are fast-running beetles that vary in size from very tiny to more than an inch in length; some of them, such as the fiery-hunter (*Calosoma*) are colored in bright metallic hues. They are all heavily armored and have powerful jaws, which they employ in capturing other insects. Many kinds feed on cutworms and other pests, and thus are definitely beneficial to man.

Perhaps the most interesting and unusual of all the carabid beetles are the bombardier beetles (*Brachinus*). These are medium-sized beetles having their heads and the front parts of their thoraxes colored rust red, the remainder of their bodies being black or dark blue. They, too, are hunters, but it is their method of defense that is especially interesting. When disturbed they emit small puffs of irritating gas from their anal openings. This smokelike gas is apparently most effective in repelling enemies.

Carabid larvae are usually flat, segmented creatures that prey on other insects as do the adults. Some kinds feed upon snails and slugs.

The water is a special habitat and the insects that have taken up an abode there have been especially adapted. The diving beetles (family Dytiscidae) hunt their game beneath the water's surface. Their hind legs are greatly elongated and set with stiff bristles which are used as oars to enable them to swim rapidly. Some of them are of considerable size and they are energetic predators, capturing and eating almost any small aquatic creature. These include mosquito wrigglers, mayfly larvae and other insects as well as small tadpoles and fish. They also practice cannibalism. They are often seen hanging head downward in water with only their tails touching the surface film through which they obtain air. When alarmed, they dive rapidly to the bottom and hide beneath the mud or sand. Some kinds have stridulating organs with which they make sounds both in water and in the air. Even though these air-breathing beetles have taken to the water and make their living there, they still leave the water occasionally and fly—sometimes they are attracted to bright lights.

Larval diving beetles, too, are predators that capture and devour aquatic insects and other animals. They are of slender form and have long, sicklelike jaws. Sometimes they are called water tigers, an apt name since they are well fitted for the chase.

It is the nature of many beetles to prey on other insects. For example, the fireflies (family Lampyridae) feed during both adult and larval stages on small insects and snails. The water-scavenger beetles (family Hydrophilidae) are mostly scavengers, as their name implies, yet some kinds are hunters like their cousins, the diving beetles.

Just as modern nations have taken to the air in military offense and defense, so many insects long ago took to the air to battle each other. No one knows for sure which insect was first to hunt from the air, but it seems probable that the ancestors of the dragonflies have that honor. Many millions of years ago there were great dragonflies, as large as small hawks, that darted through the archaic forests, presumably capturing flying insects as do modern dragonflies.

Of all flying insects the dragonflies and damselflies (order Odonata) are the most adept flyers. Their grace and precision in the air are unequaled by any flying creature. Like all flying insects, the dragonflies and damselflies begin life as wingless, crawling nymphs or immature forms. They live beneath the surfaces of ponds and streams where they are predaceous on small animals. When these nymphs are fully developed they crawl up above the water's surface and transform into the winged stage. From that time on they inhabit the aerial realm. The underwater world was their cradle, but they never again return to it, except to lay their eggs.

The Odonata capture their food on the wing or, sometimes, pluck it from plants. They have been observed searching the trunks of trees or the leaves of plants for hiding insects. An observer in Bavaria once saw a large dragonfly (*Aeschna grandis*) capturing and eating small frogs on the ground.

These winged hunters are well equipped for capturing food on the wing. Only time and the slow processes of evolution could have fitted them so perfectly for this method of feeding. Their vision is very acute, and they can discern moving objects several hundred feet away. If their eyes are carefully examined under a hand lens, it is found that the facets on the upper portion are larger than those on the lower portion. In other words, the upper parts of a dragonfly's eyes are especially fitted for distant vision while the lower parts are fitted for nearby vision. The eyes of these insects, like those of a horsefly, can be compared to bifocal glasses worn by humans. In most dragonflies there is a gradual reduction in facet size toward the lower portions of the eyes, in contrast to the damselflies in which there is a sharp demarcation between the two facet sizes. This adaptation fits them well for the capture of flying insects which are almost always approached and captured from below.

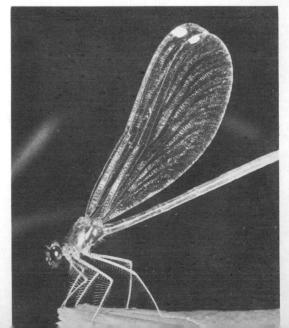

Dragonflies and damselflies capture prey on the wing. Their spiny legs are often used to scoop up flying gnats and other small insects. The young or nymphs are also predaceous and live in water.

Some tiny wasps deposit an egg in a caterpillar and, by a process of division called *polyembryony,* many larvae are produced. These feed upon the inner tissues of the caterpillar and eventually emerge and spin cocoons.

The actual seizing of the prey is done by the legs, which are fitted for the task. The legs are located far forward on the dragonfly's body and bear numerous spines. When capturing flying insects, the legs are held in such a position that they form a small basket in which prey is scooped up. After the capture is made, the prey is consumed while the dragonfly is in flight or it alights and eats at leisure. Dragonflies often establish themselves on tall weeds or twigs, making short forays to snatch up flying game, and returning to the perch after each capture. Sometimes dragonflies take up perches near bee hives and capture large numbers of honeybees. However, since they usually feed on gnats and mosquitoes, they are actually beneficial to man.

Dragonflies are usually seen flitting about over the surfaces of ponds or along streams. These individuals are usually not hunting game as such flights are a part of the mating behavior. Most hunting flights are made away from water over fields or around trees. Sometimes they travel long distances from water, often flying at high altitudes, frequently above the tops of trees.

So far we have said nothing about those insects which have taken up parasitic habits and live, usually during their larval stages, within the bodies of other insects. The parasitic habit occurs in several insect orders, but is especially common among the fly and wasp tribes. Parasites vary greatly in size and habits. There are wasps so tiny that they can lay their eggs in the eggs of larger insects where their larvae mature. Other wasps deposit eggs within the bodies of caterpillars and, in some species, these eggs, instead of producing only one larva, produce many larvae by a process of division. This process is called *polyembryony* and by it one egg may produce hundreds of larvae, all of the same sex.

Among the more interesting of the parasitic insects is the *Pyrgota* fly that attacks May beetles. In spring when these large, heavy-bodied beetles are on the wing, the *Pyrgota* fly singles out a female beetle, darts in with lightning speed and thrusts an egg into the soft membrane on the beetle's back. This is precision dive-bombing at its best. The fly must make her attack while the beetle is in flight since it is only then that the tender membrane on its back is exposed. When the beetle is at rest, this portion of its body is well protected by the hard wing covers. After the egg is laid in the May beetle's body the beetle resumes her normal leaf-eating habits, but in the meantime the fly's larva is feeding and growing within her body, slowly destroying her stored food. Eventually, the beetle dies and the fly larva transforms into the pupal stage. The winged *Pyrgota* fly does not emerge until the following spring. Other flies use similar tactics in depositing their larvae on the bodies of flying grasshoppers. In studying the habits of these flies, paper pellets have been flipped through swarms of flying grasshoppers and then retrieved. Upon examination, many of the paper pellets were found to have parasitic fly larvae attached to them. The speed and precision of these flies are almost unbelievable.

The courtship habits of animals are often of great interest. Some male penguins present small pebbles to desirable females; if the gift is accepted the male knows that his courtship has been successful. Strangely, there are certain predaceous flies with somewhat similar habits. In this case, however, there may be a rather gruesome reason for presenting the gift. When the males of dance flies (family Empidae) approach prospective mates they usually bring gifts in the form of captured insects. Dance flies of the genus *Hilara,* found in New Zealand, have silvery "bladders" on the sides of their abdomens which can be inflated, enabling the insects to float in the air. Dance flies are named from their habit of flying in small swarms that move up and down over the surfaces of land or water. There are silk glands on the forelegs of these little flies, which is a most unusual location. When a male Empid has the urge to go courting, he first captures a tiny midge and encloses it in a silken "balloon." On approaching his prospective mate he presents this "wedding gift" to her. This choice morsel keeps her occupied during the mating act; otherwise she would eat him instead! In the realm of questionable ethics, we might consider another empid fly, *Hilara maura.* The males of this species merely pick up some plant fragment or flower petal and, after encasing it in silk, present it to the bride. Naturally, it takes the female some time to discover that she has been duped. Similar habits are found among some robber flies (family Asilidae).

chapter eight

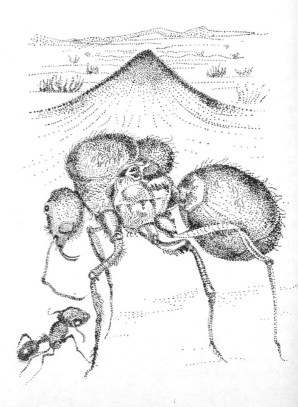

The Farmers

MAN was originally a hunter—he stalked wild game and killed it
with arrows or spears. To supplement his diet he dug edible roots
with crooked sticks or gathered wild fruit. Life was a continual struggle
to satisfy his hunger. For countless centuries it never occurred to him that
edible plants could be cultivated or that the wild beasts he slew could
be domesticated. The habits of these primitive hunters eventually changed
and man took up a more or less sedentary agricultural life. Under such
conditions life was more stable and stores of food could be accumulated.
As a result, human populations tended to increase and living became less
strenuous.

In many ways, the evolution of some insects has paralleled that of the
human race. This is especially true of certain ants that have abandoned
the carnivorous diet of the hunter and taken up agricultural pursuits. The
more primitive hunting ants lived in small colonies and obtained their
food wherever they could find it. This mode of life still prevails among
many ants, but some kinds have developed agricultural habits that are
amazing in their similarity to their human counterparts.

Among the most interesting of the ants that follow agricultural pursuits
are the harvester ants. These ants do not actually raise plants; they merely
harvest and store seeds. Several investigators at various times have sug-

This shows a bisected nest cone of the prairie harvesters. Note the various chambers or galleries which are used for brood rearing and seed storage.

gested that these ants actually plant seeds, raise the plants, and then harvest the seeds, but this extraordinary possibility, unfortunately, has been disproven.

True harvester ants occur in several parts of the world and are all closely related. Generally speaking, these ants inhabit barren regions of sparse vegetation and deficient rain, though there are exceptions. It is probable that their remote ancestors were forced to abandon an insect diet because insects are scarce in the desertlike areas of their origin. Plant seeds, on the other hand, are comparatively abundant at certain times of the year and can easily be stored for future consumption.

Harvester ants have the distinction of being the first insects recorded in human writings. They occur around the Mediterranean, southward to the Cape of Good Hope and eastward to India. They were abundant in the ancient Biblical lands. The seed harvesters of this region belong to the genus *Messor,* and it was undoubtedly to these ants that King Solomon referred when he advised the sluggard to go to the ant and consider her ways. Ants closely related to these are found in the southwestern United States. Besides Solomon, other ancient writers, too, referred to the seed-gathering habits of these ants. These include Hesiod, Aesop, Plutarch, Horace, Virgil and Pliny. Between the time of the ancient observers and writers, and more modern scientific studies, there is a gap of hundreds of years. During that time seed-harvesting ants were often referred to, but, apparently, only in quotations from the ancient writers. No new observations were made. The first of the modern observers to study the habits of seed-gathering ants was Lieutenant-Colonel W. H. Sykes, who saw *Pheidole* ants drying their stored seeds at Poona, India, in June 1829.

The most interesting and widespread of the seed gatherers in North America are the *Pogonomyrmex* ants. The name means "bearded ant," in reference to the bristles on the undersides of their heads. These are the true harvester ants that build the neat conical mounds, resembling miniature volcanos, often seen on the Great Plains from the Dakotas south across Texas to Patagonia. A closely related species is found in sandy areas of the more humid Southeast, but these do not construct high, sandy mounds as do their prairie cousins. The economy of the harvester ants is based almost completely on the seed-yielding plants of the vicinity, though the ants often supplement their diet with captured insects.

If one excavates a prairie harvester ant mound, it will be found that within the cone are many connecting galleries located at various levels. These galleries continue down into the earth, often to depths of six feet or more. It is within these galleries that the harvesters live and carry on their daily activities. The colonies are often very populous; more than 12,000 ants were counted in one colony in Arizona.

Each nest cone is situated at the center of a circular cleared space about ten feet in diameter within which the ants carefully remove every sprig of vegetation. The southeastern and the California harvesters allow weeds and grasses to grow up to the edges of the ant hills. Just why the prairie harvesters should go to so much trouble to maintain the cleared space surrounding the nest cone is unknown. Perhaps it helps in eliminating enemies, such as horned toads, that might creep up and ambush the ants at their labors. It probably also helps to keep the area dry and eliminates the penetration of roots into the underground nest area.

In many respects these colonies resemble miniature feudal kingdoms set in a hostile environment. Each morning, while droplets of dew still glisten from the sparse prairie vegetation, the entrance to the nest cone is opened. Among some kinds of harvester ants, this entrance is situated near the base of the southern or eastern slopes of the cone; with other kinds the entrance is at the top. At dusk it is barricaded with small pebbles to keep enemies out, and any late returning workers are forced to spend the night in the open, clinging to weeds. As soon as the entrance is opened, worker ants begin streaming out; they hurry across the open

Close-up of harvesters in one of their granaries. The seeds in this case are those of *paspalum*.

courtyard and follow tiny ant trails extending away into the grassy jungle. Each ant forages by itself; it searches for fallen seeds wherever they have dropped from prairie plants. The ants may often travel a hundred feet or more away from the nest.

Many kinds of ants lay scent trails as they walk, enabling other ants to follow and take advantage of food sources discovered by the first ant. The harvesters, however, lay no scent trails and there is apparently no transfer of information between individual ants. Each ant searches for seeds and, when one is found, hurries home with its booty. Where harvester colonies are abundant, most of the area's plant seeds may be gathered by these ants. This may be quite harmful since few seeds remain and many of the plants do not reproduce themselves.

Harvested seeds are carried into the nest and deposited in galleries located near the ground level, and, in time, a considerable store of seeds accumulates here. When harvested, most of the seeds are still enclosed in husks, and other ants, probably the younger adults, remove the chaff, carry it out and discard it at the outer edge of the cleared courtyard. This is called the "kitchen midden," and here sizable heaps of chaff may accumulate. Here also are deposited ants that die within the nest. This habit can easily be observed in an artificial nest; dead ants are carried as far from the nest site as possible and piled in a "cemetery" heap. The writer kept one such colony in an artificial nest in his office and noticed how the dead ants were carried out, one by one, and dropped on the cemetery pile. At last there was only one ant left.

Now you may wonder why the seeds so carefully gathered and stored by the industrious harvester ants do not germinate in the damp, underground environment. The answer is that they often do. Some writers, including Pliny, have stated that the ants cut the germ ends out of the seeds, thereby preventing germination. Apparently, this is not always so since I have been able to obtain germination of most of the seeds collected from the harvesters' grain bins. Apparently, the ants sometimes do cut the germ ends out after they have begun to sprout. After periods of rain some varieties of harvesting ants carry the seeds out and dry them in the sun, after which they are carried back and again placed in storage. This has been observed many times. It may often happen, however, that during prolonged periods of damp weather the seeds do sprout in the subterranean bins and form large clumps which, in time, mildew and decay. In some cases the ants are able to carry sprouted seeds out and discard them on the kitchen midden, and, here, if conditions are favorable, the seeds grow into plants. As a result, the courtyard is often surrounded by a dense fringe of plants. This gave early observers the idea that the ants "planted" seeds around their nests in order that they would have convenient sources of seed-producing plants. Of course, the end result is the same, but the fact remains that the ants do not actually "plant" crops. The fable of ants and their alleged crop-planting habits was given credence by an observer in the mid-1800's, who stated that the Texas harvesters actually planted the seeds of "ant-rice" or awn-grass (*Aristida*) around their nests. This observer also believed that the ants cultivated and cared for their crop much as a human farmer might do. But the myth has now been exploded, and modern biologists do not believe that the ants take any active part in crop production. We might philosophize by saying that perhaps in a million years or so the harvesters may eventually develop crop-cultivating habits like those of the fungus-growing

When excessive moisture causes the seeds to sprout, the ants take them out on the surface of the mound to dry in the sun. Some of them are then carried back and stored, but those that have reached an advanced stage of sprouting are discarded.

ants today. Insects' habits change slowly, however, so such an instinctive behavior, if it ever does develop, is far in the dim future as far as the harvester ants are concerned.

The plant seeds so carefully gathered and stored by the harvester ants constitute the staple food supply of the colony. The seeds are cut up by the worker ants and the starchy material rasped off by their filelike tongues. This material not only serves as food for the worker ants but is regurgitated and fed to the queen and the white larval ants. In some species of harvesters, there is a large-headed caste in addition to the normal workers. There are never very many of these in a colony, and they are probably descended from the ancient soldier caste that was important in colony defense in the days before the harvesters abandoned their carnivorous habits and became grain eaters. As far as defense is concerned, these large-headed ants no longer have any use; they wander about in the vicinity of the nest area but never seem to be doing anything very useful. Within the nest, however, their powerful jaws are still of value —they use them to cut up the flinty seeds. For this reason they are called the "miller" caste. These "millers" are not produced in young colonies. They appear only in colonies that are older and well established. Like normal worker ants and queens, the large-headed soldiers or "millers" arise from fertilized eggs, and their differences result from the diet they receive during larval development. It has been found that if young worker larvae are fed a diet high in proteins, such as that derived from captured insects, they will grow into soldiers. As in the case of honeybees, males arise from nonfertilized eggs.

Like all ants, the harvesters pass through four stages of development: egg, larva, pupa and adult. The larvae which hatch from the eggs pass through several periods of growth, gradually becoming larger. They resemble small crooknecked squashes, the smaller ends being the heads. During the larval stage they are fed and cared for by the worker ants, their food consisting of material regurgitated by the workers. When fully developed, the larvae are about one-quarter inch long and are ready for transformation into the inactive pupal stage during which their larval tissues are slowly rebuilt into organs fitted for active adult life. Once the adult stage is reached, the ants pass through periods of apprenticeship; workers that mature in spring serve first as nurses and later in the summer join the field labor force. The workers that mature in autumn assume nursery duty at once, but do not become foragers until the following spring. During cold weather or periods of rain, all activity is confined to the interior of the nest; field work comes to a halt.

The architecture of the prairie harvester ant nests is quite interesting when considered in respect to its suitability to the region. The high plains constitute an inhospitable environment. In winter, temperatures often drop far below freezing, and during summer the land is seared by desertlike heat. Between these two extremes is the period of spring when rains sweep across the prairies and the vegetation comes to life for a relatively brief period. The deep subterranean galleries enable the ants to escape both winter's cold and summer's heat. The conical mounds are shaped to shed the spring rains, and it is in the galleries located in the mounds above ground level that seeds are stored and brood is reared during the cooler and damper parts of the summer and spring. If one of the cones is cut in half with a shovel, the honeycombed nature of its architecture can easily be observed. The investigator should be warned, however, that the harvesters do not take lightly the destruction of their home. They sting painfully.

The nest entrance is less than an inch in diameter and opens into a vestibule with a smooth floor. A few worker ants are almost always present here in the capacity of guards, and it is through this portal that the ant labor force passes on its foraging expeditions. As stated previously, the gate is closed at night by a barricade of pebbles. Beyond the entrance, a tunnel extends into the nest cone, where it connects with other tunnels extending from one enlarged gallery or chamber to another. It is here that the young ants or larvae are kept and seeds are stored. Seeds and young in various stages of development are kept in separate galleries. Near Kit Carson, Colorado, I found that the larvae were located in the upper galleries near the tops of the cones. This was in June and apparently the young ants were placed in that location to take advantage of the sun's warmth. Seeds were stored in lower galleries. It is probable that the larval ants are shifted from one level to another as the weather

This is a lead cast of a harvester ant nest. It shows the interior architecture of the nest. The rods were added to give support to the cast.

changes. Galleries used as granaries may be near the surface or deep in the earth. Reverend Henry C. McCook, who made extensive and accurate studies of the prairie harvesters in 1880, found seed storage rooms as deep as eight and a half feet. These ants are enthusiastic diggers and seem never to tire of excavating new tunnels and galleries. Some nests may contain over 400 separate galleries. In artificial nests they dig continually; if there is no space to dig new tunnels they fill in old ones and dig again. In their digging operations they resemble tiny fox terriers, loosening the grains of sand with their mandibles and tossing them back with their legs. In their excavating activities the harvesters are constantly bringing bits of gravel and sand from deeper in the earth, and it is said that prospectors in New Mexico sometimes plot the courses of manganese veins by observing the subsurface gravel deposited on the tops of harvester ant craters. On the Atacama Desert of Chile, veins of copper, silver and gold have been traced by mineral-bearing gravel excavated by these ants. Of course, the busy ants are not interested in precious minerals; it's all "gravel" to them! Herodotus long ago stated that ants often dragged grains of gold from deep in the earth.

Any creature with the ability and ambition to gather and store food is apt to attract star-boarders who move in to share the bounty. The harvesters are no exception. They have many "guests." These are called *myrmecophiles,* which means "ant lovers," but this term does not exactly describe their relationship. The most interesting of these "guests" are tiny crickets that took up life with the ants so long ago that they have been modified by the semiparasitic existence and can no longer live anywhere else. These little crickets are wingless, but they have large hind legs well fitted for jumping. They stand about "knee high" to their host ants, who tolerate their presence in the nest galleries. In fact, the relationship is somewhat analogous to the presence of cats and dogs in human homes. The crickets actually nibble at the bodies and legs of the ants, apparently to obtain oily secretions. Occasionally, the ants become irritated by this attention and snap at the worrisome crickets, but otherwise they are not disturbed. The crickets are very agile and seem able to escape harm. It is an interesting fact that these crickets are found associated with a number of different kinds of ants, and there is a direct relationship between the sizes of the crickets and their host ants. For example, there are very tiny species of these crickets found in fire ant nests, medium-sized species in harvester ant nests and much larger species in the nests of the large, black carpenter ants that nest in wood.

Harvester ants have several social parasites that live with them. Sometimes these are treated like "pets." Here is shown an ant-loving cricket. These tiny crickets live upon secretions which they lick from the bodies of the ants. In this case, the cricket is licking the hind leg of a harvester worker.

The abundant food supplies in the harvesters' nests also attract thieves. Their granaries are often robbed of their stores of seeds by kangaroo rats that dig into the nest cones. These attractive little rodents are naturally seed eaters, so the grain stored up by the industrious harvesters is an irresistible source of food. Thief ants (*Solenopsis*) often locate their nests close to those of the harvesters. The thief ants are very tiny, and their tunnels are correspondingly small. They dig tunnels to connect with those of the harvesters and steal in to rob them of food, but, because of the small diameters of the tunnels, the harvesters are not able to pursue them.

Harvesters are preyed upon by other kinds of ants. *Dorymyrmex* ants often nest in the area surrounding the harvesters' nest sites and feed upon insects brought in by the harvesters to supplement their grain diet. These ants are hijackers and not only waylay the busy harvesters for the food they carry but often attack the ants themselves. Beyond the fringing grassy jungle surrounding the harvester nests there are still other enemies. Horned toads hide in the vegetation and gobble up foraging ants as they pass by, and birds, of course, take their toll.

Like all ants, new harvester colonies are established by queens that swarm out of the nest, mate and settle down to domestic life. At several periods during spring and summer, large numbers of winged males and females (queens) are produced. These emerge from the nest, and the males climb up on weeds or other places and take off in flight. Soon they are followed by the females. Mating may take place high in the air or on the ground, depending on the species. During these nuptial activities many of the males and queens are captured by birds that gather around for the feast. Each mated queen that survives the nuptial flight selects a nest site, severs her wings, for which she has no further use, and begins excavating a hole in the earth. This hole is several inches deep and connects with from one to four dome-shaped chambers. She next deposits about 50 eggs and, when these hatch, the larvae are fed on material secreted by her. As they grow she cares for them, moving them from one chamber to another so that they will have proper conditions of temperature and humidity. These first workers are smaller than normal because of their limited supply of food, but succeeding generations are fed and cared for by the worker ants and develop normally. From that time on the queen's only function is that of egg-laying. Year by year the colony grows larger as the population increases and new tunnels and chambers are excavated.

While the harvester ants discussed previously do not take any active part in producing the crops they harvest, there are other insects that do actually grow their own food crops. These include several species of ants, the ambrosia beetles and certain African termites. These insects cultivate fungi as food crops. The fungus-cultivating habits of these insects were probably evolved as natural results of their close association with fungi in the locations where their ancestors lived. Fungi are commonly found in soil, so it is natural that ants nesting in subterranean locations should sometimes have used them as food. The next evolutionary step would logically be the development of habits involved with the care and cultivation of the fungi.

The most spectacular of all the fungus growers are ants of the genus *Atta,* found in many areas of the American tropics. One species, *Atta texana,* has extended its range into southern Texas and Louisiana. Other, but smaller and less spectacular, fungus-growing ants are found as far north as Canada. One of the most common of these belongs to the genus *Trachymyrmex.*

Of all the fungus or mushroom growers, the *Atta* ants are by far the most fascinating. Early settlers and travelers in the American tropics often saw the foraging columns of these ants carrying leaves into their

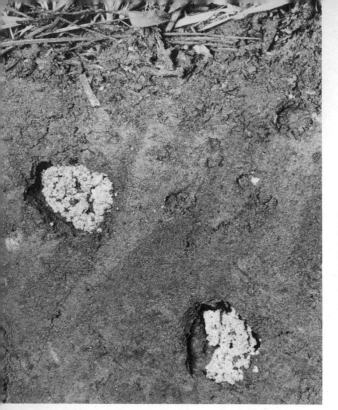

This shows the fungus gardens of the *Trachymyrmex* ants. The cavities in which these fungus gardens are located are from three to six inches below the surface of the ground. Tunnels lead up to the surface. The compost upon which the fungus is grown consists of bits of vegetable debris and caterpillar droppings.

underground nests. The ants follow well-marked trails through the forests to the trees or plants where they cut circular pieces from leaves and carry them back to their nests. Each returning ant carries its piece of leaf held vertically over its head; for this reason they are often called parasol ants. The early observers had no idea to what use the ants put the great quantity of leaves they cut and carried home. H. W. Bates, one of the first naturalist-explorers in South America, who wrote *The Naturalist on the River Amazon,* published in 1892, stated that he had come to the conclusion that the leaves were used to thatch the nest. He evidently thought the leaves were used like wallpaper! Any idea as to their true use was just too fantastic to even consider, yet T. Belt, author of *The Naturalist in Nicaragua,* had excavated one of the underground nests of the leafcutters many years previously and found that none of the large chambers was actually thatched with leaves. On the other hand, he found that the chambers, each the size of a small watermelon, were partly filled with a grayish mass of fungus that seemed to be growing upon a compost made up of vegetable material. He found thousands of ants busily work-

ing in this mass of fungus; apparently, they were cultivating it and feeding on it. After careful investigation, Belt came to the conclusion that
the ants were using the leaves to make a compost upon which they cultivated fungus or mushrooms for food. These observations were made in
1874, but they were too fantastic to be accepted by the scientific world.
Many years later, however, other biologists made careful studies of the
Atta ants and found that Belt had been right all the time; they did cultivate and feed on fungus.

In the regions where the Atta ants are abundant, they are considered
to be serious pests. They have been known to completely defoliate a tree
or destroy a garden overnight. I have seen this occur in southern Louisiana, where I studied the leaf-cutters in their native habitat. A farmer
told me that the ants had also carried off a sack of chicken feed in one
night. Almost any vegetable material is used in their fungus gardens. In
Louisiana their foraging trails can be followed for long distances through
the forest. The trails are about two inches wide and quite distinct,
worn smooth by the feet of countless hurrying ants. If one of these mean-
dering trails is followed, it will be found that it eventually enters a tunnel
about an inch in diameter. After going underground these tunnels continue just beneath the surface for perhaps a hundred feet before angling
downward to the main nest chambers. These so-called "feeder tunnels"
radiate away from the nest area in every direction and afford the ants
easy means of travel to the surrounding foraging areas.

The actual site of the underground nest cavities is easily located. The
surface of the ground is dotted with many flat-topped nest cones, each a
foot in diameter and a few inches high. At the center of each crater is a
large entrance hole. In a way, the area looks something like a prairie-dog
town and may often cover a space several hundred feet in diameter. In
parts of the South, the Attas are called "town ants." Beneath the surface,
at depths ranging from 4 to 20 feet, are located the numerous nest chambers where the ants cultivate their fungus or mushroom gardens. These
chambers vary in size but are usually about 18 inches long and 8 or 10
inches high. They are oval and are interconnected by smooth-walled
tunnels.

The description of the physical aspects of a typical Atta colony might
seem to indicate a relatively simple form of communal life like that of
other ants. The truth is that the daily activities of the Attas are complex
in the extreme and, at present, only partly understood. The logical place
to begin a study of the Attas' agricultural activities is with their harvesting

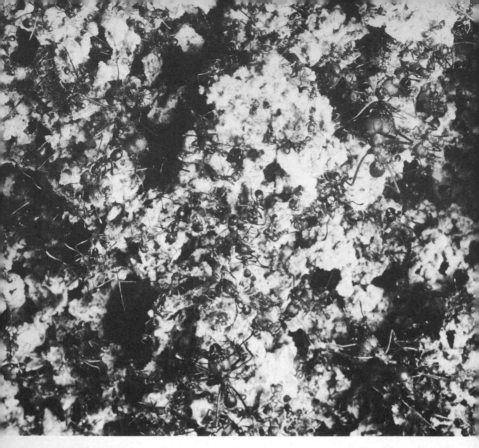

Close-up of *Atta* ants working in their fungus garden. Note the small minim ants that care for the garden and weed out the foreign fungi. Note also the medium-sized ants. These form most of the labor force concerned with harvesting leaves. The largest ants are the warrior caste, whose function is the protection of the colony.

of leaf fragments which constitute the raw agricultural product. The ants set out on leaf-gathering safaris at various times of the day—the time seems to be governed by weather conditions. Usually, these safaris occur at night, but the *Attas* have been known to work during the daylight hours, especially during cloudy weather. Usually, they do not gather leaves during periods of drought. My own observations of the leaf-gathering habits of these remarkable ants were made at night. I watched the returning columns of ants, each with a piece of leaf held over its head. They hurried along the well-worn path, now and then bumping into obstructions such as small roots, and there was a definite urgency about their actions. In the column were ants of several sizes, but it was the

Atta ants carrying leaf fragments toward the nest. These may be harvested several hundred feet from the nest and carried over well-marked trails to the entrance.

medium-sized ants that carried the loads. The largest ants, or soldier caste, did no work but followed along with the rest. Most of the soldiers, however, remain in the nest, perhaps for colony protection. I followed the columns until they came to the tunnel entrances and disappeared underground. What mysteries lay beneath my feet I could only guess. No biologist has ever studied closely the activities within the undisturbed nest, though the nests have often been excavated and many of the details of their lives observed.

After being deposited within the nest chambers, the leaves are chewed up into fine pieces and placed in the masses of growing fungus. Bits of the fungus *mycelium* are planted on the leaf fragments, and these grow rapidly, soon covering them with a gray, cottony growth. This fungus garden is cared for by very tiny castes, or forms, of the ants, called *minims*. These are midget workers. As might be expected, the leaves brought in by the foragers contain numerous fungus spores, and if these foreign fungi were not weeded out they would soon contaminate the pure culture of the special fungus cultivated by the *Attas*. This fungus has been cultivated by the ants for so long that it seems, in most cases, to have lost its ability to produce true fruiting bodies. For this reason it cannot usually be classified. The fungi cultivated by some other ants have been identified and found to be the *mycelium* stages of mushrooms or *Basidiomycetes*. They are not mold fungi. Large mushrooms or toadstools have been found growing out of abandoned fungus and nests, and these, presumably, were the fruiting stages of the ant fungus. While under control of the ants, however, the fungus is never allowed to develop into the mushroom stage. Actually, the ants do not feed upon the cottony mycelium; their food consists of small capsules or clumps formed on it called bromatia or "kohlrabi clusters." Since these are not normal to the "wild" fungus, evidently the ants do something to the fungus to cause their formation.

In the dark subterranean caves the minims toil endlessly, cultivating, pruning and weeding the cottony garden. During dry spells the outside nest entrances are closed to regulate the humidity, an important factor in the proper growth of the fungus. During foraging periods, loads of fresh leaves are brought in. Sometimes a few of the minims go out with the foragers, stimulated, perhaps, by a half-forgotten instinct from the ancient days before they became gardeners and weeders. On rare occasions some small enemy, such as a mouse, may attempt to invade the nest, but the ants quickly sound the alarm through the dark passages by means of their stridulating organs, producing a small squeaking sound. The enemy is soon destroyed or driven out by the sharp jaws of the soldiers, which can easily pierce the skin of a human. They have no stings.

In addition to toiling in the fungus garden the minims assume the role of nursemaids. The white, helpless larvae are fed and cared for with great solicitude. They rest in the soft fungus garden and are moved about now and then, perhaps to more suitable levels within the fungus mass. In time, they transform into the pupal stage and, later, into the adult form.

The founding of new *Atta* colonies is similar to that of the harvesters, but is on a grander scale because the colonies are larger, often containing nearly a million ants. During spring, winged male and female ants swarm out of the subterranean nests and mate. These mating flights usually occur during moonless nights following rainstorms. They begin precisely at 3:40 A.M. and continue until dawn. There are usually enormous numbers of these males and females and, in Louisiana, small piles of dead ants often accumulate under bright lights such as are found at service stations. Each mated queen that survives the wedding flight, like the harvester queen, severs her wings and excavates a cavity in the sandy soil. She then seals the entrance and goes into a period of isolation that lasts about 40 days. Her first act after closing the nest entrance is the depositing, from a special pouch in her mouth, of a bit of fungus she has brought with her from the parent nest. She fertilizes this with material from her own alimentary canal. Her large flight muscles are slowly broken down into a form useful as nourishment, thus helping her to survive. She now begins laying eggs and, when these hatch, the larvae are fed on fungus and also on subsequently laid eggs. She must sacrifice some eggs to feed the growing young. In time, the young transform into adult workers who open the nest and begin gathering plant material to nourish the garden. A new colony is founded that will slowly expand as the years pass.

During later years newly mated queens are often taken into the colony and adopted. Thus, the life of the colony continues to thrive far beyond the life-span of the original queen.

Like the harvester ants, the *Attas* have a "house guest," that long ago moved in to share their bounty. This is a tiny, wingless cockroach (*Attaphila fungicola*) that lives with them in apparent harmony. Interestingly, this little cockroach is the only "guest" found associated with the *Attas,* which may indicate that these ants do not tolerate unbidden boarders. There is one strange fact concerning these little cockroaches that has never been explained. Every one of these "guests" always has its antennae clipped off short. They do not feed on the fungus cultivated by the ants but feed by licking secretions from the bodies of the ants. Like other myrmecophilous insects, these cockroaches are never found anywhere but in the underground nests of the *Atta*. The way the cockroaches become established in new ant nests is a marvel of adaptation to a life of social parasitism. When virgin queens are ready to leave the parent nest on their nuptial flights, the tiny cockroaches attach themselves to the queens and cling to them until they excavate cavities in the earth and establish new colonies. Thus, the *Atta* queens take their "pets" and a "start" of fungus with them when they leave the family nest and start out in the world on their own.

The *Trachymyrmex* ants mentioned previously also cultivate fungus gardens. These ants are closely related to the *Attas* and are actually miniatures of them in many respects. They are much smaller in size and their bodies are covered with numerous spines. They are very timid ants and, unlike the *Attas,* make no effort to defend their nests, which are located in subterranean cavities about the size of oranges. While the fungus gardens of the *Atta* rest upon the floors of the caves or cavities, those of the *Trachymyrmex* ants are usually suspended from small roots that penetrate the nest spaces. Instead of gathering large pieces of leaves, the latter ants gather caterpillar droppings, small flower petals or vegetable debris. I have successfully kept *Trachymyrmex* colonies alive in artificial nests for long periods by supplying them with finely chopped up leaves or rose petals. There are several species of these ants, and they occur in many parts of North America.

We might expect to find agricultural habits among the social insects, but we would certainly not expect to find them in the beetle tribe. Yet, there are certain wood-boring beetles that have developed fungus-growing habits quite similar to those of the *Attas* and other ants—the ambrosia beetles of the genus *Xyleborus*. They are closely related to the engraver beetles which excavate tunnels of intricate designs beneath the bark of many trees. These beetles both belong to the family Scolytidae.

Ambrosia beetles are quite small. They are hardly over a quarter of an inch in length, and the tunnels they excavate in trees are not much larger than the lead in a pencil. The male and female beetles—or sometimes, just the females—bore tunnels straight into the solid wood of living or recently cut trees. First, a main tunnel is excavated, then short side chambers are hollowed out. These latter are the "cradle" chambers in

Like the harvester ants, the *Attas* have at least one "guest" or social parasite. In this case it is a tiny cockroach which lives in the fungus garden. Strangely, the antennae of these little roaches are always clipped off short.

each of which an egg is laid. There are actually a number of different species of ambrosia beetles and the forms of their nests vary somewhat. Like the *Atta* queens, the female beetles carry a "start" of fungus when they leave the parent colony. In the case of the ambrosia beetles, however, the fungi they cultivate are molds and not the mycelial stages of mushrooms. Instead of carrying bits of the fungal threads, as do the ants, the beetles carry spore-bearing *conidia*. The spores are "planted" in beds of wood chips cut from the tunnels, producing abundant fungus growths. Apparently, these fungus gardens are also fertilized by excrement from the beetles. Both larvae and adults feed on the tender shoots of the fungus.

In those species of beetles that excavate cradle chambers, each larval beetle occupies its own chamber where it is fed and its waste removed by the adult beetles.

In the tropics, there are ambrosia beetles that live in the wood of casks used for holding water or wine. Naturally, the tunnels excavated by the beetles allow the liquid contents to leak out. One of these, *Xyleborus perforans,* is known as "Tippling Tommy."

Termites are strange creatures of the darkness that feed, in most instances, upon wood. They are an ancient race, far older than the ants or bees. Because of their wood-eating habits, they have incurred man's ire, and people are usually more interested in destroying them than in studying their habits. Like the ants, they are social insects, living together in large colonies. The termites that invade our houses in the United States tunnel into the timbers and eat the wood. This wood is not digested by the termites but by certain microscopic protozoa that live in their intestines. The nourishment obtained from the wood by the protozoans is then absorbed by the termites. It is a necessary and complicated arrangement, for the protozoans cannot live outside the termites' bodies and the termites cannot get along without the protozoans.

The continent of Africa might be called the Termite Capital of the World. There, termites of many kinds are found, some with very unusual habits. Among these are termites that cultivate fungus gardens after the manner of the *Attas*. Perhaps it is not too surprising to encounter the fungus-growing habit among these insects for they have dwelled for millions of years in situations where fungi abound. In Africa, some of the most serious termite pests are those that cultivate fungi. For instance,

Macrotermes natalensis has habits quite similar to those of the *Atta* ants. These termites chew up wood and use this as a medium or compost upon which they cultivate small, honeycombed fungus gardens, each about the size of a walnut. Like the *Atta* fungus, small clumps or bromatia are formed here and there on the surface of the garden. Bromatia are a special food, however, and are fed only to the chosen few. This ambrosia is reserved for the young termites and for the royalty, or kings and queens. As in the case of the fungus-growing ants, special workers tend the gardens, but, as far as is known, the workers do not feed on the fungus. Perhaps, nature balances the economy within the nest in this way; the termite colonies contain so many workers that there would probably not be enough of the ambrosial food to go around.

chapter nine

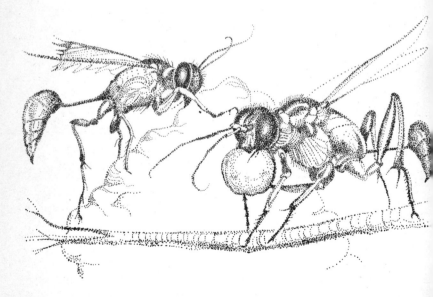

The Builders

USUALLY we think of insects as being mere automatons unable to do anything except what instinct dictates. Yet many insects seem at times to be almost endowed with human intelligence. The insects, through their long evolution, have developed and refined instinctive behavior to an astonishing degree. By instinct alone insects are able to carry a multitude of complex procedures to successful conclusions. A number of these require tremendous skill and it is almost incredible to us that mere insects could accomplish results so difficult and complex.

Some insects seem often to show glimmerings of learning ability—the ability to adapt their actions to new circumstances. In the case of the caddis larva, each pebble it attaches to its case presents a somewhat different problem since no two pebbles are ever exactly the same shape and must be fitted together. On the other hand, a caddis larva that normally constructs its cases of pebbles cannot build one out of sticks if no pebbles are available.

Many insects have developed skills in the structural trades that parallel those found in human societies. Most of these insect artisans belong to the most advanced insect order, the Hymenoptera, which includes the ants, wasps and bees, and yet the caddis insects, which are also craftsmen, are quite primitive, belonging to one of the most lowly of the insect clans, the Trichoptera.

In general, these insects use their skills to construct homes or shelters for themselves or for their future young which, in most instances, they will never see. The materials used are usually those that are readily available; these include clay, mud, wood, leaves, wax or resins collected from plants. These basic structural materials are often mixed with saliva or other secreted substances to give them added strength and durability. Silk secreted by silk glands is frequently used for fastening building materials together.

Mason wasps, of which there are many kinds, use clay or mud for the construction of cells in which their larvae develop. At least two wasp families are involved—the family Eumenidae to which the potter wasps belong and the family Sphecidae which contains the so-called mud daubers and related wasps. These wasps are of wide distribution, various species being found in many parts of the world. They are all solitary, never forming colonies as do the hornets and many bees.

Some of my most interesting experiences have been those involved in recording the habits of mud daubers on film. I recall a small pond surrounded by muddy margins where yellow-legged mud daubers (*Sceliphron caementarium*) were busily collecting pellets of clay and carrying them by air to a shed a few hundred feet away for use in cell construction. The banks surrounding the pond were about six feet high, so the wasps carrying the heavy pellets often had some difficulty in air-lifting them. They buzzed straight up from the collecting sites, and it apparently required all their flight power to clear the bank. Once over the bank, however, they seemed to have no difficulty in flying with their loads.

Photographing the wasps presented a problem since they were rather shy and easily frightened by the camera. I eventually solved the problem by using a long-focus lens which enabled me to obtain a large image at a distance of more than a foot. Even so, they viewed the camera with suspision. Upon alighting on the bank, each wasp almost always faced the camera and pranced back and forth in indecision. Having at last made up her mind that all was safe, the wasp would select a spot where the clay seemed to have the proper consistency, tip up her body to an almost vertical position and begin scraping up a ball of clay with her mandibles. Sometimes the work was complicated by the presence of small roots, and then the wasp found it necessary to tug this way and that until the ball was clear. The front feet were used to help hold it. These balls of clay were about the size of small peas and, while the wasps were in flight, were held between the wide-spread mandibles and the front feet. Once the clay pellet was collected, the wasp did not hesitate but at once spread her wings and buzzed upward. She arose slowly at first but gradually gained speed like a helicopter taking off. Now and then a wasp accidentally dropped her pellet and had to return for another load. The task of collecting and forming the clay pellets took only about five or six seconds, within which time it was necessary to locate the wasp on the groundglass, carefully focus and then take the picture. The day was very hot and apparently the toiling insects were affected as much as I was. Upon returning to the pond for another load of clay, many of them first visited the water's edge and drank before resuming work.

I also saw many metallic blue wasps drinking water, but these insects never made any effort to collect and carry clay. After filling up with water they flew away in the direction of the old shed. They were blue burglar wasps (*Chalybion caerulium*) which use the water they imbibe to soften the walls of mud dauber nests so they can break in and toss out all the spiders so laboriously collected by the rightful owners. The blue burglars then restock the cells with spiders they, themselves, have collected and lay their own eggs inside before resealing them. In addition to other spiders, they often stock the cells with black widow spiders. The burglars,

however, are poor craftsmen and their skill as masons is far inferior to that of the mud daubers. In resealing the clay cell, the blue burglar does an amateurish job. Perhaps this is a result of her long habit of living as a lazy parasite. Once, perhaps a million years ago, she may have been as skilled as the mud dauber in cell construction, but she has now degenerated to a plunderer of other wasps' nests.

The sites chosen by mud daubers for the construction of their cells may be almost anywhere, the chief requirement being shelter from the rain. Before the coming of man and his wooden buildings the wasps probably built their nests in hollow trees or beneath stone ledges. Structures built by man, however, turned out to be a boon to mud daubers. Never before in all their history had the wasps had such choice locations, and they immediately began taking full advantage of them. Rarely are mud dauber nests now found anywhere except in man-made structures. Only two basic things are needed by mud daubers for nest construction, a source of clay or mud of the proper kind and a nearby, sheltered location for the cells. The wasps are very particular about the kind of clay or mud they use. It must be smooth-flowing and of the proper consistency; if it contains too much coarse sand the wasps will not use it. I know of a group of abandoned buildings which would seem to be ideal as sites for nests, but I have never seen nests there. This puzzled me for a long while until I realized that even though there are ponds and streams nearby, the area is very sandy and contains no clay or mud. It is an interesting fact that the clay used by mud daubers is of about the same quality as that used by human potters. A number of years ago, for example, a number of mud dauber nests were collected in the vicinity of Pigeon Forge, Tennessee, and burned in a kiln. These nests showed that the clay from which they had been constructed had all the qualities needed for making pottery. When tapped with a steel instrument, these burned nests rang like china. As a result, a very successful pottery industry was founded there. Pigeon Forge pottery is now rather well known in the Great Smoky Mountains.

Mud daubers are always searching for mud and will quickly find any small mud puddle, such as that made by a leaky garden faucet. Realizing this, I recently made an artificial mud puddle in a large, shallow pan and was pleased when mud daubers in large numbers found it and began air-lifting the mud. What I did not know until later was that the wasps were using the mud to construct nests on all my neighbors' porches. For some reason they ignored my own porch.

Mud dauber wasps construct their clay cells under bridges or other sheltered locations. Shown here are cells built by organ pipe wasps (*Trypoxylon politum*) and by the common mud daubers (*Sceliphron caementarium*). Many of the cells show exit holes where adults or parasites have emerged.

In building their cells the female wasps—only the females build clay cells—first smear the selected surface with thin coatings of clay. The cells are then formed, each load of clay being applied with consummate skill in a definite pattern. In her work the wasp uses her front feet and her head to smear and shape the clay. The cell itself is constructed by applying succeeding clay pellets first on one side and then on the other in a series of arches. The finished cells show ridges where each successive load was shaped into the desired form. There are always the same number of diagonal ridges and, because of these, the cells often look like tiny mummies complete with spiral wrappings. About 30 loads of clay are needed to construct a cell. During the entire process of cell construction the wasp works by instinct. It is almost as if she were being guided, step by step, by a set of detailed instructions, except that she cannot go back and do any part of the job over. It must be right the first time or not at all. Once she has passed one stage she must go on to the next without question. First comes the selection of the site, then, probably, the search for clay, then the step-by-step construction. When the cell is completed, her instinct tells her to hunt spiders. These must be of moderate size, though she is not too particular as to species. She paralyzes these by plunging her sting into them and injecting a special narcotic poison.

After the first paralyzed spider is placed in the cell the wasp then lays an egg on it. Some observers, however, state that the egg is laid on the second or even the third spider. Apparently, it is never placed on the last one. If darkness interrupts the task of stocking the nest with spiders, the wasp constructs a thin curtain of clay across the nest entrance to keep out enemies. This is removed the next morning. When the cell is filled with six or eight paralyzed spiders, the wasp flies away for more clay to seal the entrance. This is her final act and she may then spend some time sipping nectar from flowers, as the males have been doing all along since they take no part in constructing or stocking the nests. She may then construct other individual cells or return and build other cells alongside the first one. Often clusters of cells as large as a person's fist are built. Such cell clusters are presumably the work of individual females. It is of interest that there is considerable variation in the manner in which individual wasps finish the outer surfaces of their cells. Some seem content to leave their cells unadorned while others decorate them with blobs of clay. Sometimes, too, these blobs are of contrasting colors. It seems almost as if some mud daubers deliberately seek clays of contrasting hues

When the cell is finished the mud dauber stocks it with paralyzed spiders, lays an egg in it and seals the entrance. The wasp larva feeds upon the spiders.

'or this final decoration, but only occasionally do they use clay of more than one color for building the main portions of the cells. After examining large numbers of mud dauber cells, it becomes obvious that they exhibit considerable individuality in their surface architecture. I wonder whether the evolution of instincts that govern the building of these cells has reached the point where the glimmerings of intelligence guide the final acts of nest construction?

It will be noticed, too, that there are many unfinished nests. No doubt these are the result of little tragedies since wasps have many enemies that often capture them during the process of nest building. This is undoubtedly the reason that each cell is built and stocked individually. But even after the nest is completed, stocked with spiders and sealed, there is still no assurance that a wasp will develop there. In rearing these insects from collected cells we are always surprised at the small number that eventually produce wasps. Usually the percentage is below 25 percent and may be much lower. Phil and Nellie Rau (1916) collected 4,397 nests from which only 175 adults, or 4 percent, emerged. Many cells are built and stocked but few result in future wasps. Insect parasites and predators of many kinds break into the cells and lay their eggs or devour the larval wasps. These enemies of the mud dauber include several kinds of parasitic flies and wasps as well as scavenger beetles. Not all of the nesting failures can be laid to enemies; in many instances the mother wasp is at fault. Sometimes she stocks the nest with insufficient spiders to supply the larva and it dies before maturity; in about an equal number of cases the mud dauber eggs fail to hatch.

Shortly after the cell has been sealed, the wasp egg attached to one of the spiders hatches into a small larva that immediately begins feeding upon the helpless spider. The larva grows rapidly as it consumes one spider after another. This rapid development is a special adaptation since the store of living food will not remain in proper condition for very long. Usually the spiders will all be consumed and the larva full grown in from two to five days. Mud dauber larvae, like many other insect larvae that develop in closed spaces, do not void excrement during their growth. Indeed, their mid- and hindguts are not connected until the time arrives for the formation of the cocoon and subsequent pupation. At this time all the accumulated waste material is voided at one time. After transformation to the pupal stage there is an interval of about three weeks during which the larval tissues are broken down and changed into adult tissue. When the time for emergence arrives the adult wasp chews its way out through the clay cell and flies away; the life cycle has been completed. There are two or three generations a year. Some complete their cycles during the summer, but the larvae that develop in autumn do not emerge until spring; winter is passed in the protective earthen cells.

So far we have considered only the yellow-legged mud dauber which builds her cells as separate units or in clusters, but there is another kind, the organ-pipe builder, *Trypoxylon politum,* with equally interesting habits. The shiny black organ-pipe wasp constructs her cells in the form of tubes partitioned off into sections, each of which is stocked with spiders and sealed off, one at a time. Sometimes these nests consist of single tubes, but usually they are in groups placed side by side. Now and then one finds instances where additional tubes are constructed on top of those previously constructed. It is from the nest form, of course, that the organ-pipe wasp gets its name. While the habits of the two mud dauber wasps are quite similar, there is one interesting difference. Whereas the male yellow-legged mud dauber is a lazy fellow whose only interest, beyond mating, is sipping nectar, the male organ-pipe wasp actually remains with the female and guards the cell while she is away gathering clay or hunting spiders. He hides in the cell and presumably drives away potential enemies. Although he never actually takes an active part in domestic labor, when one remembers the many enemies and parasites that infest mud dauber nests, he does seem to serve a useful purpose.

As might be expected, the abandoned cells of mud daubers are often used as nests by other insects. They are ready-made homes that save the labor of construction. Some wasps are so specialized that they apparently cannot build their nests anywhere else. Probably the most interesting of these are the tenant wasps or "house-renters" (*Trypoxylon clavatum*) that nest in old nests of both the yellow-legged and organ-pipe mud daubers. Other tenant wasps are so small that they must construct partitions across old mud dauber cells in order to adapt them to their own use.

In addition to the mud daubers there are many other species of *Trypoxylon* wasps that use any small cavity, such as a key-hole, wood-borer tunnel, knothole or even the depressions in carvings. Such cavities are stocked with spiders and the openings sealed with clay. They are not skilled masons and represent, perhaps, more primitive nest-building habits than those of the true mud daubers.

Recently it was my privilege to visit Oak Ridge National Laboratory to observe some interesting mason wasp research being done there. A rather amazing discovery regarding mud daubers has been made by Dr.

Alvin F. Shinn of the Radiation Ecology Section. Sometime ago it was discovered that yellow-legged mud dauber wasps were collecting highly radioactive mud from waste pits and using it to construct cells in nearby electronic equipment. Since some of these cells were found to be emitting gamma rays at rates as high as one roentgen per hour, the proper functioning of the electronic equipment was being interfered with. This led to studies of the wasps, especially the yellow-legged mud dauber and the organ-pipe wasps. It has now been established that, while the yellow-legged mud daubers will gather and use the "hot" mud for nest construction, the organ-pipe wasp will not do so. This is most interesting since it indicates that in some way the organ-pipe wasps can detect radiation. This is the only case known where any animal has been found capable of detecting radioactivity. While at Oak Ridge, I visited one of the "hot" waste pits where gamma rays were being emitted so strongly that the safe human exposure time was only a fraction of a minute. Yet, the yellow-legged mud daubers were busily gathering the mud! By contrast, the organ-pipe wasps were completely absent.

Of all the wasps, however, that build with clay, the potter wasps (*Eumenes*) are the most skillful. There are many different species in the United States and other lands, but their habits are all quite similar. Almost everyone has seen the cells of the potter wasps; they are beautifully formed and resemble small jugs complete with necks and flaring, funnel-like tops. They are delicate little structures and it would seem that rain water would quickly dissolve them, yet they are often built in unprotected places. Sometimes they are found in little rows on twigs or attached to the sides of trees. I once watched a potter wasp building her masterpiece on the side of a cypress deep in the Everglades.

Potter wasps are of moderate size and black with yellow, orange or red markings. As a craftsman—or perhaps we should say craftswoman— she is without equal in the insect world. In building her jug, she plasters each load of clay along the rim and then smoothes it down between her mandibles and forelegs in a manner quite similar to .that used by the mud dauber. She is a better craftsman, however, and the walls of the cell are very thin. The inside walls are smooth, but there are raised lumps or tubercles scattered over the outside, resulting, apparently, from the fact that not all of the loads of clay are smoothed off. Perhaps this is done as a means of camouflage.

After the jug has been finished, complete with flaring neck, the wasp then inserts her abdomen into the open neck and lays an egg. The egg

The potter wasp (*Eumenes*) constructs her delicate jug of clay and then stocks it with paralyzed caterpillars which serve as food for her larva.

is suspended on a slender thread like a ceiling droplight and hangs down in the cell. This is probably done to make sure that it will not be injured by the partially paralyzed, but still quite lively, caterpillars with which the cell will be stocked. You will recall that the mud daubers, by contrast, lay their eggs on one of the first spiders placed in the nest. The caterpillars captured by the jug builder are of small size, usually not over a quarter of an inch long. After being stocked the neck of the jug is sealed with clay. There is an interesting variation, however, in the habit of an African species which does not mass-provision its nest but leaves the cell open so that fresh caterpillars can be supplied to the growing larva each day.

One of my earliest studies of insects was one concerning caddis insects that dwell in water and construct stone cases within which they dwell secure from most enemies. I collected these insects during winter in a warm spring that emerged from the side of a mountain and placed them, along with aquatic plants, in a jar. Through the walls of this makeshift aquarium I watched them reconstruct their stone tubes after I had removed portions of them.

In many ways the caddis insects (order Trichoptera), of which there are about 750 kinds in the United States, are the most fascinating of all

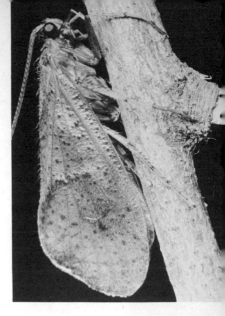

Adult caddis insects are moth-like and are often attracted to lights in the vicinity of lakes and streams.

insects that nature has endowed with structural skills. The mud daubers and potter wasps belong to the most advanced order, the Hymenoptera, so the presence of craftsmen among them might be expected, but it is a little surprising to find such skill in a low order of insects such as the caddisflies. The Trichoptera received their name from two Greek words meaning "hairy wings" which certainly describes the adults. They are closely related to the Lepidoptera or butterflies and moths, with which they probably have a common ancestry. The ancestors of the Lepidoptera and Trichoptera probably had hairy wings and it required only a moderate amount of evolutionary change to transform their hairy wings into the scaly wings of butterflies and moths. The Trichoptera or caddisflies did not make the change; their wings are still covered with hair.

The common names of these interesting insects, caddis insects or caddisflies, probably came from their original name, "caseflies," which was applied to them because of the stone cases within which the larval forms live. There is, however, the possibility that the word comes from the Celtic word "caddis" which was applied to heavy cotton twill, a fabric often used for robes worn by clergymen. At any rate, the caddis insects constitute the largest group of aquatic insects and are found in almost all parts of the world, though they are most abundant in the cool waters of the lakes and streams of the Temperate Zone. A few kinds are even found in salt water. The adults resemble small moths, but they are not at all colorful, most kinds being gray or dull yellowish. Usually the adults

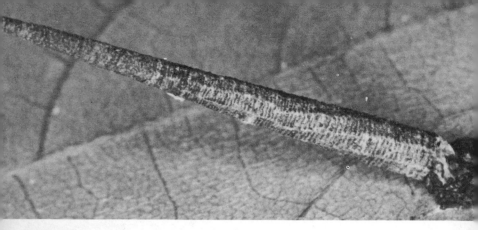

The caterpillar of a small moth (*Coleophora octagonella*) constructed this case. It resembles some caddis cases. The caterpillar builds its case of its own droppings and feeds upon leaves.

are most active at dusk when they leave their hiding places in vegetation near streams to engage in nuptial flights. Sometimes they are very abundant in such places, where they may often be seen skimming back and forth over the surface. Their mouthparts are fitted for taking liquid foods, but the adults do not normally seem inclined to feed to any extent. Some species, however, do visit flowers for nectar.

Caddisflies usually lay a large number of eggs, which offsets the high mortality rates of the young larvae. The number of eggs varies from 300 to 1,000. In some species the females crawl beneath the surface to deposit their eggs, while others merely push their abdomens below the water. Some species drop their eggs on the surface of the water; in other species the eggs are laid on plants or stones above the surface. During rains the gelatinous coverings of the egg masses swell and liquefy; the young quickly hatch and are carried down into the water by raindrops. Eggs laid in water are usually in strings, but one species, *Phryganea interrupta,* lays its eggs in a doughnut-shaped mass. Caddis eggs are almost

A caddis insect (*Phryganea*) in its case under water. These caddis insects build their cases of pine needles and grass stems.

This caddis case from the Great Smoky Mountains was built of bits of bark and sticks. This species always constructs its cases in the same way: two twigs are attached to the sides.

always enclosed in a gelatinous matrix which makes them adhere to aquatic plants.

The habits of caddis larvae are quite varied. In some kinds such as *Rhyacophila* the larvae are free-living and build no cases until the time for pupation arrives. In other kinds the larvae are free-living for only a short time and then settle down and construct cases. In some species the caddis larvae drag their cases about with them; in other species the cases are permanently attached to large stones. In general, those species that live in rapidly flowing water, such as tumbling mountain streams, have heavier cases than those that dwell in sluggish rivers or in lakes. This, of course, prevents their being tossed about in currents. For building their cases, caddis larvae make use of a wide variety of building materials such as are available in their aquatic habitat. These include pieces of leaves, grass and bark as well as twigs. Many kinds use gravel or fine sand. Each species usually has its own special style of architecture; thus the shapes and forms of the cases vary widely.

It is always interesting to watch caddis larvae build their cases. Soft materials, such as bark fragments or pieces of leaves and grass, are cut to size by the larva's jaws but sand and pebbles are, of course, used as they are found and fitted onto the case. New materials are attached at the front ends of the cases and cemented in place by a gluelike substance secreted by glands in the forepart of the body. In some kinds, old cases

177

This square case was constructed by caddis insects of the genus *Brachycentrus*. The structural materials are bits of aquatic plants or wood.

are abandoned and new ones built as the larvae increase in size. In the selection of structural materials the larvae often show very interesting preferences. Usually their choices are quite definite and they will not accept substitutes; however, if they are carefully removed from their cases and placed in an aquarium where only "foreign" material is available, they will often attempt to use it for case building. For example, a lady in England succeeded in getting caddis larvae to construct cases of gold dust. When several caddis larvae are moved from their cases and placed in an aquarium along with an amount of building material that is insufficient for all, they are not above stealing from each other. This is often accompanied by considerable fighting. When given only foreign building material some individuals seem better able to adapt themselves to its use than others, which would seem to indicate differences in "intelligence" or adaptability.

If a large number of caddis cases are examined it will be found that they often use unusual materials, even in their natural habitats. These include small snail shells, grains of wheat, various plant seeds and other artifacts. In one instance it was found that caddis larvae that normally build cases of small pebbles seemed to show a preference for small opals that were scattered among the other gravel at the bottom of the stream.

I was once collecting caddis insects in a small stream at the foot of the majestic Teton Mountains in Wyoming. When these were examined it was found that one of them had used a piece of quartz containing a fleck of shiny gold! Other caddis collectors, too, have found gold, as well as other rare metals, in caddis cases, but these, of course, had been picked up and used by the industrious insects along with other materials and do not necessarily indicate special preference. To a caddis a gold nugget is the same as a piece of gravel.

The larvae themselves are more or less caterpillarlike but have special adaptations for aquatic life. Their forelegs are the stoutest and are used for case building or for holding prey. In most species there are rows of gill filaments along the sides of the body. Since they live in cases there are three "spacing humps" on the first abdominal segment to center the larvae in their tubes and allow water to flow freely through their gills. This flow of water is created by undulatory movements of the insects' abdomens. Case-bearing caddis larvae cannot swim in most instances but crawl about over the bottom or among aquatic plants. Some species feed upon algae or other plants while others capture small crustaceans, worms or insect larvae. Some kinds, as we shall see later, spin seines in which they trap food from flowing water.

In view of the unusual habits of the caddis insects, it is of value to present a brief survey of the family groups and the types of cases constructed by them.

Family Philopotamidae—The Silken-tube Spinners. These caddis larvae live in swift mountain streams where they construct silken tubelike nets within which they live. These nets are attached to rocks, with their front ends upstream, so that water flows continuously through them. The larvae feed upon organic materials strained out of the water. They are somewhat gregarious and large numbers often live close together.

Family Hydropsychidae—The Seine Builders. In many respects these are the most interesting of all caddis insects. It is a large family, many species being found in various parts of the world. I have collected and photographed them in mountain streams in both the Rockies and the Great Smoky Mountains. In Australia and Tasmania there is a species called the snowflake caddis because of the white wings of the adults which often fly over the water in clouds. It is the larval habits of the seine builders, however, that are of special interest. These larvae fabricate small seines from silk secreted by glands. They are beautifully woven and resemble very closely the seines used by fishermen. Those belonging to the genus

Probably the most interesting of the caddis insects are the seine builders (*Hydropsyche*) that live in pebble tubes attached to rocks. Alongside their cases they construct silken seines that strain bits of organic matter out of the water. It is upon this that they feed.

Hydropsyche are probably the most skillful of the seine weavers. Their seines are placed at right angles to the current and the larvae live in retreats located alongside. These retreats are constructed of small stones cemented together and here the larvae live, safe from enemies. As the water flows through the silken seines, various bits of organic material or small aquatic animals are trapped. Periodically the caddis larvae crawl out and feed upon the bounty so conveniently deposited at their doors.

Family Hydroptilidae—The Micro-Caddisflies. These are small insects that construct bean-shaped or flask-shaped cases which are dragged about as the insects crawl. They are found in lakes as well as streams and feed on algae.

Family Pharyganeidae—The Large Caddisflies. The adults of these caddisflies are quite large, often measuring over an inch in length, and the larvae and their cases are proportionately large. They favor marshes and lakes, but a few live in streams. Their cases are constructed of bits of leaves or sticks placed end to end and usually arranged in spirals. When ready to pupate, the larvae of some species burrow into submerged logs. The adults often have wings marked by contrasting colors.

Family Limnephilidae—Northern Caddisflies. This is one of the largest families, there being about 200 species which are found mostly in northern and western North America. In some species the adults are quite large and, like those of the previous family, have "pictured" wings. The cases built by the larvae are of many forms, and in some species the cases built by the young larvae are different from those built by older larvae. For example, in a Canadian species, *Limnephilus combinus,* the young larvae build log-cabin cases with small sticks placed crosswise, but when they grow older an entirely different type of case is built consisting of bits of bark and snail shells. There is great variation in the cases built by

This caddis insect is found in the Rocky Mountains. It fits and cements small pebbles together to form the case. (family Limnephilidae)

Sometimes snail shells are cemented to caddis cases. In some instances the living snail is inside.

the caddis insects of this family, and they use a wide variety of building materials, including sand, bark, sticks or snail shells. Some members of the genus *Limnephilus* construct their cases entirely of small snail shells. Actually, small shells are used by many caddis larvae and they are not too particular as to whether the owner is "home" or not. It is amusing to watch a tiny snail whose shell has been firmly cemented to a caddis case attempt to crawl one way while the caddis larva crawls off in another direction. The members of this family are usually found in ponds and slow-flowing streams and are often called "rockworms."

Family Leptoceridae—Long-horned Caddisflies. This is a large family whose members occur in many localities. The adults, as their name implies, have unusually long antennae; sometimes these are several times as long as their bodies. The architecture of their cases varies widely; some are constructed of bark fragments while others are of fine sand. The cases of those that use sand are often cornucopia-shaped as are those of the

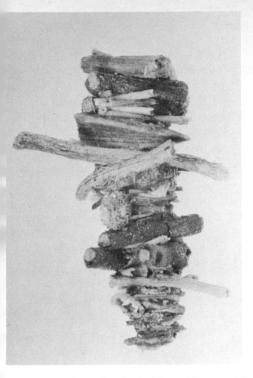

This caddis case was constructed of twigs and grass stems attached crosswise. Cases of this type are built by the log-cabin caddis insects (*Oecetis*).

Front view of another log-cabin caddis case. This shows how the "logs" are fitted together.

genus *Leptocella*, but in others, such as the genus *Leptocerus*, they are shaped like slender ice cream cones. One widely distributed leptocerid, *Athripsodes ancylus*, constructs its case of sand in the form of a shield, on the underside of which is a pocket in which the larva lives. Included also in this family are the log-cabin builders of the genus *Oecetis*, found in quiet streams and pools in many places. Their very characteristic cases are constructed of tiny twigs or spruce needles attached crosswise so that they look like little log cabins. The larvae are predaceous.

This unusual case was built of sand grains by the snail-shell caddis insect (*Helicopsyche*). Such cases are about one-eighth inch in diameter.

Family Brachycentridae—The Chimney-case Caddisflies. This is a small family, but its members are interesting in that they construct small, tapering cases, square in cross-section, built of plant fragments. They may often be found under stones or upon water-logged pieces of wood.

Family Helicopsychidae—Snail-case Caddisflies. This is a small family containing but a single genus, *Helicopsyche,* but they are of unusual interest, however, since the larvae construct their sand-grain cases in the form of small, spiral snail shells. Indeed, they resemble snail shells so closely that they are often confused with them. They are usually found in clear, swift streams.

chapter ten

The Paper and Tent Makers

THE insect artisans that build nests of clay and stone are, at least in North America, all solitary insects. They work individually and their nests, or cells, are not the results of community effort. Often these insects build their nests close to each other, but each nest is an individual project. The paper and tent builders, on the other hand, usually construct their shelters as cooperative projects and these serve as homes for colonies, all individuals of which hatch from eggs laid by a single queen that, presumably, founded the colony. They are thus *social* insects and belong to the order Hymenoptera, which includes the wasps, bees and ants. The paper and tent makers are either wasps, hornets or ants. There are a few insects of other orders that also construct tentlike shelters, but these are the dwelling places of individuals, not colonies. Among these are leaf-rolling caterpillars, webworms, bagworms and the unique leaf-rolling crickets.

In our modern economy, paper and related products of almost endless sorts are made of wood fiber obtained from pulverized wood. Most of the commodities we use in our daily lives are either made of this wood fiber or come enclosed in containers made from it. It is one of the most versatile of all natural products, and we would have difficulty getting along without it. As an example of the enormous amount of paper we use, we might mention that one Sunday edition of *The New York Times* uses 800 cords of wood, which requires the cutting of about 80 acres of forest. It is estimated that each person in the United States uses about five hundred pounds of paper a year.

While wood fiber has been used by us for paper making for only a few hundred years, there are a number of insects that, millions of years ago discovered its value in fabricating snug homes. The most skillful of these are the hornets that collect fiber from weathered trees and chew it into paper of excellent quality. This paper is formed in thin sheets and may actually be typed or written upon. In making their paper the worker was search for weathered wood on fence posts and dead limbs. Sometimes they will even use fiber from discarded paper cartons or paper bags. The insect tears the fibers apart with her sharp mandibles and forms them into a small pellet about an eighth of an inch in diameter, which chewed and mixed with a salivary secretion into a pulpy mass resembling papier-mâché. This is transported back to the nest where the wasp straddles the edge of the paper sheet that is under construction and applies her ball of pulp to it. Now, moving back and forth, she gradually forms the moist fibers into a thin addition to the edge of the sheet. While the wasp is away collecting more building material, the newly added layer hardens and by the time she returns it is in condition to receive another addition. If a wasp nest is closely examined, these layer-by-layer zones can be distinguished because the fibers collected on various trips vary somewhat in color. In some wasps, such as the yellowjackets, the fiber is applied in half-circles, which gives the finished nest a characteristic pattern. Other wasps, such as the bald-faced hornets, apply the fiber in straight line. Wasp paper is usually gray, but there are often bands of contrasting hues which more or less—perhaps accidentally—camouflage the nest. recently had occasion to relocate a large hornet nest in a deep forest for photographic purposes. Even though the nest was more than a foot in diameter it was very difficult to find.

Probably the most spectacular of the paper-making wasps is the bald-faced hornet (*Dolichovespula maculata*). These black and white wasps or hornets build paper nests that are often of large size. A few years ago one of their nests was found in Florida that is said to have measured thirty feet high! In most instances, however, their globular nests seldom reach a size of much over two feet in diameter. In the cooler parts of their range, where freezing temperatures occur, these elaborate nests are one-year affairs; as soon as late summer or autumn arrives the wasp society

This is a cutaway view of the paper nest of bald-faced hornet colony. The multiple-walled construction affords insulation against both heat and cold. Young hornets are reared in the paper comb cells.

breaks down and the inhabitants all wander away and die. The queens seek hibernating places, where winter is passed. I suspect that the large hornet nest in Florida was the result of several years occupation by the same colony that had survived the mild winters.

When the queen emerges from hibernation in spring she selects what she considers a suitable location for nest construction. This may be in a tree or under a shed. She collects wood pulp and constructs a nest consisting of a stem at the lower end of which are a few paper brood cells shaped like the wax cells of honeybees. Next, a paper envelope is built, enclosing the brood cells. This outer envelope is more or less egg-shaped and the entrance is at the bottom. Usually, there are several layers of paper enclosing the nest for added protection and insulation. When this structure is completed, the queen hornet lays an egg in each cell. When the small larvae emerge from the cells they stick to the tops of the upside-down cells by a thick mucus which they secrete; without this they would fall out of their cells. Later, after they have become larger, they appear to be anchored in their cells by friction alone. When the time for pupation arrives, they spin silken cocoons and close the cell entrance with the same substance.

After the larvae hatch from their cells, the queen must begin feeding them, so she now turns into a hunter. Insects are captured and dismembered and the softer parts of their bodies are chewed into hamburger-like food pellets. These are fed to the growing larvae. They are probably also fed regurgitated food from the queen's digestive system. The adult hornets that arise from this first batch of eggs are smaller than normal, probably because their food supply is limited to what the queen working alone can supply.

Once the little colony is established and there are workers to take over the labors of construction and feeding young, the queen gradually settles down to the domestic duty of laying eggs. In time she even loses the ability to fly. During the one summer that she lives she may lay as many as 25,000 eggs. As the number of inhabitants increases, the paper nest is gradually enlarged and additional tiers of brood combs are added, one below the other. In laying eggs the queen lays in concentric zones radiating outward, the oldest larvae are thus toward the inside. As the nest grows in size there is much rebuilding and remodeling to make more space available. The outer walls are enlarged and added to until at last there are many paper walls separated by air spaces. These air spaces form an excellent insulation against the heat of the days and the cold of the nights, and there is much less temperature variation within the nest than there is on the outside. When the temperature within the nest becomes too hot, currents of air are created through the passages by the fanning of workers' wings as in the case of honeybees. Some paper wasps apply water to the walls of the nest to cool them by evaporation. They were thus among the first creatures with air-conditioned homes. Just as in the case of honeybees there is a division of labor among the workers of various ages. The young individuals remain in the nest, receiving food and paper pulp brought in by the "field hands." The young also perform guard duty at the entrance and fan the nest. When the workers become older, they leave the nest on foraging expeditions. Hamburger pellets are fed to the larvae, but the adult workers feed only upon liquid food because their throats are too small to admit solid particles. Paper hornets and wasps hunt by sight and kill their game by biting it, not by stinging it as do mason wasps and other solitary wasps.

We like to think that the purposes of such social insects as wasps, ants and bees are similar to our society. However, biologists have gradually come to realize that the solicitous care given the young is the result of selfish motives and not of any devotion to duty. During their larval period, wasps secrete a sweetish substance from their salivary glands and this appears as small drops on their lower lips. The adult, nurse wasps lap this up at the time they feed the larvae. Thus, in effect, they are paid or rewarded for the care they give the young wasps. This relationship of care to food reward is called *trophallaxis* and apparently is an important social factor in binding together all insects that live in colonies.

During late summer the hornet workers start building larger cells in which the queen lays fertilized eggs. She also lays nonfertilized eggs in other cells. The fertilized eggs hatch into larvae which develop into queens; the nonfertilized eggs develop into drones or male hornets. In this respect they are very similar to honeybees since there are three castes —workers or imperfect females, queens or perfect females and drones or males. In nature's economy the queens and drones are not produced until late in the season; if they were produced earlier they would constitute a useless drain on food supplies. Just what it is that causes fertilized eggs to develop into queens rather than workers during late summer is not fully understood. In the case of honeybees it has been known for a long while that a special material called royal jelly, secreted by the glands of nurse bees, causes larvae from fertilized eggs to develop into queens. Whether or not some similar substance causes the difference between the wasp workers and queens is unknown. It has been found, however, that when the wasp adults were kept cold at night the larvae they fed developed into workers. The temperature at which the larvae were kept seemed to make no difference. It is thus possible that temperature may in some fashion affect hormone secretions given off by the worker wasps. Just how this fits into the seasonal wasp cycle is as yet not clear. At any rate, after emerging from their cells the queens and drones mate, some queens mating with drones from other colonies. The drones soon die, but the mated queens seek protected locations where they hibernate to continue the chain of hornet life from summer to summer.

The founding of a hornet nest always has a sad ending. The queen toils to establish her small queendom, and during the happy days of summer her realm increases in size and in the number of inhabitants who defend it with their fiery stings. But as summer comes to a close, the old queen wears out and, at last, stops laying eggs. The populous colony is now doomed. In an instinctive effort to survive, some of the workers lay eggs, but, since they are imperfect females and unmated, these eggs hatch only into drones. The community that functioned so well during the summer now breaks down and some workers even turn to cannibalism, feeding upon the young larvae. By the time of the first frosts about all that re- mains is the paper nest that once housed a teeming hornet colony, although a few workers may remain in the nest until cold weather kills them. Just what it is that causes the degeneration of wasp societies and the premature dying of larvae in their cells has been the subject of considerable research. Apparently, the dying of larvae is caused by some deficiency in their food, but whether this is a glandular secretion from the workers is unknown. There is evidence, however, that larvae fed by old workers fail to mature. Seemingly, the aging of workers is influenced by temperature.

Closely related to the hornets are the common *Polistes* wasps that also construct their nests of plant fiber. The name *Polistes,* by the way, comes from Greek, meaning "founder of a city." Unlike the hornets, the *Polistes* wasps do not enclose their nests in paper envelopes and are considered to be more primitive, otherwise their habits are quite similar. Strangely, there seems to be no special popular name for these common insects except "hornets" even though they are usually much more common than the true hornets that enclose their nests in paper envelopes. All of these insects fold their wings lengthwise when at rest.

The abundance of these wasps varies from year to year—during some years their nests seem to be everywhere, while during other years there seem to be very few. Just what factors bring about "wasp years" has been the subject of considerable speculation. It seems that early, warm springs followed by late freezes are harmful to the queens who are then in the process of nest founding. During one recent summer following such a cold spring I noticed that the *Polistes* population in my locality was very low.

There are a number of different species of *Polistes* wasps, and they vary greatly in coloration from rust to black. Some kinds are banded in contrasting colors. All of them sting viciously. A typical *Polistes* nest consists of a disc-shaped group of inverted brood cells suspended by a central pedicel. The fiber mixed with saliva, of which the nest is constructed, is surprisingly tough and can be torn apart only with difficulty. That it was once a favorite material for muzzle-loading gun wadding is evidence that this wasp paper is very tough.

Usually, *Polistes* nests are built in sheltered locations such as porch ceilings or thick shrubs, but I have also found them suspended from the under sides of large leaves. Like their relatives, the hornets, the individual societies break down in late summer and only the queens survive the winter to found new colonies. *Polistes* queens have one very unusual habit. Several queens may construct a nest on a cooperative basis. These

Polistes wasps build clusters of cells in sheltered locations. This one is attached to the underside of a ragweed leaf. They are never enclosed in paper envelopes as are those of bald-faced hornets.

gregarious queens sometimes continue their cooperation during the full period in which the colony is a going concern; usually, however, the queens shift from colony to colony during early spring. Sometimes queens actually desert their brood to join nearby colonies where there may be more activity. Such a deserted brood soon dies.

Some interesting studies of wasp social behavior have been made by biologists who had the fortitude to invade their private lives. These studies concerned the relationships of queens to each other where several were present in the same nests. In some *Polistes* species there are almost always three or four queens present, and there is considerable fighting among them for the dominant position of true queen. Eventually, there is established a regular order of dominance with the most aggressive queen at the top. Those lower in the scale give food to those higher up, but when the first workers appear the queens of inferior status leave the nest. It may be interesting to call attention to the fact that this social behavior among *Polistes* queens resembles closely the remarkable "peck order" found to prevail among domestic chickens. It has also been found that there is a difference in the development of the ovaries of the queens in the "peck order." The queen at the top of the scale has fully developed ovaries, the next one down has smaller ovaries, and so on down the social scale.

While most *Polistes* queens usually retire from all work and devote their time to egg laying after there are workers present, there is at least one species, *Polistes hunteri,* of the Southeast that continues to take part in nest building. She takes the moist pellets of fiber brought in by field workers and begins construction of cells in which she lays eggs. Later, the workers finish the construction of these cells by elongating them.

Like true hornets, *Polistes* larvae are fed hamburger pellets made up of captured insects. After being brought back to the nest they are received by nurse wasps and given to the larvae, which exude droplets of fluid that the nurses find delicious. The hamburgers are thus traded for the droplets, so here again we see in operation the interesting principle of trophallaxis. The wasp larvae are fed, but they must pay for it; few things in nature are given freely. The nurse wasps place the hamburger pellets in the cells and each larva is allowed to feed for several seconds, after which the pellet is removed and offered to another. One pellet is usually sufficient to feed about four larvae.

Just as some queen ants practice social parasitism, having found that it is easier to take over colonies already established than to found their own, so do certain species of *Polistes* queens lay their eggs in the nests of other species of *Polistes* wasps. The original inhabitants rear the foreign larvae, unaware that they are not their own. The parasitic *Polistes* larvae all develop into queens and drones, the worker caste having been discarded along the evolutionary path. In time the original *Polistes* wasps all disappear and the nest then consists only of parasitic queens and drones that continue their species by mating and laying eggs in other *Polistes* nests again. Wasps having this habit occur in both Europe and America, and are often called cuckoo wasps, for obvious reasons.

While all our *Polistes* wasp colonies come to sad ends in autumn, those species that inhabit the tropics continue to thrive, new colonies being formed by swarming just as with honeybees. Some of these tropical wasp nests become very large and consist of thousands of individuals. In some species the brood cells are exposed, and in others they are enclosed in paper or fiber envelopes as are our hornets. The walls of the nests of these tropical wasps are formed of heavy cardboard-like material and some are provided with thin parchmentlike "windows" to admit light.

To most of us the word "yellowjacket" brings to mind vivid memories of hot-tempered wasps emerging from holes in the ground. Unlike the

Close-up of yellowjackets on their paper combs. The large yellowjacket with back to the camera is a queen, the rest are workers.

other paper-building wasps and hornets, the yellowjackets, *Vespula,* excavate cavities in the earth in which they construct their paper mansions. The paper they fabricate is of excellent quality but thinner and less durable than that made by those wasps that dwell above ground, which is understandable when one considers the sheltered location of their nests. In forming their paper sheets, yellowjackets apparently rotate their bodies in half circles so that the grain of the finished paper consists of a patchwork of concentric arcs resulting from the various colors of the wood fibers used.

As in other paper-making wasps, it is only the queens that live through winter to found new colonies. Nature is usually economical—why, then, is there always this waste of wasp life? Honeybees survive the winter by forming tight clusters to conserve heat, but the paper wasps never have mastered this technique. The paper wasp clan had its origin in the tropics where wasp colonies can thrive all year. As they extended their ranges northward, only the queens seemed able to survive the cold of the temperate climate. This was the price they had to pay for life in the northern habitat. In autumn the mated yellowjacket queens, which are considerably larger than the workers, seek out protected locations to spend the winter. These may be crevices beneath bark, beneath pieces of rotten wood or other places more or less insulated against the cold. The queen makes herself a nest or cell by arranging bits of wood or other available material in a circle. It is not a very substantial structure, but it seems to be adequate for her need. Having finished her meager preparation, she then tucks her antennae behind her forelegs and folds her wings beneath her abdomen. Thus composed for the long sleep of hibernation, she settles down to await the coming of spring. Snow may cover the ground and bitter winds may blow, but the queen sleeps on, her life processes slowed down to near the zero point. Like groundhogs and chipmunks, she knows nothing of winter. Frost often penetrates her hiding place and glistens on her body, but she sleeps on until the warmth of spring arrives. Then, like many other hibernating creatures, she slowly "comes to life" and her life processes return to normal. She crawls forth into the sunshine, flexes her wings and flies away seeking a suitable place to found her queendom. This may be a gopher hole, mouse nest or other cavity in the earth. The

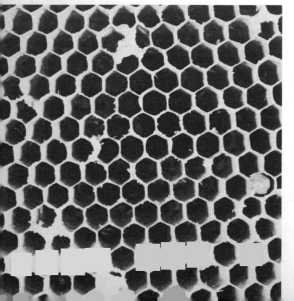

Close-up of yellowjacket comb. The cells are quite similar to those of honeybees, but the latter insects build theirs of wax.

size seems not to be important since it will be gradually enlarged as the size of the colony grows. Her next act is locating a source of water and taking a long drink. Back at the nest site she moistens the hard earth and removes it pellet by pellet until there is a cavity of suitable size. Next, she collects wood fiber and constructs a small nest with a few cells. This is not very large since she toils alone. When the cells are finished she lays an egg in each and when these hatch she hunts insects to feed them. As in the case of other paper wasps, captured insects are reduced to hamburger pellets. Yellowjackets are more or less omnivorous and are also fond of nectar or ripe fruit juices. Like the other paper wasps, the larvae pay for their board by secreting a sweet substance that is lapped up by the queen. Slowly the larvae grow, and at last they transform to the pupal stage—white ghosts of the future yellowjackets into which they eventually will transform.

Once this first generation of workers has emerged and taken over all the work details, the queen becomes simply a layer of eggs. More earth is removed and the cavity is enlarged. More wood fiber is collected and more tiers of brood cells are added, one below the other. Paper walls always enclose and protect the entire structure. The tiny nest constructed by the queen is only an inch in diameter, but by autumn the nest may be as large as a pumpkin and contain several thousand hot-tempered inhabitants all enthusiastically working—and ready at any time to defend the colony. But, alas, the time comes when cold penetrates the earth and food is no longer available. New queens and drones are produced and these fly away and mate; the queens seek places to hibernate and the drones die. Within the parent colony a few workers may linger on for a time, but eventually they all die. Another yearly chapter in the life of the yellowjacket clan has come to a close.

While most yellowjackets lead exemplary lives, there are some kinds that live as social parasites. For example, the queens of *Vespula squamosa* and *Vespula austriaca* have developed the lazy habit of laying their eggs in other yellowjacket nests. Eventually, of course, all the original workers are replaced by those of the parasitic species.

While the members of the wasp tribe are famous for their paper-making habits, there are a number of ants, too, that are quite skilled in this craft. Most of these occur in the tropics, but there is at least one such species found in various parts of the United States. This is the acrobatic ant (*Crematogaster lineolata*), a species that feeds on honeydew collected from aphids and mealybugs. The nests of these ants are often fabricated from paper pulp formed into small cardboard-like structures that usually surround twigs. These are actually "cow sheds" since they are built to shelter aphid or mealybug colonies. The ants, of course, feed on the honeydew secreted by these insects which they protect from enemies. These ant nests are sometimes quite large considering the size of the ants. While the nests are, in most cases, used merely as protective coverings or sheds for their "herds," ants sometimes actually live in such *carton* nests, as they are called. Somewhat similar sheds are often constructed by the imported fire ant (*Solenopsis saevissima richteri*) in the southeastern United States. These latter sheds are poor structures, however, being fabricated by loosely attaching bits of dead plant debris. In Madagascar there is a species of acrobatic ant that constructs carton nests up to a foot in diameter. Seemingly, the carton-making habit is rather widespread among various species of the acrobatic ant clan, especially in tropical lands. In the tropics there are many other ants that also build carton nests. Among these are ants of the genera *Dolichoderus* and *Azteca* that construct nests that are either suspended from limbs after the manner of hornets or built around twigs. The nests of *Azteca* are sometimes four feet high and exist for many years. Like our acrobatic ants, these ants also construct carton sheds over aphids and scale insects. Other species of *Azteca* construct small "ant gardens" in the forks of twigs by bringing soil up from the ground. In most cases the seeds of plants either lodge in these balls of soil or are accidentally carried up along with soil particles. Here they germinate and grow so that a little cluster of living plants eventually results; the roots probably help to hold the soil together. Within this "ant garden" the *Azteca* colony lives. I often saw these "gardens" on jungle trees but did not at first realize what they were.

Silk, secreted by various glands, is one of the most useful materials employed by insects. Usually, it is secreted by immature forms such as larvae for cocoon making, but it may also be produced by some adults for special purposes. Silk glands are usually modified salivary glands. In the case of caterpillars these are often quite large since an abundant supply of silk is needed for spinning cocoons. The silk glands of the commercial silkworm (*Bombyx mori*) are about five times as long as the body within which they are coiled, but those of our native *Polyphemus* larvae are even longer. In such caterpillars the silk from the two glands empties into paired silk reservoirs, where it is stored in a liquid condition. From these reservoirs ducts emerge which join together and conduct the silk to a spinneret in the mouth. When the insect is in the act of spinning, it is forced out through a minute opening that controls the size and shape of the strand. When the liquid silk, which is a colloidal solution, emerges from the spinneret it hardens almost at once. This is not, as was once thought, a matter of hardening on exposure to air for it hardens just as quickly under water. Actually, it is a chemical process brought about by the physical flow or stress forces within the liquid. The solidified silken strand consists of a crystalline central fiber (*fibroin*) surrounded by a coat of silk gelatine (*sericine*). This latter material is water soluble and when commercial silk is processed it is removed by washing.

Sericulture or the commercial culture of silkworms is an ancient craft that began in China about 1800 B.C. The perfection of methods of rearing silkworms on mulberry leaves and obtaining their silk is credited to Si-ling-Chi, wife of Hoang-ti, and the secret of sericulture was closely guarded for several thousand years. While the commercial silkworm was originally a native of Asia, it probably does not now occur in the wild state. Each cocoon spun by the larvae consists of a single silken strand about 1,000 feet long, more than 25,000 cocoons being required to produce a pound of silk. Silk is now produced commercially in China, Japan, France, Spain and Italy. Silk produced by American saturniid larvae has been experimented with but found not to be practical for commercial purposes.

The ability to spin silk is widespread among insects. Beneath the water it is used by caddis insects for cementing stones together and for spinning seines. Caterpillars, wasp larvae, ant larvae and numerous other immature insects use it for making cocoons. The silk glands of the embiids are apparently located in the legs. These small and little-known insects occur

A tiny caterpillar (*Coptodisca splendoriferella*) built this case in which it lives upon apple leaves and other plants. In time, a tiny moth emerges from the case. It is called the resplendent shield-bearer.

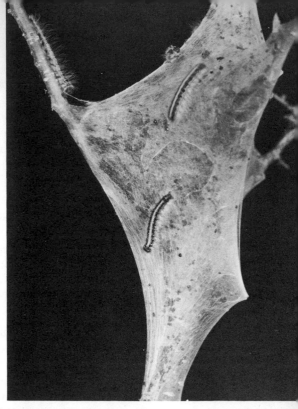

Forest tent caterpillars (*Malacosoma americana*) construct silken nests on trees in early spring. During the day they hide within these retreats. They feed on nearby foliage at night.

in some warm countries where they live in silken nests. The larvae of beetles and nerve-winged insects, such as antlions, have their silk glands in the posterior portions of their bodies. Actually, these silk glands are modified Malpighian tubes or excretory glands corresponding more or less to kidneys. Apparently, almost any insect gland may be modified into a silk-producing organ.

Of all the ants that build tentlike nests, those that bind leaves together with silk are probably the most remarkable. The ants that practice this method of nest construction inhabit the vast tropical region from India down to Australia and parts of Africa, and they belong to the genera *Oecophylla* and *Polyrhachis*. Actually, the nests of the latter genus are usually not very elaborate, consisting of silken retreats covered with debris. Sometimes, however, several leaves are fastened together with silk. It is in the ants of the genus *Oecophylla* that the making of leaf nests reaches its highest development. The workers of some species are green or reddish. The queens are grass-green and the males are black. This alone is very unusual among ants, which are usually black or reddish.

Since these ants use silk to fasten leaves together to form their nests, it is obvious that they must have a ready source of this material. No adult ant has silk glands since the ability to secrete silk is lost when it transforms into the adult stage. Neither do all ant larvae secrete silk, but those that do usually use it to spin cocoons. In the case of *Oecophylla* larvae the silk they secrete is not used for cocoon spinning but is diverted to use in nest building in a most interesting manner. The obtaining of silk by non-silk-spinning adults would seem to be an insurmountable problem, but nature, with millions of years in which to experiment, has come up with a unique solution that seems almost like science fiction. In nest construction, worker ants grasp the larvae and, using them like bobbins, "sew" tree leaves together with the silken strands the larvae emit. The larvae are held in the ants' mandibles, front ends forward, and moved from one leaf to the other while silken threads issue from the larvae's mouths. Each larva is grasped by its middle and apparently squeezed, perhaps to stimulate the production of silk. In this respect it is not unlike applying pressure to a tube of glue.

In nest building the worker ants line up and pull the edges of leaves together while other workers hurry into the nest and emerge with young larvae which produce the binding material. For a first-hand account of the manner in which these remarkable ants work, we can do no better than quote, directly, the observations of F. P. Dodd, who watched them in Queensland, Australia, more than half a century ago. He says:

> If the foliage is large or stiff, scores or even hundreds of the ants may be required to haul a leaf down and detain it in place until secured, both operations taking considerable time. It is quite a tug-or-war matter to bring the leaf into position and keep it there. The insects holding it have a chain of two or three of their comrades fastened on to them, one behind the other, each holding its neighbor by its slender waist, and all at full stretch and pulling most earnestly. What a strain it must be for poor number one! When the leaf is far apart the ants form themselves into chains to bridge the distance and bring it down; many of these chains are frequently required for a single leaf. [In attaching the leaves together] the soft and tiny grubs are held by the larger ants, who slowly move up against those pulling. Each grub is held by the middle, with head pointing forward, its snout is gently made to touch the edges of the leaves where they are joined, it is slowly moved backwards and forwards and is undoubtedly issuing a thread during the operation, which adheres to the leaf edges [and pulls them together].

The above is a first-hand account of the manner in which *Oecophylla* ants "sew" leaves together. Here we have instinct of the highest order in operation. If the ants had been endowed with the ability to reason they could hardly have solved the problem more efficiently or imaginatively. Here is a case where another insect, besides the tool-using *Ammophila wasp,* uses a tool in its work, but the "tool" is its own larva.

In the United States there occurs a number of species of ants of the genus *Camponotus* (carpenter ants) which excavate their nests in wood. These ants have a relative in Africa, *Camponotus senex,* which weaves its nest in a manner quite similar to that of *Oecophylla.*

Plant leaves are a good building material and are used by a number of different animals for nest construction. They are even put to use by humans in thatching houses, especially in tropical areas. Some spiders construct cells by bending grass blades into the form of little boxes. We have already seen how tropical ants make use of leaves, but there are many other insects which make use of this readily available structural material. One of these is the leaf-rolling cricket (*Camptonotus carolinensis*). This cricket is unusual in at least two respects: it hunts aphids at night and is, thus, carnivorous; it also uses silk to fasten leaves together to form a shelter in which it hides from birds and other enemies during the daylight hours. This cricket's ability to secrete silk is unique among the cricket clan, but silk glands, as we have seen, may occur where least expected among insects.

The background of our knowledge concerning this cricket followed the usual sequence of events in entomology. First, the insect was discovered and given a scientific name, and much later its unusual habits were observed and recorded. A dead insect on a pin in a museum usually gives no clue to its habits however unique and interesting they may be. In the case of the leaf-rolling cricket, however, some indication of its unusual

The leaf-rolling cricket (*Camptonotus carolinensis*) uses silk to "sew" sections of leaves together to form a daytime shelter. A new shelter is constructed each day. At night this unusual cricket emerges from its shelter and feeds upon aphids.

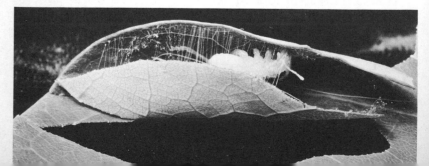

habits might have been seen in the length of its antennae, which are more than twice the length of its body. Long, sensitive antennae are most often found in insects that are active at night. This cricket was first described and given a Latin name in a German scientific journal more than a hundred years ago. The specimen from America then lapsed into obscurity in a German museum. It was merely a dried specimen with nothing to indicate its habits. The years passed and eventually A. N. Caudell of the U.S. National Museum in Washington, D.C., found one of these same crickets in a rolled-up pawpaw leaf. Realizing that he had discovered an interesting cricket, Mr. Caudell searched out more specimens and studied their habits. It is now known that these crickets occur in many places in the eastern United States.

During the hours of darkness the leaf-rolling cricket crawls and jumps about among vegetation searching for aphids upon which it feeds. Long before dawn, its appetite satisfied, the cricket selects a leaf and sets about constructing a tent in which it can hide safely from enemies during the daylight hours. There is some variation in its method of tent construction, depending on the shape of the selected leaf, but, in general, the cricket, using its jaws, first cuts slits along the margin of the leaf, the form and direction of the cuts varying, apparently, from leaf to leaf. This done, the cricket next places its body between the slits and pulls the severed section of the leaf around itself with its feet, an action requiring considerable force. When the edges approach each other, the cricket then begins "sewing" them together with silk which issues as a fine thread from its mouth. Back and forth it moves, attaching the silk first on one side and then on the other. The silken strands slowly harden and contract, drawing the leaf edges together as more and more silk is added. Sometimes the cricket finds it necessary to emerge from the rolled tube in order to pull the edges closer together. At any rate, the cricket eventually finishes its cylindrical tube and settles down inside with its long antennae coiled lengthwise about its body. Here it remains all day awaiting the coming of another night when it again goes on the prowl. New shelters are constructed each night. In making the accompanying photograph the writer spent most of one night in his studio with his nervous specimens. It was easy to observe the manner in which they fastened the leaf edges together since they always cooperated by repairing shelters that had been pulled open. It has also been found that these crickets will construct their tents of transparent sheet plastic if leaves are not available.

It is a common habit among caterpillars, too, to use leaves for the construction of shelters of various forms. My first observation of the way in which a caterpillar causes a leaf to roll over and form a tube was made while horseback-riding down a mountain trail in the mountains of the Northwest. I had broken a leafy twig off a quaking aspen as I passed and happened to notice that a caterpillar was busily at work on one of the oval leaves, so as I rode along I watched its activity with great interest. The caterpillar was moving its head rapidly back and forth across the leaf, laying down a silken mat. The process did not make too much sense until I noticed that the leaf had begun to curl over due to the contraction of the silk as it hardened in the air. Eventually the leaf curled over and completely enclosed the caterpillar.

There are many kinds of caterpillars that "roll their own," and the forms of their finished shelters are endless. Usually these leaf tubes are occupied by a single insect that lives within it, emerging at times, especially at night, to feed on nearby foliage. Sometimes pupation takes place in the shelter. Entomologists usually consider that there are two types of leaf shelters: those constructed in the form of rolled leaves (the insects that make them are called leaf-rollers) and those made by merely bending over edges of leaves (the insects that make these are called leaf-folders). Both types are quite common and their shelters can be seen on almost any tree or shrub.

More unusual are the portable shelters constructed by the bagworm moths that often infest junipers and cedars as well as some other trees. The common bagworm, *Thyridopteryx ephemeraeformis,* is quite often a serious pest of ornamental junipers. Because of the camouflaged nature of the shelters constructed by the caterpillars, a favorite juniper may be almost defoliated before the homeowner realizes that the pests are present. Needless to say, the homeowner is usually more interested in exterminating them than in studying their habits.

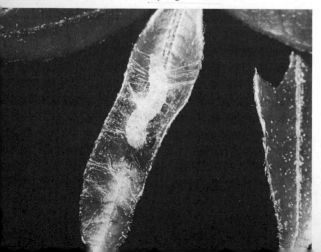

A leaf-rolling caterpillar in the act of rolling up a leaf to serve as a shelter. Silken strands are spun from edge to edge; as more silk is added the edges of the leaf are drawn together.

These sac-like structures were constructed by bagworms (*Thyridopteryx ephemeraeformis*). The bags consist of bits of cedar foliage held together with silk. The enclosed caterpillars eventually become full grown and pupate. The males are winged and leave their cases. The females never acquire wings; they deposit their eggs within the case.

The cases constructed by bagworms closely resemble those built by some caddis insects, especially the log-cabin builders. There are several species, and the bags built by them vary somewhat in architecture and in the materials used. Some kinds use twigs, attached either lengthwise or crosswise with silk. The cedar bagworm mentioned above builds its case of cedar leaves, or "needles." If one of these cases is cut open (they are too tough to pull apart with the fingers), a plump caterpillar will be found inside. The open front end, by the way, is usually closed by a loose flap of silk. The bagworm pushes its head and the forepart of its body out of the case and crawls about feeding on the green foliage. Since their cases are covered with the same plant material as the plant upon which they feed, they are well camouflaged. The caterpillars feed all summer and become full grown before autumn, at which time they attach their cases to twigs, seal the entrances and pupate. Very shortly those pupae which are destined to be males push themselves out of the lower ends of their cases and the adult moths emerge. These adult, male moths are clear-winged and grayish. Strangely, the females never acquire wings and never leaves their bags. The males visit the bags containing females and insert their long copulatory organs, fertilizing them. Soon after this, the females lay large masses of eggs in the lower portions of their bags and then die. With the arrival of spring the eggs hatch and the young bagworms emerge and begin feeding. At first their cases are constructed of tiny bits of debris cemented together with silk, but later larger leaves are used. No doubt, birds such as jays sometimes tear the tough nests open and feed upon the fat larvae, so the bagworms have developed the ability to repair torn bags. If one is cut open, the caterpillar will at once set about sewing it back together again with silk.

chapter eleven

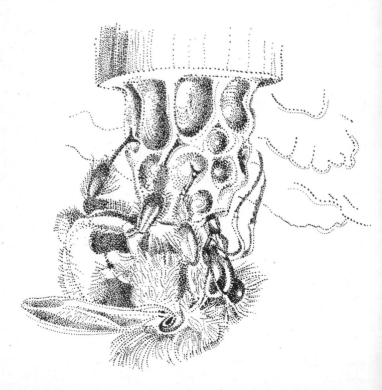

The Nectar Gatherers

MANUFACTURING honey from flower nectar is an ancient profession practiced by several species of insects. The nectar produced by flowers is secreted especially to attract insects. Its production is one facet of many plants' methods of enticing insects for their aid in pollination. Flower nectars contain varying amounts of several sugar types, chiefly sucrose (cane sugar), fructose (fruit sugar) and glucose (grape sugar). In addition to sugars, nectar contains organic acids, plant pigments, minerals, essential oils and enzymes. All these are dissolved in water, the amount of which varies considerably among the various plants. The total solids in nectars vary from 4 to 65 percent. To show the wide variation in sugar content of nectars we might list a few examples as follows:

Willow—60 percent
Dandelion—51 percent
Sweet clover—35 to 60 percent
Sunflower—31 percent
Eucalyptus—13 percent
Apricot—5 to 25 percent
Pear—4 to 30 percent

These figures, obtained from California, illustrate very well the wide variation in sugar content of nectars, even within the same species of plant. The relative percentages of the various types of sugars is also subject to considerable variation. For example, it was found that honeysuckle nectar contained 6.9 percent sucrose while that of red clover contained 27.5 percent.

It is obvious that flower nectars have high food value and it is little wonder that honeybees can subsist and work on it during their entire adult lives. During their immature stage worker bees are fed on other food.

Of all the world's nectar gatherers the domestic honeybee (*Apis mellifera*) is the best known. It has been kept under domestication for thousands of years and is now a common "domesticated" animal in almost every land. It was mentioned in Sanskrit writings as long ago as 3000 B.C. and was well known in ancient Greece and Rome. Inscriptions on early Egyptian tombs prove that these industrious insects were kept for their honey at least 4,000 years ago. The Babylonians used honey for food and medicine, as well as for offerings to their gods. Honeybees are semitropical insects that have adapted themselves in temperate climates where they survive cold weather by forming themselves into winter clusters or balls within the hive, hollow tree or wherever the colony has taken up residence. These clusters are formed whenever the temperature within the hive falls to 57°F. or lower. Within the cluster, a temperature of about 90°F. is maintained by the bees fanning their wings, thereby creating heat by muscular activity. This temperature is remarkably constant

Honeybees often go back to their ancestral homes in hollow trees to establish colonies. They are not actually domesticated animals and their habits have changed little, if any, during their association with man.

and is one of the rare instances among the cold-blooded insects where any effort is made to control temperature.

To many people, the terms nectar and honey are more or less synonymous, but there is a great difference. Nectar is the raw material gathered from flowers; honey is the product manufactured from it by honeybees. Nectar is gathered from flowers and carried into the hive in the honey stomachs of the worker bees. When a worker bee sucks up nectar from a flower, it passes through its esophagus and into the thin-walled honey stomach located in the bee's abdomen. A valve prevents the nectar from passing on into the posterior part of the digestive system. Upon returning to the hive, the worker delivers her load of nectar to younger workers or "house bees." It is apparently passed back and forth between the bees several times, and it is believed that during this process certain enzymes are added that digest the natural sugars. After this ritual the nectar is placed in the cells where it is fanned and evaporated. The final result is honey. If comb containing honey that has not been properly evaporated is removed from the hive, it will ferment or sour. There is no other food quite like it, and it was once considered to be a great luxury since other sources of sweets were scarce. In ancient Europe honey was made into a potent drink called "mead" by fermentation. The term "honeymoon" is said to have arisen because of an old German custom of drinking mead for thirty days after a wedding.

In addition to nectar, honeybees gather pollen from flowers and carry large quantities back to their hives where it is stored in the cells. Nectar, as we have seen, contains much sugar and is thus high in carbohydrates, but larval bees must also have protein in order to grow. Pollen, which contains about twenty percent protein, in addition to oils and other foods, fills this need. It is estimated that one pound of pollen is needed in rearing 4,500 bees. During one summer an average hive will use about a hundred pounds of pollen.

In collecting pollen the bees must often visit many flowers, though usually not as many as for nectar. Some flowers produce pollen abundantly so that a bee can obtain a full load from one flower. On the average, however, a bee visits a hundred or more flowers. Some flowers, such as those of white sweet clover do not produce much pollen, so bees must collect from many. In one case a bee was followed as it collected clover pollen and found to visit 585 blooms to obtain one load. The number of visits bees must ordinarily make range from 50 to 1,000 flowers on a trip.

Studies have also been made to determine how much pollen a bee can carry. On the average, this ranges from one-fifth to one-third of its own weight, or about twelve milligrams. Pollen from different flowers varies considerably in weight, but the weight of pollen is not what determines the amount carried by a bee, rather, it is the amount that its pollen baskets will hold. These baskets are located on the outer surfaces of the hind legs, the pollen being held by the surrounding bristles. In the process of collecting pollen the bee uses her body as a brush to sweep up pollen from the anthers of flowers. The front legs are then used to brush the pollen from the eyes, antennae and head while the middle legs are employed to brush it off the thorax. Pollen adhering to the abdomen is swept off by the hind legs. The pollen thus collected is transferred to the pollen baskets for transport back to the hive. The legs of a worker bee contain a whole set of "tools" especially designed to facilitate her work.

In the case of nectar, the maximum load is about seventy milligrams, but, here, too, it is not the weight of the nectar but the capacity of the honey stomach that determines how much is carried. The weight of an "empty" worker is about 80 milligrams, and it has been determined, by attaching small weights to bees, that they can fly with loads of more than their own weight. From the standpoint of aerodynamics, this is remarkable wing-loading performance.* It has been found that bees can carry heavier weights in warm weather than in cold. I have often seen individual bumblebees that had imbibed so much nectar that they could not fly, but I have never seen an instance of this in honeybees. Honeybees take on larger loads of nectar when it is being carried from a greater distance. Perhaps this is a case of a "lazy man's load."

Just as an airplane uses large quantities of fuel in flight, so does a worker honeybee. A bee in flight consumes about 40 milligrams of sugar per hour. When we recall that a bee weighs 80 milligrams, it is evident that it is burning up sugar equivalent to its own body weight every two hours. At this rate a man, if he could fly, would use about 80 pounds of sugar an hour!

Honeybees, like the ants, hornets and bumblebees, have three castes—workers, queens and drones or males. The workers and queens are both females, but only the queens are fully developed reproductively and capable of laying fertile eggs. While workers do occasionally lay eggs, the resulting offspring are all males since workers are incapable of mating.

* The term wing-loading refers to the amount of load carried in relation to wing area.

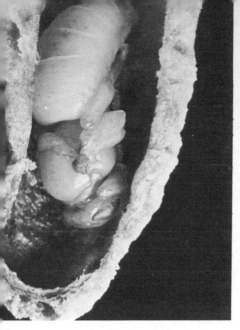 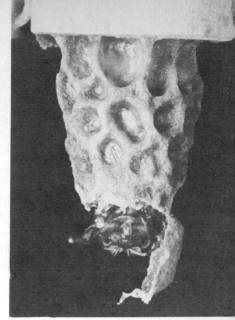

Queens are reared in special elongate cells. Here such a cell has been cut open to show the white pupal queen ready to emerge.

Her head is now emerging.

Drones arise from nonfertilized eggs. Thus, we find here an instance of parthenogenesis, which also occurs in some other insects. (In the case of white-fringed beetles, for example, no males have ever been found; the females reproduce continuously without mating.) As the queen honeybee goes from cell to cell depositing an egg in each one, she apparently has control over the fertilization of her eggs. At certain seasons the bees construct enlarged cells and the eggs she deposits in these cells are nonfertilized and develop into drones. On the other hand, the difference between queens and workers has another explanation. Young worker and queen larvae are exactly alike—which caste they will eventually develop into depends upon the food they receive. For the first day or so, both worker and queen larvae are fed royal jelly, a special substance secreted by glands in the workers' heads. In the case of larvae that are destined to develop into workers, their diet is changed after the first day or two to a mixture of pollen and honey. Queen larvae, on the other hand, are fed continuously on royal jelly, and it is apparently this highly nutritious diet that enables them to develop into perfect females capable of mating and laying eggs. The unique properties of royal jelly have led to its being used for human consumption in the supposition that it would do many things, such as increasing beauty and prolonging life. The idea that royal jelly has the ability to prolong life has arisen because queen bees live so much longer than the other castes. While royal jelly—called "bee milk" in England—is high in proteins and B vitamins, it is doubtful if it is the miracle food it is sometimes alleged to be. It has been used in all sorts of concoctions from face creams to quick cures for hangovers. Since it sells for about twenty dollars an ounce, it is a very expensive source of vitamins. Small jars of face creams have appeared on the market selling for as high as fifteen dollars. Actually, such jars contain only minute amounts of royal jelly, amounts too small to do any good even if it had any value in external application, which seems doubtful.

Beekeepers, of course, are aware of the potential profit and increase the production of queen bees for the market. Day-old worker larvae are placed in special queen cells that have previously been stocked with small supplies of royal jelly. The bees continue to feed these larvae with royal jelly and they all develop into queens.

The queen was once called the "king bee" in the erroneous belief that she was a male. It is now known, of course, that she is normally the only functional female in the colony and as such is attended at all times by a retinue of workers—her ladies-in-waiting—that continually. groom and feed her. Even though her duty is confined to that of laying eggs, this is an arduous task since she lays from 1,500 to 2,000 eggs a day during summer. The eggs laid by queen ant and termite are received by workers and carried away to nurseries, but the honeybee queen must insert her long abdomen deep into each separate cell and cement an egg to the bottom. It is a tribute to the care she receives from the the nurse bees and to her own metabolism that the total weight of the eggs she lays each day may exceed her own weight. Like the workers, the queen has a well-developed sting, but she uses this only on rival queens. As previously stated, the fertilized eggs laid by the queen may develop into either workers or queens depending on the food they receive. The unfertilized eggs laid by her develop only into drones. It has recently been found, however, that in rare cases unfertilized eggs laid by queen honeybees may also develop into workers. How or why this occurs is, so far, a mystery.

The queen has considerable control over her subjects. Recent research has revealed that the queen has a very definite governing influence over the colony through glandular secretions which are passed on to the workers by their mouths. This secretion, often known as the "queen

Queen on comb surrounded by her retinue of workers. She is always surrounded by these ladies-in-waiting who groom and feed her.

substance" is passed from worker to worker so that everyone receives a small but continuous supply. It is secreted by large salivary glands located beneath the queen's lower mandibles. It is, in effect, a chemical messenger that coordinates almost all the bees' activities. Such substances, that regulate the lives of many social insects, are now called *pheromones*. The pheromones secreted and passed along by the queen honeybee control, in turn, the development of the workers' glands, causing the workers to do various things. For example, as long as the queen is healthy and producing these pheromones, the growth of the workers' ovaries is inhibited, but when the queen becomes old and decrepit and her glands slow down, the workers' ovaries begin to develop and eventually they may even lay eggs. These eggs, however, develop only into drones since these laying workers have not mated. If the queen dies or is killed, this, of course, cuts off the supply of pheromones and all the workers are at once aware of the fact. If a hive is opened a short time after a colony has become queenless, it will be noticed that the bees are not reacting normally. They rest on the combs and buzz in a characteristic manner. They have received "word" that their queen is dead. If a queen's glands are removed, her power over her subjects quickly disappears.

While the queen governs her subjects by means of chemical secretions, she is herself a slave to her own glands and is devoid of any "mothering" instinct. She has no interest in her offspring; all her instincts center in laying eggs and eating. She is tied to her workers by a tenuous chemical bond, and while she may not have the authority of a royal despot, her influence is felt throughout the hive at all times. The usual life span of a queen is about three years, but some have lived for as long as ten years. Most beekeepers, however, requeen their hives each year to make sure of having young, vigorous queens.

Bees of the worker caste constitute the teeming labor force of the hive; their number varies from a few thousand up to 60,000, depending on the strength of the colony. Except for the laying of eggs, the busy workers do all the work of the hive, such as feeding young, secreting wax, building comb, gathering nectar and pollen and cleaning the hive. They also gather resin from trees, which is used as a cement or glue for various purposes, such as making the hive watertight. This material, called *propolis,* is also used for encasing foreign objects, for example, a dead mouse, that cannot be removed. Propolis is sometimes known as "bee glue."

Close-up of worker bees on comb. At the left, below center, larval bees can be seen in their cells. At the extreme lower right is a queen cell.

After emerging from the cells where they have passed their larval and pupal periods, worker bees pass through distinct stages of apprenticeship governed by their ages and the development of their glands. During the first two days of their adult lives the workers spend their time cleaning the hive. Bees are quite clean insects and no one need ever fear that honey has been produced under unsanitary conditions.

On the third day the worker bees are promoted to the task of feeding the older larvae and they continue to do this until the fifth day when they begin feeding the younger larvae. They continue in this duty for about two days. This work is very arduous since each larval bee must be fed about 1,300 times a day or about 10,000 times during its growth. Human mothers should, indeed, be grateful that their charges do not require such attention. As a result of the constant feeding of the larvae, they increase in size 1,570 times in the first six days out of the egg.

At about ten days of age the worker bees begin the task of receiving food from the field bees and placing it in the cells for storage. They serve in this capacity until they are about 16 days old, at which time they are again promoted and begin other duties. One of these consists of standing at the hive entrance and fanning their wings to cause currents of air to flow through the hive. It is during this period of their lives, also, that they begin making little exploratory or orientation flights in the immediate vicinity of the hive. On their seventeenth day they take up guard duty at the entrance and continue in this important capacity until their twenty-first day out of the cell. At this time their lives change and they graduate to the status of full-fledged field bees. Scout bees are continually out seeking new nectar sources, and when these are located the scouts return to the hive and do charadelike dances on the combs. These dances tell the field bees the exact direction and location of nectar-bearing flowers. The field bees then go out and harvest the crop. Rarely do the worker bees go out on nectar-gathering flights without first receiving information from the scouts, which are older field bees which have been collecting nectar for a long time. Field bees also collect pollen when it is needed in the hive, but they much prefer to gather nectar. Some individuals gather pollen in the morning and nectar in the afternoon, but others appear to devote their entire lives to collecting either one or the other. They do not collect both on the same trip afield. The field bees also collect propolis and, during periods of warm weather, they carry in water. The water is spread on the combs to cool them by evaporation—a simple system of air-conditioning. During summer while the bees are working hard they live for only about five weeks. Usually, they die afield, but those that die within the hive are tossed out without ceremony.

Worker bees begin their lives as janitors and end them as scouts and dancers. All the successive changes in their duties are the results of instinct and the secretions of internal glands. Workers are subject only to the chemical messages that filter down from the queen.

Few of us realize fully what an amazing little "machine" a worker bee really is. In a single day a worker may collect nectar from 250,000 blooms and, in order to obtain enough nectar to make a pound of honey, the workers must make a total of about 37,000 trips afield. The life work of a worker is but a spoonful or two of honey. In the process of gathering the nectar for a pound of honey, bees may sometimes fly a combined distance of 300,000 miles—more than the distance from the earth to the moon. Think of this the next time you buy a pound of honey in the super-market.

The production and use of wax is one of the basic functions of honey-bees. Without this remarkable material a colony of bees could not live. It is out of wax that they construct their comb just as the hornets use wood fiber. Honeybees begin their lives in wax cells and, if they die in the hive, end them in these same cells. Chemically, beeswax is composed of a complex mixture of esters, fatty acids, higher alcohols and hydro-carbons.

When wax for comb building is needed, young workers from 10 to 17 days old form groups which hang from the top of the nest site. These workers have previously filled themselves with honey and, as they rest quietly, their wax glands begin secreting wax scales. These glands are located in the abdomen and open on the last four sternal or abdominal plates, which have shiny surfaces called "mirrors." The wax is in liquid form when first secreted, but rapidly hardens. Usually, it is light yellow in color, but there is some variation. After the scales of wax have formed, the worker then removes them with her hind tarsi and they are then grasped by the "wax pinchers" located between the tibias and the first (largest) tarsal segments of the hind legs. The scales are then carried forward to the mandibles. In using the wax for comb construction, the scales are formed into shape by the mandibles and the cells are gradually "drawn out" by the addition of more and more wax. While the walls of the cells are thin their outer edges always bear a thickened rim or coping. This strengthens the cells so that they are not injured when the bees walk about over them.

The wax cells constructed by honeybees are extraordinary structures when one considers that they are built by an insect that depends only upon instinct and works in the total darkness of the hive. They are hexagonal in form. In worker brood cells, which are also used for honey and pollen storage, there are 55 per square inch of comb. Mathematicians have determined that the shape of the cells is such as to hold the largest amount of honey with the smallest amount of structural material. They are very accurately built, there being less than three or four degrees of variation in their angles. Réaumur, the well-known French naturalist of the eighteenth century, conceived the idea of using the diameter of these wax cells as an international unit of measurement. It was never adopted, but this idea is an indication of their uniformity in size. The walls of the cells vary from about 1/230 to 1/500 of an inch. One pound of wax will build about 35,000 cells which will hold about 22 pounds of honey. In order to secrete a pound of wax it is usually estimated that the bees will consume about eight pounds of honey—the production of this necessary structural material is rather expensive to the hive's economy.

Beeswax also has many uses in human industry; it is used in making floor waxes, candles, cosmetics and many other things. As human food, beeswax has no value, but there is a bird in Africa that appears to subsist on a diet of wax and bee larvae. There are 11 species of these birds, the honey-guides, all sharing similar habits. They are related to the woodpecker clan. Two species will unerringly guide both humans and honey badgers to wild bee nests. These unique birds are about the size of small starlings and rather demurely colored. Another strange habit of the honey-guide is their practice of laying eggs in the nests of other birds as do cuckoos. When the eggs hatch, the young honey-guide attacks the other bird's young, kills them with its hooked beak and pushes their remains out of the nest.

When the honey-guide locates a nest of wild bees, it then finds either a honey badger or a human being and, alighting on a bush, begins to chatter. If the chosen party shows interest in following it, the honey-guide flies farther off and chatters again, always in the direction of the wild bee nest. When the bird has lured its "guest" to the bee nest and the colony has been plundered of its store of honey, the bird then gorges itself on the comb containing both wax and larvae that has been exposed or scattered about. Honey-guides have no interest in the honey, but can apparently digest and assimilate the wax. Probably the first person to become acquainted with the wax-eating propensities of the honey-guides was a Portuguese missionary in the sixteenth century, who was astonished to see one of the birds fly in through an open window in his chapel and begin devouring one of the beeswax candles. Truly, this is one of the world's most remarkable instances of symbiosis, a cooperative arrangement between two animals whereby each is benefited.

In addition to the common domestic honeybee, there are a number of other bees that also gather nectar and manufacture it into honey, though in much smaller quantities. For this reason they are not of value as commercial sources. Probably the best known of these are the bumblebees (*Bombus*) of which there are many species found in almost all parts of the world, especially in the cooler zones. Like their cousins, the domestic honeybees, the bumblebees live upon nectar and pollen harvested from flowers, but their nesting habits have many differences.

Whereas the entire honeybee colony survives the winter in the form of a warm cluster, all the bumblebee workers die in autumn. Only the mated queens survive by retiring to small cells they excavate in the ground. When spring arrives these queens emerge from their winter quarters and begin feeding upon nectar and pollen. During cool spring nights they retire to sheltered places again. This continues for several weeks during which time their ovaries are developing. They then seek places to found colonies, such as deserted mouse nests in the ground, which are formed of dried grass, or other nesting sites, including haystacks or even old bird nests. During early summer, queen bumblebees can often be observed as they buzz about among vegetation, alighting now and then to investigate cavities and holes in search of suitable places to nest.

Having at last found a situation that meets her needs the queen clears a small space inside and settles down to wait for her glands to develop. Occasionally, she leaves the site and gathers food. In time she begins secreting wax after the manner of honeybee workers and uses this to construct a cup-shaped cell. This is often stocked with pollen which she gathers from flowers. This done, she then lays a number of eggs in it—usually about eight—and seals it over with wax so that its final shape is that of a sphere. The queen next begins the construction of a honey pot consisting of an open receptacle about the size of a thimble, located just inside the nest entrance. Some species build the honey pot first. In this receptacle she places a store of nectar which will be used to feed the larvae during periods of bad weather when she cannot harvest it from flowers. This, in effect, is her "money in the bank." In three to five days the larvae hatch and the queen mother makes an opening in the wall of the spherical cell and feeds them nectar. In some species a store of pollen has already been placed in the cell. As the larvae grow, the queen enlarges the original cell so that eventually there are a number of cells, all connected together. When not out collecting food, she spends her time "brooding" the larval cells—keeping them warm with the heat of her own body. In about seven days the larvae transform to pupae and, in about twelve days, to adult worker bumblebees which emerge from their separate cells.

When the workers have emerged, the colony becomes a social unit somewhat like that of a honeybee colony. The first workers, which are smaller than normal, take over the field work while the queen now remains in the nest. It is interesting, however, that, unlike the queen honeybee, she does not become merely an egg layer but continues to help feed the brood and to engage in other activities within the nest. Brood cells are not reused for brood rearing, but after the young emerge they are used for food storage. Stored nectar thickens by evaporation and the cells are then capped.

As the summer advances, more young are reared so that the colony eventually numbers from a few hundred to several thousand workers, depending on the species. As in the case of honeybee workers, they live for only a few weeks. During late summer when the colony has become populous and food abundant, a number of queens and drones are produced.

In this picture two bumblebee cells have been cut open to show white pupal workers.

Unlike larval honeybee queens, those of bumblebees do not apparently receive glandular food comparable to royal jelly, although food for bumblebee queens does seem to differ in both quantity and quality. Once the production of queens and males has begun in late summer, no more worker brood is reared. In the economy of the bumblebee colony, this would be a waste of effort since, with the coming of autumn, they all die anyway. In late summer the virgin queens and males mate, but only the queens survive the winter to found the colonies of another year. In this respect they resemble hornets.

Bumblebees are often confused with carpenter bees (*Xylocopa*) which make tunnels in wood. Carpenter bees, however, are not social insects and do not belong to the same tribe as the bumblebees. While the robust bodies of bumblebees are usually black marked with contrasting colors, especially yellow or orange, the bodies of carpenter bees are usually black. Carpenter bees have no pollen baskets on their hind legs even though they collect pollen.

While bumblebees, like honeybees, often impress us with their industry, some kinds have degenerated into the role of social parasite. One of these is the parasitic bumblebee (*Psithyrus*) which resembles the ordinary bumblebee but has no worker caste. Somewhere along the evolutionary line the queen *Psithyrus* lost the ability to found her own colony. She is now a chiseler and instead of going to the trouble of rearing young she seeks out a bumblebee nest and lays her eggs in it. The bumblebees rear these "cuckoo" young, which turn out to be only males and queens. They leave the bumblebee nest and, after mating, the females seek other bumblebee nests to parasitize. When the female *Psithyrus* enters a bumblebee nest she may be killed at once, but often she is more or less accepted and may live in peace with the rightful queen for some time.

Most people are aware that both honeybees and bumblebees gather nectar, but it may come as a surprise to learn that some wasps, too, collect and store nectar. Most of the species of these honey wasps are native to tropical areas, where natives often rob them of their honey or nectar stores. Whether the substance they produce should be designated as honey is questionable, but in places where these insects occur the sweet material they store is known as honey and the insects themselves are known as honey wasps. They are apparently quite common in Mexico, but one species, *Brachygastra* (*Nectarina*) *lecheguana,* is found in the vicinity of Brownsville, Texas, and is part of our native fauna. These wasps—perhaps they should be called hornets—construct paper-enclosed nests resembling closely those of our native hornets. However, their nests are about 20 inches high and elongate in shape. Usually, they are constructed on low shrubs, such as Mexican mahogany, and their interior architecture is not much different from that of nests built by our common hornets. They are apparently quite docile and do not usually sting in defense of their nest, although they will sting severely if handled or sufficiently aroused. But, curiously, they may be robbed of their honey or have their nest cut down with impunity.

Honey is stored in the paper cells which, like those of other hornets, are in horizontal layers with the cells extending downward. In a typical colony there are about 50,000 cells. The cells in which honey is stored are not capped. Not much seems to be known about the biology of these wasps, but the colonies apparently survive more than one year, as do most other tropical wasps. Instead of the new colony being founded by a mated queen, those of the honey wasps are founded by small swarms consisting of several queens and a few workers.

In studying insects, we should always be prepared for the unusual. Just as certain tropical hornets store honey, several ants, too, store honeydew or "honey." One kind occurs in North America and another in Australia. Those occurring in Australia are named *Camponotus inflatus* while those in our country all belong to the genus *Myrmecocystus* of which there are a number of species. The curious aspect of these ants is that they all dwell in arid regions where they can harvest their sweets only during short periods of the year. Under such conditions some method of storing the liquid food becomes a necessity—a method in this case which is most unusual. Ants cannot secrete wax to build combs like bees, so they have evolved another storage method. They use their own bodies as honey casks. Not all individuals serve in this capacity, but those that do so are called "repletes," and their abdomens become so greatly distended with contained "honey" that they resemble small grapes. After becoming repletes they are comparatively helpless and spend their time clinging to the ceilings of the underground galleries by their feet. The *Myrmecocystus* ants of our Southwest are found over an area extending from southern Idaho to deep into Mexico, usually at altitudes of from 5,000 to 7,000 feet.

My own experience with these unusual ants consists of two trips to Colorado's Garden of the Gods to observe and photograph them first-

This is a close-up of a honey ant replete. Note the abdomen swollen with amber honey. The plates or sclerites that once covered the abdomen exist now only as isolated islands on the globular abdomen. When these ants become repletes they are quite helpless.

hand. The red, sandy ridges contain their underground colonies. Since they are nocturnal in habit, the identification of their nests is somewhat difficult because there are many other ground-nesting ants in the area. The entrances to honey ant colonies are nearly half an inch in diameter, larger than might be expected for ants of moderate size. In my first search for these ants I dug up several harvester ant colonies which I mistook for those of honey ants. However, I at last recognized a honey ant nest when I glimpsed one of the slender, yellowish ants in the entrance. Excavating the nest down to the galleries where the repletes were housed constituted a major undertaking since the gravelly soil was very hard and the sun was hot. About three inches beneath the surface I encountered a gallery containing pupal ants in gray cocoons. It was not until I had dug downward about a foot in the hardpan earth that my trowel at last encountered a gallery that proved to be one of those where the repletes were kept. Clearing away the earth revealed a startling sight. As far as I could see back into the dark gallery, dozens of repletes were suspended from the ceiling, their distended abdomens glistening in the light. In color they were translucent amber and, when examined under a lens, it could be seen that, in the process of expansion, the original sclerites or abdominal plates existed as mere islands on the globular surfaces of stretched membrane. They were almost completely helpless and when I dislodged them from their perches they lay on their backs waving their legs in the air. In the meantime the normal workers rushed about in vain efforts to defend their nest. However, they have no stings and they make no effort to bite. The first gallery or chamber I excavated was about an inch high and about eight inches across. When other, lower, chambers were excavated a total of several dozen repletes were unearthed.

In former years the Indians often dug into honey ant nests for the repletes, which they ate for their sweet contents. The Australian honey ants are also eaten by natives. The swollen abdomens of honey ant repletes are very delicate and burst very easily. As a matter of fact, I noticed that when some of them fell from their perches to the floor of the gallery—a distance of only about an inch—their abdomens ruptured and the liquid contents soaked into the gravelly soil. When this occurred the normal workers gathered around and attempted to salvage the sweet contents. I tasted some of this ant honey, but found it rather sour, not nearly as palatable as that from honeybees.

In order to observe their nocturnal activities, my wife and I returned to the Garden of the Gods after dark when a full moon hung over Pikes Peak. After locating a honey ant colony we waited until they began emerging and crawling away across the ground toward scrub oaks. They climbed up these and began imbibing the droplets of honeydew exuded from galls on the twigs. This is the source of their honey and explains its relatively poor quality. These galls, each about the size of a small marble, are produced by the activities of cynipid gall wasps whose larvae develop within them. The droplets of honeydew that form on the surfaces of the galls result, probably, from the excess sugar that accumulates within them. We noticed also that some of the ants were obtaining honeydew from aphids on nearby wild rose bushes.

The honeydew gathered from oak galls or aphids is carried back to the underground nest where it is "fed" to the repletes. Later, whenever a worker ant is hungry it approaches a replete which regurgitates a drop of honey. Thus there is always a readily available source of food in the honey ant nest. Here in this relatively barren region, honeydew sources do not last long, only from late June through August. Thus, the ants must have a safe means of food storage for the remainder of the year. Theirs is a remarkable solution to the storage of food in an inhospitable region.

chapter twelve

The Carpenters, Miners and Gall Makers

WHILE many insects, probably the majority of plant-feeding kinds, obtain their food by eating leaves or siphoning sap from them, there are numerous others that have "gone underground" and dwell within the tissues of plants. This type of existence has many advantages: it affords protection from both enemies and weather, and places the insect in an abundant supply of food. Such a life might be compared to that of a small boy living in a cooky jar! There are so many advantages to life within plants that almost every insect order is represented. Some of these, especially the beetles, ants and termites, tunnel through the wood of living or dead trees. Others, such as the immature stages of certain beetles, moths and flies, excavate mines between the surfaces of leaves. These latter insects are necessarily of small size and are known collectively as leaf-miners. Still other insects create their own plant structures within which they live in the midst of abundance. These are the gall-making insects. Here, too, many insect orders are represented.

While a tree is alive and growing it is host to many kinds of insects, but, in many cases, the insects that tunnel within its tissues are specific to the kind of tree. When the tree dies it at once becomes the abode of a new insect population, consisting chiefly of boring beetles. When the tree finally falls to the earth and begins rotting there is yet another shift in population as new insects take over and hasten the processes of decomposition. Actually, more insects live within dead wood than in living wood. A tree, living or dead, is a teeming world of life that thrives in amazing diversity.

Foremost among the insects that tunnel through living wood are the beetles, of which several families are represented. First, there are the long-horned beetles (family Cerambycidae) whose larvae or grubs tunnel through living or dead wood. Some kinds are called "sawyers." The adult beetles are characterized by having very long antennae that are often longer than their bodies. They vary in size from tiny beetles to giants such as *Titanus giganteus,* a tropical species measuring five inches long found in the Amazon area of South America. While the majority of the long-horned beetles are dull colored, there are some species, such as the splendid long-horned borer (*Callichroma splendidum*) which is dressed

The grublike larvae of the long-horned beetles (family Cerambycidae) bore in wood. There are many different species.

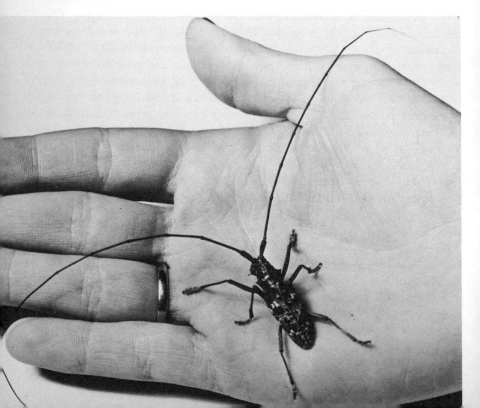

Record of a small woodland tragedy. This twig which has been split open shows that a woodpecker drilled a hole into it to capture the larva of a beetle that was boring at the center.

in beautiful shades of metallic blue and green. There are about 13,000 species of long-horned beetles in the world.

As adults many long-horned borers feed upon flower nectar, but the larvae usually tunnel through the wood of trees or shrubs. Many of the adults have stridulating organs and make squeaking sounds when picked up. Possibly because of the nature of their food, some kinds spend long periods in the larval stage. Adults often emerge from furniture that has been in use for twenty or more years. The borers were undoubtedly in the trees before they were cut into lumber and then made into furniture. The tunneling activities of the larvae often injure trees.

While it might seem that these hidden larvae would be completely safe, the truth is that they have many enemies. Woodpeckers often drill holes into trees where their tunnels are located and spear them with their long tongues. Apparently, the birds locate the grubs by the clicking sounds made by their mandibles as they chisel through the wood. If you place your ear against the end of a sawlog, you can often hear these sounds. They can more easily be heard if a medical stethoscope is used.

While the tunnels of the long-horned borers are round, those of the flat-headed borers (to be discussed later) are oval in cross section. Among the more interesting types is the twig-girdler (*Oncideres cingulata*). When ready to lay her eggs, the female of this beetle cuts a deep groove around a twig of hickory, elm or other tree and then inserts her egg in the twig beyond the girdled portion. As a result of the girdle, the twig dies and

This is the flat-headed larva of a metallic wood borer (family Buprestidae). These larvae usually tunnel beneath the bark of trees.

falls to the ground, usually during a wind storm, and the larva develops there. Trees are often severely damaged by the girdling activities of these beetles.

Often, in autumn, the ground beneath oak trees is found to be covered with small limbs that appear to have been neatly sawed off. This is the work of a long-horned beetle grub, the oak pruner (*Hypermallus villosus*). The adult beetle lays her eggs in a small twig and the young larva feeds in the succulent wood for a time, then works down into a larger branch where it feeds on the harder wood. Eventually the grub makes a circular cut in the limb so that it falls from the tree during a wind storm. On the ground, the grub completes its development.

Similar in habits to the long-horned borers are the metallic wood-boring beetles (family Buprestidae). These are flattened beetles both in their adult and larval stages, and, as their name implies, the adults, in most cases, are colored in metallic hues of green and blue though some kinds are dull colored. Some species have contrasting markings. The larvae are well adapted to life beneath the bark of trees since the fore parts of their bodies are enlarged and flattened. When the bark falls from dead trees the tunnels made by these beetle larvae can almost always be seen. When I was a boy we often fished through the ice on Lake Henry in Idaho. Prior to chopping a fishing hole we obtained a supply of "grubworms" from dead pines surrounding the lake. These were the larvae of metallic woodborers. Some kinds such as the flat-headed apple tree borer (*Chrysobothris femorata*) often injure fruit trees.

Of special interest are the engraver beetles (family Scolytidae) because of the pretty designs they make, as both larvae and as adults, beneath the bark of many trees. The female adult beetles, which are only about a quarter of an inch in length and of cylindrical form, bore in through the bark and excavate galleries between wood and bark. In these galleries the females lay eggs at regular intervals. When these eggs hatch the young grubs tunnel away beneath the bark, the size of their tunnels increasing as they bore along. As a result, when the bark peels away these characteristic heiroglyphics can be seen on the trunk of the tree. The patterns of the tunnels vary with the species. Some kinds of engraver beetles damage trees irreparably.

To this same family belong the interesting ambrosia beetles that cultivate fungi or "ambrosia" in their galleries. The story of these beetles was told in the chapter The Farmers.

These are the "engravings" made by engraver beetles beneath tree bark. The large tunnels are those of female beetles that laid eggs as they bored along. When the eggs hatched the larval beetles tunneled away, growing in size as they bored through the wood.

We usually think of the caterpillars of moths as feeding upon leaves, and most of them do, but there are a number of curious members of the moth tribe whose caterpillars have taken up unusual habits. For example, the aquatic pyralids (*Nymphula* and *Elophila*) during their larval stages live in water, where they feed upon submerged vegetation. Another unusual case is that of the carpenter moths (family Cossidae) whose larvae tunnel in the living wood of various trees. The adult moths are dagger-winged and gray in color with dark wing markings. Their wing-spreads are about two inches. The larvae or caterpillars are plump and nearly devoid of spines or hairs and live for several years in wood before pupating. When ready to pupate the caterpillar pushes itself out of its tunnel in the tree before the adult emerges. As a result, the empty pupal skins can often be seen protruding from trees.

Another of the more interesting wood borers are the large carpenter bees (*Xylocopa*)—there are nearly a dozen species—that tunnel through hard wood to establish nests. These bees are robust and resemble bumble-bees, but the upper surfaces of their abdomens are shiny and devoid of hair and their hind legs have no pollen baskets as do the bumblebees. Actually, carpenter bees are quite closely related to the common honey-bee, but the female has no worker caste to "rule." However, for the purpose of our discussion we will confer upon her the courtesy title of queen.

In spring the males can often be seen flying about old barns or out-buildings. These males hover in the air like hummingbirds, now and then chasing off some flying insect that chances to enter their domain. Such males are waiting for the emergence of the unmated queens that have spent the winter in the old nests. After mating, the queens choose loca-tions for nests, usually on the undersides of rafters or timbers. In the forest they excavate their tunnels into the undersides of dead limbs or fallen trees. As the queen cuts away the wood with her mandibles, she becomes covered with sawdust, but this does not appear to bother her. The tunnel she excavates is about the size of a dime in cross-section and, after extending about an inch into the wood, turns at right angles and follows the grain. When finished the tunnel may be a foot in length. Sometimes the tunnel forks just inside the entrance, one branch running up the timber and the other down. After the work of excavating the tunnel is completed, the queen then goes shopping. She gathers pollen from flowers and carries it back to the nest and places it at the end of the tunnel.

The nest tunnel of the carpenter bee (*Xylocopa*) is partitioned off into separate cells, each stocked with a mixture of pollen and nectar (lower left), and an egg is laid in each. When the eggs hatch the larvae feed upon the stored food.

The pollen is carried in brushes on her hind legs. When she has accumulated about a thimbleful, she then lays an egg on it and constructs a partition using wood chips cemented together with saliva. In a similar fashion she constructs more cells, each separated by a partition until about a dozen are finished. The construction and stocking of the nest is an arduous task, especially the excavation of the tunnel. The amount of labor that goes into the construction of an insect's nest is quite often amazing. The need for providing their young with quarters that are as safe as their means can devise is great, for enemies are everywhere, awaiting the chance to rob and plunder.

When the carpenter bees' eggs hatch, the larvae feed upon the stored food and grow. When mature they transform into pupae and then into adults. Now the matter of timing comes in. Naturally, the first egg laid hatches first and this bee reaches the adult stage soonest. But it is at the far end of the tunnel with its escape route blocked by the other cells. As the adults emerge successively from their pupal cases they simply settle down and await the last one. Then the queen leads her children out on their first flight. In some species the first adults to transform simply break out of their cells and crawl over the others which are not as yet mature. After emerging, the daughters then aid their mother in cleaning out the old tunnel, and one of them eventually uses it to rear her own brood. From this it is apparent that the carpenter bee has reached the point in evolution where the social habit is just beginning. Given sufficient time, it is possible that a true worker caste might eventually develop. The common large carpenter bee in eastern United States is *Xylocopa virginica,* but there are other species in the West, such as *Xylocopa californica,* which ranges southward into Mexico. The eastern species bores in such relatively hard woods as pine, cedar and magnolia while the western species uses softer woods such as Sequoia, yucca and agave. There is apparently a definite preference among the various species for certain woods.

The excavation of these tunnels in wood is indeed an arduous task, and it is not at all surprising that other insects avail themselves of the ready-made shelters as nesting sites. One of the most common of these house-renters is a wasp closely related to the jug-builder wasp (*Eumenes*). These "carpenter" wasps (*Monobia quadridens*)—they have no other common name—are black, marked with white and can often be seen loitering about places where carpenter bees are nesting. As might be expected from their close affinity with the jug wasp, the nest partitions are constructed of clay and the cells stocked with paralyzed cutworms.

Like the carpenter bees, carpenter ants also tunnel through dead wood creating a honeycomb of interconnecting galleries within which the colony lives. The common North American species, *Camponotus herculeanus pennsylvanicus,* is our largest ant, the workers averaging nearly a half inch in length. They are black in color and highly carnivorous in food habit. I once kept a colony of these ants in captivity in order to observe and photograph them. For food I gave them bits of hamburger meat upon which they fed ravenously like tiny wolves tearing at a dead carcass. In the wild state the workers are continually out on individual hunting expeditions seeking game. They are not specialists and will capture and carry back to the nest almost any small insect and will also feed upon honeydew secreted by mealybugs. I have seen large numbers clustered on colonies of mealybugs on alder where they were in competition with buzzing clusters of hornets and bees all bent on collecting the amber droplets of honeydew. In their native habitat these large ants often excavate their nests in partially dead trees, invading only the dead wood. They sometimes tunnel in the timbers of houses, where their destructive activities are frequently confused with those of termites.

Probably because of their safe home sites and relatively abundant food, a number of "star boarders" have taken up residence in carpenter ant nests. One of these is *Atemeles,* a beetle belonging to the family Staphylinidae. These beetle house guests are treated almost like pets, being cleaned and fed from the mouths of their hosts. These remarkable beetles bear tufts of yellow hairs on the sides of their abdomens. Beneath these hairs are glands which secrete a druglike substance upon which the ants feed. Their larvae are also tended and fed along with the ants' larvae. Amazingly, also, when a carpenter ant nest is broken into, the ants dash to the defense of the *Atemeles* larvae in preference to their own larvae. In this respect the ants are behaving very strangely since the *Atemeles* feed upon the larval ants! Among the other guests found in carpenter ant nests are small ant-loving crickets (*Myrmecophila*) whose hind legs are swollen with muscles which enable them to hop about and avoid the jaws of their vicious hosts. These miniature crickets are merely tolerated and the ants occasionally turn upon them and eat them. On the other hand, the crickets are often allowed to nibble or lick the ants' legs and bodies for oily secretions. The crickets avoid the forelegs and heads of the ants, thus remaining as far as possible from the mandibles.

Of all the insects that tunnel in wood the termites are of first importance and interest. While these insects are primarily inhabitants of tropical lands, there are many kinds that have extended their ranges into the temperate zones of the world. The termites belong to the insect order Isoptera, an ancient group of insects that had its beginning hundreds of millions of years ago. Winged termites have been found in Baltic amber in which they were imbedded about fifty million years ago. Their remains are also found in the shales of Colorado. A termite wing has been found in middle-Permian shales of the Sylva River Basin in the Ural Mountains. It has been named *Uralotermes permianum* and is the most ancient of all known termite fossils. This is the wing of a termite that fluttered through an archaic forest on its nuptial flight about two hundred million years ago. The venation of this wing shows that the insect had a close affinity to the ancient cockroaches from which it had evolved.

It is probable that the termites of those ancient days were little different from those that live today. The termite tribe is far older than the dinosaurs and older than the ants and bees. Their social organization antedates any other. There are nearly two thousand species in the world, most of which occur in Africa and the Orient. In the United States and Canada there are less than fifty species. To the home owner, termites are pests which destroy the timbers of his home and necessitate expensive repairs. In general, there are two types of termites here in the United States that are destructive to wooden structures. There are the subterranean termites (*Reticulitermes*) which nest in moist ground and build tunnels up into houses, and there are the dry-wood termites (*Kalotermes*) which live and nest in dry wood, needing no connection with moist soil.

Like the ants, bees and hornets, the termites have a well-developed caste system, but differing considerably from that of these insects. The termite social structure is generally far more complicated. Termites have an incomplete life history, there being no pupal stage. The eggs hatch into nymphs which gradually grow into adult winged termites. In this respect they show their affinity to the cockroach clan. When first hatched, the young all look alike, but within a few days some of these begin to show differences. Some of them are small-headed reproductive types and others are large-headed sterile types or "workers." When fully developed the reproductive types are winged. The life cycle and colony organization given here is that of the common subterranean termite (*Reticulitermes*), but other termites have similar life histories. In contrast to bees and other social Hymenoptera in which workers are all imperfect females, the individuals of the termite worker caste are potentially either males or females. However, they do not usually reproduce. They are blind and repelled by light and, because they have evolved and live in a moist, protected habitat, they are soft bodied. These workers gnaw away at solid wood with their jaws and swallow the cellulose-containing fiber. Perhaps the most remarkable thing about these small insects is their manner of digesting the wood fiber. Cellulose is very difficult to digest, but the termites have evolved an interesting way of doing it. Within the intestines of all termites are enormous numbers of special protozoa which produce cellulose-dissolving enzymes that break the cellulose down into sugar that can be absorbed and used by the termite. A similar symbiotic relationship exists between protozoa and certain primitive cockroaches which also bore in wood. If the intestine of a termite worker is crushed and the contents examined under a microscope, these protozoans can easily be seen, still in a living condition. The young termites become "infected" with the helpful protozoa from the older termites. Research has proved that termites cannot exist without these living aids to wood digestion. It should be noted in passing, however, that not all species of termites contain protozoa. For example, the mound-building termites of Africa (*Macrotermes*) cultivate fungus gardens in a manner similar to that of the *Atta* or leaf-cutting ants. Since these termites feed upon fungus, they have no need for symbiotic protozoa.

In addition to the numerous workers in a termite colony, there are many soldiers which, like the workers, may be either male or female. Like the workers, the soldiers are sterile. They have elongate heads and large mandibles which are supposedly of use in defending the colony. However, when the nest is broken open the soldiers appear to be of little help in defense. It is only when a tunnel is breached that the soldiers are able to keep enemies out. Ants are the ancestral enemies of termites, and it is likely that the soldiers are able to defend the nest against these insects when they attempt to enter the galleries. If a piece of wood containing termites is broken open so that the inhabitants and their galleries are exposed, it can usually be seen that the soldiers strike their hard heads rapidly against the floor of their tunnels. This is probably a means of communicating an alarm through the colony.

While the soldiers of our native termites defend their nests by means of strong jaws, those of some termites, especially many tropical species, have noselike projections extending out from the fronts of their heads. This is called a *nasus* or "nose" and it is the opening of a gland that secretes a fluid that is either repellent or sticky, depending on the species of termite. In some termites (*Nasutitermes*) the soldiers repel ants by squirting them with this fluid. In other termites (*Coptotermes*) the secretion is sticky and when squirted on ants so gums up their bodies that they are rendered helpless. Termite soldiers with such squirtgun heads are also found in other genera, including *Armitermes* and *Rhinotermes*.

In a honeybee colony, only the queen has the ability to lay eggs, and this is her sole function throughout life. In the case of termites, there are two functional kinds of egg-laying females in addition to the primary queen. The first two kinds have short wing pads that never develop into true wings. One of these has shorter wing pads than the other. The primary queen thus has help in producing the enormous number of eggs required to keep the teeming population of the colony going. In our common subterranean termite the primary queen is difficult to locate. Usually, she is situated in a cell deep within the nest site and is accompanied by the king (male). In these termites the primary queen is about a half inch in length, but the queens of some tropical termites reach enormous size, some measuring four or five inches. Such queens are helpless and are merely great reproductive sacks. Some of these queens are 160 times as large as the males or kings and 2,400 times the size of the workers! It is believed by some that these large queens may be 40 or 50 years old! Some have actually been observed living in nests for 25 years.

After a termite colony is established the queen loses her wings and develops an enormous abdomen filled with eggs. She never again leaves the nest.

In spring and early summer an established termite colony produces a large number of winged males and females. These emerge from the nest through exit holes opened by the workers and fly out in a swarm. Sometimes these winged sex forms are carried to high altitudes by air currents. They have been trapped at 3,000 feet by special devices on airplanes. Such an emergence often attracts many birds that gorge themselves on the defenseless insects. I recently observed such an occurrence. A large number of mockingbirds were flying around a garden post capturing some kind of insects. Closer observation showed the insects to be swarming termites.

The termite males and females that escape enemies fly away seeking cracks in dead trees, fallen logs or crevices in the timbers of human dwellings and creep in. The males and females pair off and shed their wings. The wings of these termite sex forms have sutures or breaking points near their bases and are quite easily severed. After they have taken up a subterranean life, the wings would be more than useless—they would be in the way.

At the time of swarming the males and females are not yet sexually mature and, thus, not ready to mate. After alighting on the ground or other situation and losing their wings, the individuals pair off and the males follow closely behind the females as they crawl about seeking a location for nest establishment. Once such a location has been found, a small cell is excavated and the two eventually mate and a new termite colony is founded. In contrast to queen ants that mate and then found colonies alone, the queen termite has the male to aid her in caring for the young.

If the royal pair are successful in founding a colony it gradually increases in size if food is available and other conditions are favorable. American subterranean termites must have moisture to live. Usually, the nest proper is in the ground where ecological conditions are favorable with special regard to humidity and temperature. Extending up out of the ground the termites construct tunnels running to sources of wood. In some cases this may be to the timbers of a house. Above the ground these tunnels may follow over the surfaces of foundations. In damp basements the tunnels may be constructed upward without regard to attachment to a wall or foundation, but more often these chimneylike tunnels are built downward rather than from the ground upward. They consist of wood or earth particles cemented together and are constructed from the inside. That is, the workers carry the structural material up or down through the hollow tunnel and cement it in place at the edge, gradually extending its length. Sometimes, in dark basements where there is little air movement, these suspended tunnels may reach over three feet from wooden timbers down to the ground. They are very fragile and break at the slightest touch, but they afford the toiling termites an easy and protected means of travel from the source of their woody food to the underground nest.

While most of us are familiar with the common termites discussed above, there are many species native to tropical lands having interesting and unusual habits that deserve special mention. Many of these tropical species build carton nests on trees or earthen mounds of enormous size. Some of these earthen nests extending up above the surface of the ground are as large as small cottages. One of the most interesting of these is the "compass" termite (*Amitermes meridionalis*) of Australia. The nests of these termites extend up from the ground like large shafts, and some of them resemble conical junipers in form. They are flattened and always orientated north and south, probably to take advantage of the sun's heat. In Africa there are several kinds of termites that construct large earthen nests of more or less columnar form resembling, in a general way, those of Australia. The clay of which these nests are constructed is very hard and impervious and the termites that live in them feed upon fungi which they cultivate upon wood or leaf fragments carried into the nest.

One kind, *Macrotermes natalensis,* uses an elaborate method of air conditioning and aerating its nest. The nests or *termitaries* of these remarkable termites are very large, often reaching heights of 16 feet and 16 feet across. The colony proper occupies a large cavity in the central portion of the termitary. The outer walls are nearly two feet thick. When viewed from the outside, it can be seen that there are many raised ridges or vanes extending down the sides. Since there are several million termites living within this nest, all using oxygen and giving off carbon dioxide, it is obvious that there must be some means of gaseous exchange with the outside air. There is also need for a method of controlling the interior temperature and humidity. If one of these nests is cut open, it will be found that, above the central nest chamber, there is an "attic" and that there are ducts leading out of this "attic." One of these ducts enters the top of each of the outside ridges and then divides into numerous small passages that continue on down through the ridge or vane to a point near the ground level where they unite again into a single large duct. These large ducts, one from each vane, then enter a "basement" beneath the central nest cavity. In operation the air conditioning and aeration system works as follows: the living processes of the termites and of the fungus they cultivate heat the air in the central nest chamber, causing it to rise. This heated air passes into the ducts leading into the ridges or vanes extending out from the sides of the nest. The air then flows downward through the small passages in the vanes. Since these passages are much-divided and near the outside surface of the vane, there is an exchange of gases and the elimination of moisture. In effect these vanes or ridges function somewhat like the cooling vanes on an air-cooled motor. Continuing on downward, the air, which has been cooled and purified, then enters the basement beneath the nest cavity. From here it then flows upward through the warm nest cavity where it again picks up heat and stale air. This cycle is continuous, of course, and the termites thus have as perfect an air-conditioning system as any modern engineer could design using the natural materials at hand. These termites have been constructing such air-conditioned nests for millions of years.

The limited space between the upper and lower surfaces of a leaf is a strange place for an insect to live, yet it is a microhabitat to which hundreds of different insects have adapted themselves, at least during a portion of their lives. These leaf miners, all of small size, infest the leaves of almost all plants, but they are especially abundant in the leaves of woody plants. Sometimes they are quite destructive. I have seen large stands of quaking aspens in the Rocky Mountains where almost every leaf contained the silvery mines of leaf-miners.

The area between the two surfaces of a leaf contains several different types of cells, the most important of which are those making up the palisade layer. Beneath this layer of columnar cells is a zone of irregularly placed cells called the spongy layer. Between the cells of this latter layer are many air spaces. Stomates or air pores, most of which are on the under surface, allow air to penetrate the spaces between the cells of the spongy layer. Both the cells of the palisade and spongy layers contain chlorophyll and are active in the manufacture of sugars by photosynthesis.

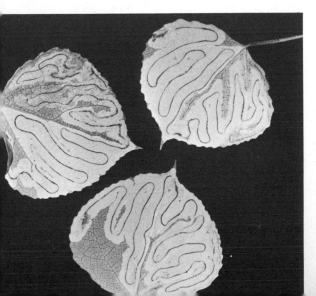

There are many kinds of insects that mine, during their larval stages, between the upper and lower surfaces of leaves. These insects are called leaf-miners. Shown here are the serpentine mines of aspen leaf-miners (*Phyllocnistis populiella*) in quaking aspen leaves.

Thus, here is a choice location where a small insect can live and feed. All of these insects are immature forms—after transforming to the adult, winged stages they leave the leaves. Four of the great insect orders are represented among the leaf-miners: the larvae of moths, beetles, flies and certain wasplike sawflies. These insects lay their eggs upon the surfaces of leaves or insert them inside and when the eggs hatch the larvae begin tunneling through the tissues, gradually expanding their feeding tunnels as they move along. As a result, the mines are usually shaped like trumpets. The entire life of the miner is usually recorded in the form of its mine. At the large end, where it completed its growth, can often be seen the pupal case or the exit hole through which it emerged. The mines, however, are of many forms since different kinds of insects feed in various ways. Some insects make blotch mines by feeding in a circle. Often the mines are so characteristic that the insects responsible for them can be identified without being seen. Leaf-miners, by the way, are most active in late summer.

In their mining operations the larvae usually assume definite positions. The fly larvae rest on their sides and move their mouth hooks up and down as they feed. On the other hand, moth, beetle and sawfly larvae rest with their lower surfaces against the epidermis of the leaf, their jaws cutting into the leaf cells as they move along. The liquid cell contents are imbibed. Some miners confine their operations to the upper or palisade cell layer, while others specialize in the spongy, lower layer; still other kinds consume all the cells from top to bottom. Not all leaf-miners spend their entire larval lives within the leaf, but in some instances they mine within the leaf during their early stages, then emerge and feed on the outside. After leaving the protection of the leaf tissues some of them construct webs while others build portable cases. One of the more interesting of those that build portable shelters is the maple case-bearer (*Paraclemensia acerifoliella*) that is often a destructive pest. During its early life the larva is a leaf-miner that excavates its mine in the form of a circular blotch. When ready to change its way of life, this larva builds a case by cutting oval sections from the upper and lower surfaces of the leaf and attaching them together with silk. This, of course, leaves a hole in the leaf. The section cut from the lower surface of the leaf is always a little larger than that cut from the upper surface. The larva, still between the two severed leaf ovals, then crawls out upon the leaf and flips the case over so that the section cut from the lower epidermis is on top. It now looks like a turtle. When the larva is feeding, this case is fastened down by silken cords attached around its edges. When the larva increases in size and a larger case eventually becomes necessary, it goes about this task in this way. While the case is still anchored to the leaf by silken strands, the larva makes a circular cut in the epidermis of the leaf beyond the edges of its old case. It then flips the case over so that the new addition is on top. The larva, of course, turns over within the case and continues feeding, protected by its turtlelike shelter.

While most insects are content to feed upon plant tissues in the form that the plants produce them, there are many insects that apparently secrete unknown substances into plants, causing them to produce special structures within which they live. These are actually new organs created by the plants as a result of stimulation by the insects involved. These insects are known collectively as gall insects and the so-called galls they produce are almost infinite in form and coloration. Altogether, there are about 2,000 different species of these insects and their galls are more or less characteristic of each.

Gall insects of many kinds produce galls or abnormal growths on many trees and plants. Sometimes these are very abundant and cause injury to the plants infested.

Insect-created galls are thus abnormal growths, only produced when the insects are present. However, it has been possible in a few cases to produce characteristic galls artificially by injecting extracts of the insects into the plant tissues. This seems to prove that the insects secrete an auxinlike substance into the plants, stimulating them to produce the special structures or galls. Not much is known about the chemical nature of the gall-producing secretion. It is a complex substance, rich in nucleic acid and protein, and hardens into a crystalline mass on exposure to air. Attention should be called to the fact that nucleic acid is the substance that conveys hereditary characteristics from one generation to the next and influences growth. Thus, the material secreted by gall-making insects apparently influences the basic growth of the plant cells involved. On the other hand, it is suspected that the irritation or other activity of the insects living within the plant tissues may be at least partly responsible for gall formation. Thus, as you can see, there is as yet considerable mystery regarding these strange growths. It may be of interest, too, that some research workers believe there is a rather close analogy between plant galls and the malignant growths of animals, such as cancer. Such evidence is found in comparing the mitotic divisions of the cells both in cancerous growths and in plant galls. Irregular mitoses or cell division occurs in both instances. The belief that the insects secreted some substance into plants, stimulating them to create galls, is not new. The great Italian zoologist, Marcello Malpighi, who lived from 1628 to 1694, was probably the first to conceive this idea.

Most galls are produced in spring or early summer while the plants are still in active growth. The insect deposits its eggs in the tissues and even before the egg hatches formation of the gall begins. It grows with the insect and apparently, in addition to a growth-stimulating substance, the insect produces an enzyme that transforms the plant starch into sugar. Many galls accumulate large amounts of sugar. For example, the galls formed on scrub oaks in the Southwest contain so much sugar that it exudes onto their outer surfaces, where it is gathered and stored by honey ants. Honeybees, also, sometimes gather and store large quantities of gall "nectar." Galls produced on oak by a gall wasp (*Dicholcaspis eldoradensis*) in one section of California produce such quantities of honeydew that honeybees may store from 30 to 40 pounds of it in each hive. The accumulation of this food material in the tissues of the galls is, of course, of direct benefit to the insects that dwell within them. In addition to sugar, many galls contain large amounts of tannic acid. For example, the Aleppo oak gall of Asia Minor contains about 65 percent tannic acid. This gall is produced by a cynipid wasp (*Cynips gallae-tinctoriae*) and the galls were once an important commercial source of tannic acid. In former years, the best inks were made from these galls. Aleppo gall ink was once the official ink specified for the writing of important documents by the United States Treasury, the Bank of England, the German Chancellory and the Danish Government. Gall extracts have also been used in medicine and as human and animal food. In Arkansas and Missouri there is a small cynipid gall that has such high food value and occurs in such numbers that it was once collected and fed to domestic animals. These galls contain 63.6 percent carbohydrates and 9.34 percent protein.

The ability to create galls is rather widespread among the insect clan— it is found among the beetles, moths, aphids, flies and wasps, as well as among many mites (not insects).

According to their structures, there are about twenty different gall types, varying from the common oak-apple gall produced by a tiny gall wasp (*Cynips*) to the beautifully tinted wool-sower gall, also found on oak and produced by another gall wasp (*Callirhytis seminator*). Both of these wasps belong to the family Cynipidae, the members of which produce a wide variety of galls on many kinds of plants. Some kinds of galls resemble flowers. For example, there is a flower-like gall produced on cypress by a tiny gall gnat (*Itonida anthici*) belonging to the family of Cecidomyiidae. To the casual observer these "flowers" could easily be mistaken for small yellowish blooms. Other galls such as the gouty oak gall produced by a gall-wasp (*Plagiotrochus punctatus*) are irregular swellings found on leaves and stems and are obviously abnormal, cancerlike growths. On the leaves of oaks are often seen the spangle-galls

These flowerlike galls on cypress were formed by a tiny wasp (*Itonida anthici*).

caused by a gall gnat (*Cecidomyia poculum*). These look like small buttons attached to the leaves. There is another gall often found in groups on hickory leaves that resembles tiny duncecaps. These also are a product of gall gnats (*Caryomyia*). Sometimes found on hickory leaves are hickory tube galls that look like tiny, pointed columns protruding up from the leaf surface. These are produced by gall gnats (*Caryomyia tubicola*).

Probably the most common of all galls are those produced on goldenrod by a pretty fly (*Eurosta solidaginis*) belonging to the family Trypetidae. These galls appear as swellings about an inch in diameter on the main stems of goldenrods and, if they are cut open in winter, a plump fly larva will be found at the center of each one. In spring these larvae transform into the pupal stage and eventually the adult flies emerge from their galls through holes previously cut almost through the walls by the larvae.

An interesting gall is produced on the leaf petioles of cottonwood by an aphid (*Pemphigus populi-transversus*). These galls appear as marble-sized swellings on the petioles. They are thin-walled and within them are found small colonies of aphids or plant lice. Here the insects develop in security until ready to emerge as winged individuals. At that time, due to a remarkable timing mechanism a transverse slit appears on one side, and slowly the lips of this slit open, allowing the imprisoned aphids to escape. Certainly, no more precise timing and apparent cooperation can be found anywhere among the plants for their unwelcome "guests." A somewhat similar gall is produced by aphids (*Hormaphis hamamelidis*) on witch-hazel leaves. This is called the witch-hazel cone-gall.

This gall produced on the leaf petiole of cottonwood has a slit in its side through which the insects can escape. It was produced by an aphid (*Pemphigus populi-transversus*).

These unusual galls, tinted in pastel colors, were produced on an oak leaf by a gall wasp (probably *Xanthoteras*).

One of our most widely distributed galls is the spiny rose gall produced by a gall wasp (*Diplolepis politus*). These galls are unique in that they are spherical with their surfaces covered with sharp spines. They are quite attractive in coloration, being tinted in pastel shades of pink and yellow. The young gall wasps, of course, feed and develop inside.

These are but a few of the vast array of plant galls, but they are sufficient to show the amazing variety of form and structure of these strange growths produced on plants by certain insects.

chapter thirteen

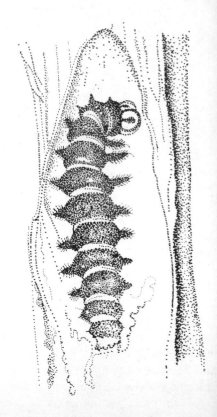

Plant Curiosities

THE relationships between plants and insects are often very complex and take many forms. Millions of years ago, when the earth was much younger than it is today and when the insect tribes were just beginning to develop, their relationships to plants were quite simple; they ate them. But as time passed some plants began subscribing to the philosophy of "if you can't whip 'em, join 'em." When this happened the relationships between insects and plants became more complicated. Some plants began soliciting the aid of certain insects in protecting themselves from other insects. Still other plants reversed the usual state of things and turned upon the insects and ate them instead. In many parts of the world—including our own country—there are strange plants that have developed carnivorous habits to supplement their diet of minerals from the soil. Most of these plants grow in boggy situations where soils are deficient in nitrogen so a partial diet of insects, whose bodies are high in nitrogen, helps them to balance the mineral budget.

Insects are lured to their doom within or upon the leaves of these unusual plants by attractive substances secreted there. Included among these insectivorous plants is the Venus fly-trap (*Dionea*), which grows only in the coastal bogs of the Carolinas. The leaves of these plants are hinged at the center and bear fringing spines. Any insect so unfortunate

One of the world's m
amazing insectivor
plants is the Venus
trap (*Dionea*) found
the coastal areas of
Carolinas. Insects crawl
across the open leaf tra
touch sensitive trigger ha
causing the traps to sn
shut and capture the
sects. Here a fly is bei
fed to a Venus fly-trap.

as to crawl across one of these leaves is trapped, as the leaf snaps shut if the trigger hairs are touched. The insect is then slowly digested, after which the leaf trap opens and sets itself again. Another insectivorous plant is the sundew (*Drosera*) found in marshy situations in many places. Its method of trapping insects is somewhat different from that used by the Venus fly-trap. Its spatulate leaves are covered by setae, each tipped with a shining globule of adhesive. Small insects such as gnats become stuck to these globules and are slowly digested. Another type of insectivorous plant is the pitcher plant (*Sarracenia*), having hollow, pitcherlike leaves and attractive blooms. Insects are lured into the hollow leaf tubes

This is the sundew (*Drosera*), a small, rosettelike plant that captures small insects by means of glue-tipped papillae. Once an insect is trapped by the adhesive the leaf bends over and holds it while it is being digested.

Pitcher plants (*Sarracenia*) grow in boggy sites in many parts of the country. Within their hollow tube-like leaves insects are trapped and digested. The overhanging lids prevent rain from entering the leaf tubes.

by an attractive odor and, once inside, cannot escape because the inner walls are covered with slippery scales or inwardly directed spines. A narcoticlike substance secreted by the plant soon kills the insects, which are eventually digested and absorbed to help nourish the cannibal plant. Closely related to our native pitcher plants is *Nepenthes,* native to Malaya but often grown in North American greenhouses. It is a climbing plant and its leaves are formed into cupshaped containers, where water accumulates. Insects falling into this fluid are killed and digested. Ironically, there are a number of insects that live happily within these leaf pools, feeding upon the trapped insects. They are apparently immune to the plant's poisons. All together there are about 450 different species of these carnivorous plants, most of which depend on trapped insects for at least part of their food supply.

Although our native pitcher plants consume large numbers of insects, there are some insects that live normally within the hollow leaves as do those previously mentioned in the case of *Nepenthes.* These include the larvae of three species of small moths that feed upon the tissues of the leaf pitchers. These are *Exyra ridingsi, E. semicrocea,* and *E. rolandiana.* These small, attractively marked moths lay their eggs within the leaf pitchers, usually only one egg in each one. If, however, more than one caterpillar should appear, cannibalism reduces the number to one so that only a single caterpillar ever matures in a leaf pitcher. These caterpillars are especially well adapted to development in pitcher plant leaves. Soon after beginning to feed on the leaf tissues the caterpillar cuts a groove around the hollow leaf near the top. This causes the top portion of the leaf to die and collapse. In addition, a diaphragm composed of silk and frass is constructed across the hollow tube. Here the caterpillar continues to feed and grow until ready to pupate. Prior to pupation, it cuts an opening in the leaf tube near the bottom to allow the escape of any water which may fall in the tube. There is some variation in the habits of these interesting moths, made necessary by growth habits and structures of the pitcher plants they inhabit. For example, *Exyra semicrocea,* which lives in the parrot pitcher plant (*Sarracenia psittacina*), has adapted itself to life in the procumbent leaves of this species which normally traps insects by means of a hood and backwardly directed spines in the leaf tube. Before pupating, this caterpillar takes the precaution of cutting a hole in the roof of the hood to enable the future moth to escape. Among the insects that feed upon pitcher plants is another moth caterpillar (*Papaipema appassionata*) that feeds on the rhizomes, constructing upright tubes up above the ground surface, possibly for air. Pitcher plants are also the homes of other creatures. Small tree frogs and lizards often hide within the leaves, where they probably subsist upon insects attracted by the plants.

In addition, there are several scavenger fly larvae that live within the leaves of pitcher plants, feeding upon the dead insects trapped there. These include several flesh flies (*Sarcophaga,* especially *S. sarraceniae*). In some locations where pitcher plants are abundant almost every leaf pitcher will be found to contain one or more of these fly larvae that are especially adapted to exist there. There is also a mosquito (*Wyeomyia smithii*) that flies into the open pitchers and lays its eggs in the small pool of water usually found there. Here, where other insects are quickly killed and digested, the mosquito wrigglers develop, seemingly immune to the plant's toxins. The hollow stems of pitcher plants are also used, sometimes, as nesting sites by hunting wasps (*Isodontia*) that stock the hollow leaves with paralyzed grasshoppers and crickets and fabricate loose stoppers of finely divided grass blades. The late William Morton Wheeler, a world authority on ants, states that a species of acrobatic ant (*Crematogaster pilosa*) often nests in pitcher plant leaves.

While the relationships between insects and plants are often complex and interesting, the most remarkable, probably, is that which has arisen between *Pseudomyrma* ants and certain acacias in tropical America.

The *Pseudomyrma* ants live within the hollow thorns of the bull-horn acacia of Mexico. Here a thorn is cut open showing a worker holding a pupal ant in its jaws.

These sprawling, shrublike thorn trees are native to a region extending from an area slightly south of the Mexican border on into South America. Their leaves are divided into many small leaflets, resembling, in a general way, those of the mimosa, to which they are related. The most remarkable thing about these plants, however, is the presence of numerous prominent thorns that resemble very strongly the horns of a bull. As a matter of fact, the thorn-pairs of some of these acacias look exactly like the horns of Texas longhorns. Others resemble those of the water buffalo. Because of the resemblance of these thorns to bull horns the plants are known as bull-horn acacias. From the standpoint of homology, these remarkable structures are modified stipules, the small leaflike structures found at the bases of the leaves of many plants. Protective thorns and spines are found in many plants and trees, such as honey locust, prickly ash, blackberry, rose and numerous others, but those of these acacias, while serving a protective function, protect in an indirect fashion. They

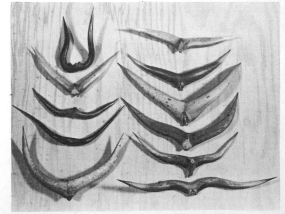

The thorns of the various species of bull-horn acacias are of many forms. Some of them resemble miniature Texas longhorns.

are the abodes of a standing army of ants that save the acacias by protecting them against leaf-destroying insects. The region to which the acacias are native is also the home of the leaf-cutting ants (*Atta*) that can, and often do, defoliate a tree over night. As was described in Chapter 8, the leaves gathered by the *Atta* ants are carried underground and used as a medium upon which an edible fungus is grown. It is probably as a defensive measure against these leaf-destroying *Attas* that the bull-horn acacias have adopted the *Pseudomyrma* ants.

Probably the first European to observe the bull-horn acacias was Francisco Hernandez, who was designated by Philip II of Spain in 1570 to study and report on the natural resources of the New World. He observed these thorn trees growing near the Pánuco River in northern Mexico and his report on them reads, in part, as follows:

> The Hoitzmamaxalli is a tree with leaves resembling those of a mezquite or tamarind, yellow flowers, edible pods, and horns very like those of a bull, growing upon the tree's trunk and branches. . . . Moreover, within the thorn there are generated certain slender ants, tawny-colored and blackish, whose sting is hurtful.

Several other early travelers to America observed that almost every thorn of these acacias was inhabited by ants, but it remained for Thomas Belt (1874), a naturalist who made many important observations on the insects of the American tropics, to determine the true relationships between the plant and the insect. He reported the results of his studies in a book published in London under the title *The Naturalist in Nicaragua*. Belt discovered that when immature the acacia thorns are green and tender and filled with pith but as time passes they dry out and turn brown. The ants then cut a circular entrance into one thorn of each pair. This hole is located near the tip and it is through this hole that the ants enter and remove the contained pith and pulp. What remains is a pair of hollow thorns with thin, tough walls, which constitute an excellent nesting site for a *Pseudomyrma* ant colony. There is never more than one entrance. Here the ants live secure from rains or enemies and rear their young. The individual colonies are necessarily small since the space within the thorns is limited. It is said that food is also stored in these cavities.

The acacia tree not only furnishes living quarters for its ants, but it also provides its ant army with food. Near the base of each leaf petiole, just above the point where it is attached to the central part of the thorn, there are several craterlike glands which secrete a sweet honeydew upon which the ants feed. Now if this were the only food available, the ants would live within the thorns and go only as far as the glands for their food. Thus, any leaf-destroying insect would probably not be repulsed since there would be no reason for the ant-protectors to be out on the leaves. In order to trick the ants into patrolling the leaflets, the plant has developed a source of food at its tips. This food consists of small, yellowish or reddish fruitlike bodies, each about one-twelfth of an inch in diameter. This "fruit" is a special growth and has no relation to seed or the reproductive organs of the acacia. They were apparently evolved as an inducement to lure the ants out to the leaves since they feed enthusiastically upon them or carry them back to their nests within the hollow thorns. In honor of Belt, who determined their function, these fruitlike structures are called "Beltian bodies." It is of interest also that these bodies do not mature all at once—by staggering their development the plant makes sure that the ants will be out hunting for them continually, thus protecting the foliage. Belt made a number of observations of bull-horn acacias to determine whether or not the *Pseudomyrma* ants actually did serve any useful function in protecting them. He also planted some acacias in places where there were no *Pseudomyrma* ants but where the leaf-cutting *Attas* did occur. He found that the unprotected acacias were quickly stripped of their foliage. On the other hand, acacias that housed standing armies of *Pseudomyrma* ants were immune to attack by most leaf-eating insects. The only insect that appeared to attack the acacias in spite of their protective ants was a beetle which infested the flowers.

While the various species of bull-horn acacias are confined to tropical regions, many kinds are grown in gardens in Florida, where they appear to do well in the absence of both their protective ants and the destructive leaf-cutting ants. In Florida the plants produce their remarkable thorns and Beltian bodies, just as they do in their native regions. They also flower and produce viable seeds in abundance.

In the tropics, where living things are growing and active the entire year, many remarkable forms of life have arisen. In addition to the bull-horn acacia and its protective ants, there are other plants also that apparently encourage ants for the protection they give, although biologists seem not to be in complete agreement as to the protective value of the ants against leaf-cutting enemies. Also growing in tropical America are cecropia trees, belonging to the family Urticacae, or the nettle family. To this same family also belong such common trees as the elm, hackberry,

Osage orange and mulberry, as well as hemp (Marihuana) and common nettle. Cecropia trees are spreading, candelabra-shaped trees with large palmately lobed leaves that, when dry, curl up into attractive forms and are silvery in color. For this reason they are much used in dried flower arrangements. The trees, which grow up to 50 feet tall, are found in many places in southern Florida, where they have been introduced. They are native to the South American Tropics and are especially abundant in the Brazilian lowlands. The trunks and branches of these attractive trees are hollow, but there are thin divisions, or septa, across the nodes, as in the case of bamboo. In their native habitat these trees are almost always inhibited by ants (*Azteca muelleri*) which make their nests within the hollow trunks just above the ground level. These ant colonies are quite large and, due to their activities in excavating the inner walls of the trunks to accommodate their nests, the trunks expand somewhat. This expansion is probably caused by the weight of the tree, since about half of the thickness of the wall is cut away by the ants. These ant nests, by the way, are constructed of plant fibers cemented together into carton-type nests. After the ants have established themselves within the trunk of the cecropia tree, they cut openings in the septa above the nest, including those in the limbs. Openings to the outside are made at various locations. As a result, the ants have protected interior runways through which they can travel to all parts of the tree. Thus, just as the bull-horn acacia furnishes abodes for its protective ants, so does the cecropia tree. In the matter of food the cecropia tree also produces fruitlike bodies, but in this case, they are found embedded in dense mats of hairs near the bases of the leaf stems or petioles. These bodies are red or yellow, about the size of millet seeds, and contain oil and other nutrients. They are called "Müllerian bodies" after F. Müller, who studied the cecropia trees and their ants about 1874. The *Azteca* ants gather this "fruit" just as the *Pseudomyrma* ants gather the Beltian bodies on the bull-horn acacia leaflets. As in the case of the acacia, the ants rush out and attack any enemy that attempts to invade their tree. They seem to be especially aggressive toward other ants such as leaf-cutters. Thus, it appears that the cecropia tree derives benefit from the presence of the *Azteca* ants even though some observers, such as von Ihering, disagree. He studied these ants in the late nineteenth century and stated that the cecropia tree needs *Azteca* ants no more than a dog needs fleas! However, even von Ihering admits that the Müllerian bodies are probably produced by the tree to encourage the *Azteca* ants. It is an interesting fact, also, that the ants are so dependent upon the tree that the colony dies if the tree is cut down or injured.

While there are no instances here in our own country of the remarkable relationships that exist between the bull-horn acacia and the cecropia trees and their respective ants, there are many plants that bear nectaries which secrete honeydew upon which various ants feed. Presumably, these nectaries have the function of attracting ants for the protection they afford against leaf-eating insects. Such nectaries are found on poplar, oak, cassia, Ailanthus, elderberry, castorbean and numerous other plants. They are even found on pitcher plants, which is ironic when one considers that these same plants are equipped to lure most insects to their doom. In most cases the nectaries are located on the leaves or the leaf petioles, and ants can almost always be found crowding around them imbibing the sweet substance that exudes from the glands. This can usually be observed in the case of the partridge peas (*Cassia*), for example.

Authorities, as we have seen, are not in full agreement as to the use of these honeydew-producing glands. It is contended by some that the primary purpose of these glands is to attract the ants *away* from the blooms, where they would plunder the nectar and serve the plant in no way. Because ants are crawling insects and do not fly from flower to flower carrying pollen, they are of no help in cross-pollination. While authorities do not all agree that the nectaries attract ants for their help in protecting the plants from leaf-destroying insects, the conclusion seems inescapable that these extrafloral nectaries, as they are called, must serve

The elderberry (*Sambucus*) has paired nectaries at the bases of its leaves to attract ants. The presence of the ants probably discourages leaf-eating beetles and caterpillars.

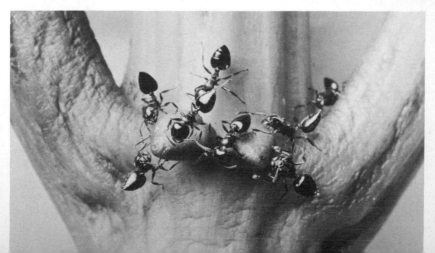

some useful function. If they had no use, the plants would not have developed them. From the standpoint of plants protecting their flowers from marauding ants, it might be mentioned that many plants have special adaptations aimed at discouraging ants. For instance, the catchfly (*Silene*) has its stems covered with sticky hairs which make it almost impossible for a crawling insect such as an ant to reach the flower. The same is true of wild lettuce (*Lactuca*), sunflower (*Helianthus*) and many others.

One of the world's most interesting associations between a plant and an ant occurs in the United States, but in this case, it is a one-sided arrangement. The plant serves as a home for the ants, but the plant is apparently not benefited. The ants involved have no common name since very few people ever see them. Technically, they are classified as *Colobopsis* ants, and this name will be used in the present discussion. They are related to the common carpenter ants that excavate galleries in dead wood, sometimes causing injury to homes.

There are several species of Colobopsis ants, all of which nest in plant cavities, usually in hollow twigs. The present discussion will be confined to the species *mississippiensis,* which usually excavates its tunnels in white ash twigs. The queen is winged and, after mating, selects a twig into which she bores a small entrance hole about the size of the lead in a pencil. The ash twig is hollow but filled with pith, which she removes and tosses out. In the resulting space she lays a few eggs and settles down to guard them. When these hatch she feeds the larvae as best she can, probably with exudations from her own body. Eventually, a small number of workers emerge and go out on food-hunting expeditions to the ash leaves, where they gather honeydew from aphids and mealybugs. As with most ants, the queen then settles down to laying eggs and does not again leave the burrow, although we have found that some colonies are queenless, indicating that a queen may go from one tunnel to another laying eggs. After the young queen produces a few more workers and the nest cavity has been enlarged by the removal of pith farther down the twig, some of the larvae develop into special workers of the soldier caste. These are larger than the normal workers and have strangely shaped heads. Under a lens it can be seen that the heads of these soldiers are distinctly plug-shaped or cork-shaped. This unique shape fits them admirably for their special function, which is that of using their heads as living doors to close the nest entrance. There are never very many—usually only five or six

Soldier ant (*Colobopsis*) in a hollow twig. Note its plug-shaped head, used to close the nest entrance.

—of these soldiers in a nest, but one of them is usually on duty with its head inserted in the entrance so that the front of the head is flush with the outside surface of the twig. When a returning worker wishes to enter, it either touches the soldier's head or is recognized by colony odor and is at once admitted. Just what password is used is not known. In any event, foreign ants are not admitted. I once collected a Colobopsis ant from another white ash and placed it near one of the entrances. It remained there for several days, apparently unable to understand why it was not admitted. At last it became discouraged and wandered away. The truth is that in a white ash tree where there are many separate colonies, there is apparently considerable mixing of individuals between colonies. We proved this by dusting all the individuals in one colony with powder which was fluorescent under ultraviolet light. Later, we split open the twigs containing other colonies on the same tree and found that they all contained the powder, as was proved by examining them under ultraviolet light. This, of course, also proved that ants from the same tree mingle freely. Apparently, the pluglike heads of the soldiers are used, quite effectively, mostly to prevent other species of ants or other insect enemies from entering.

There is another unusual association between a plant and an insect that is worthy of mention. Here, also, the plant is not benefited, so the association is a one-sided affair. The scene of this tale begins in the desert-like region of the Rio Mayo in the states of Sonora and Chihuahua, Mexico. Here, in the barrancas and arroyos grows a species of shrub, which is about 5 feet tall and bears shiny, lanceolate leaves. During early summer, when this arid region is moistened by rains, the shrub produces flower spikes. Botanically, this shrub is a euphorbia, closely related to snow-on-the-mountain and poinsettia. Its technical name is *Sebastiania pringlei,* but it is known locally as *yerba de flecha,* meaning "arrow plant." It is known by this name because its milky sap is poisonous and was once used by Indians as an arrow poison.

In spring, after the arrow plants' blooms have gone and the three-parted seed pods are developing, a small moth (*Laspeyresia saltitans*) visits them and lays her eggs. This moth looks very much like the codling moth whose larvae infest apples and is, in fact, closely related to it. When these eggs hatch, the caterpillars bore into the seed pods and begin feeding upon the food stored there. Fortunately for the plant, however, not all of the seed pods become infested with moth larvae and these complete their development. When the seeds have reached maturity and the pods are dry, they snap open, tossing the seeds a considerable distance away from the parent plants. These sound like small pebbles being tossed through the desert brush.

Those pods, however, that became infested with caterpillars do not produce seeds, since their contents have been totally consumed. When the caterpillars are mature they fill the seed pods which they have lined with silk. These pods soon fall from the plants and come to rest upon the sandy desert floor. The sand has been heated by the subtropical sun. If the pods should remain exposed to this heat, the larvae within would soon die. Here is where a special adaptation comes to their aid. When a seed pod becomes too hot, the contained caterpillar grasps the silken wall of the pod with its feet and snaps its body. Since the pod is thin-walled and light in weight, this sudden jerk causes it to move. As long as the pod is in the hot sun the caterpillar continues its activity and the animated pod hops about in a hit-and-miss fashion until it reaches the shade of a stone or other sheltered location. Here it rests quietly until the sun's rays reach it and heat it again. In time, the pod becomes lodged in a crevice or in a sandy depression and is, perhaps, lightly covered with drifting sand. After a while the caterpillar cuts a circular escape hatch part way through the wall of its pod and then transforms into the pupal stage. The cutting of this escape hatch is quite remarkable when one considers that the caterpillar has no knowledge of the use it will eventually serve. When another spring comes to the arid land and the *yerba de flechas* put forth their blooms, the pupa pushes out through the circular door that was partially cut through the wall of the pod. Out of this pupal case then emerges the adult moth and the life cycle starts over again.

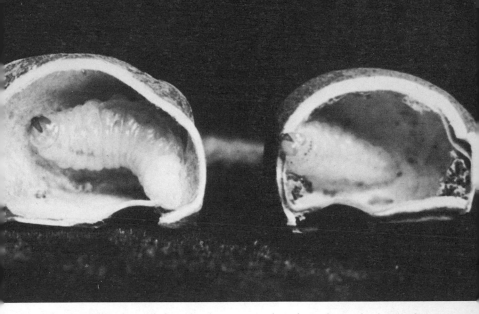

The caterpillar in each jumping bean causes it to jump by anchoring its feet in the silken lining and flipping its body.

Of course we have been talking about Mexican jumping beans. Actually, of course, they are not really "beans" at all but seed pods of the arrow plant, and the mysterious motive power that causes them to jump is the contained caterpillars. In the region where they grow, these "beans," or *brincadores* (jumpers), as they are called, are collected by small boys and sold to local dealers who, in turn, ship them to novelty stores in the United States. Many people have seen these interesting "beans," little knowing that within them were contained the larvae of small moths. Mexican jumping beans will obligingly hop about for several months, especially if they are placed on a hot surface. In time, however, the "beans" cease to hop—this is because the caterpillars have pupated. In time, too, the moths will emerge, but, in the United States, far from their native food plant, they will all die, since they cannot live on any other host. This is always the sad fate of the jumpers that are sold as novelties.

chapter fourteen

The Pollinators

INSECTS and plants existed in the world for many millions of years before the plants began to depend on the insects for help in pollinating their flowers. The primitive plants such as pines were, and still are, wind pollinated. When the ability to fly was evolved by insects, they became ideal agents for carrying pollen from plant to plant. Wind pollination is very wasteful, since sufficient pollen must be produced to literally blanket the countryside if there is to be any assurance that all female flowers will be pollinated. Insect pollination, on the other hand, is economical since insects usually fly directly from flower to flower gathering pollen and nectar. No one knows which was the first insect-pollinated flower, but it was apparently a generalized flower, such as the ancestor of the buttercup and magnolia. From this were evolved all the great host of blooms that solicit the aid of insects by color, scent and nectar. Today there are more than 150,000 species of flowers found growing in almost every climate from the Arctic to the Antarctic.

Insects, especially honeybees, are very important to the farmer and fruit grower. Many kinds of clover and fruit trees will not set seed or produce fruit abundantly unless sufficient bees are present. Bee hives are often placed in orchards and in clover fields for this purpose. In the Utah area various wild bees are depended upon for the pollination of alfalfa, since the flowers of this plant must be tripped—the pistils must be forced out of the flower keel to bring about pollination. However, there is often a scarcity of wild bees in alfalfa fields so hives of honeybees must be placed in such fields. Usually five or six hives per acre are used. Bumblebees are the most efficient pollinators of red clover, and when this crop was first introduced into New Zealand, it was found that no seed was produced. It was only after bumblebees had been introduced from England that this clover began producing seed in commercial quantities.

Long after the habit of insect assistance in pollination had become well established many plants reversed their evolution and turned again to the wind for pollen transport. For example, the ancestors of the grasses, walnuts, maples and ragweeds were insect pollinated. Seemingly there are advantages in each method. There are not enough bees to pollinate all the grass on a prairie or to pollinate each flower in a walnut forest.

Flowers are, of course, the reproductive structures of plants and they may contain both male and female organs or only those of one sex. In the process of pollination the male cells or pollen grains are transferred from their containers (*anthers*) to the female organs (*stigmas*). If the pollen is transferred from the male organs of one plant to the female organ of another plant, the process is called *cross-pollination*. If, on the other hand, the pollen is transferred from male to female organs on the same plant, or in the same flower, it is called *self-pollination*. Pollination, like animal fertilization, is necessary to the perpetuation of the species. While self-pollination of flowers will usually result in viable seeds, cross-pollination has a number of advantages. More seeds and better fruit are produced and the offspring are usually more vigorous and variable, which, from an evolutionary standpoint, affords a much greater degree of adaptability.

Nowhere are the relationships between plants and insects as complex as in the processes of pollination. There is probably no method of enticing insects for their aid that some plant has not adopted—and some of these methods are truly amazing in their invention. Flowers seem to specialize not only in their techniques of attracting insects but in the types of insects they solicit. Many flowers depend on bees, which they lure by means of nectar and pollen, which are the insects' rewards for services rendered. Such flowers are known as "bee flowers" and include such common examples as mint, snapdragon, clover, columbine, pea and numerous others. All these have colorful blooms and abundant nectar to attract various species of bees. Most of these flowers are either yellow or blue, since bees are colorblind to the red end of the spectrum. Bees, of course,

Honeybee coming in to a landing on a passion flower. In this case the bee is collecting pollen—note the filled pollen baskets on the bee's hind legs.

are day-loving insects, and the flowers they pollinate open during the daylight hours.

Flowers of another type specialize in butterflies and these often have rather deep throats where their nectar can only be reached by the long tongues of these insects. Butterflies, like bees, are day-loving and their flowers open during the hours of sunshine, but whereas the bee flowers are shades of yellow or blue, those that cater to butterflies are often tinted in shades of orange and red, since these colors are visible to many butterflies. Among the common butterfly-pollinated flowers are the carnation, red catchfly, daylily and butterfly weed.

In contrast to the flowers that seek the aid of butterflies, there are the night-blooming flowers that attract moths. Most of these flowers are pale or white, since these are most easily seen in the dusk. A brightly colored flower may be very conspicuous in the sun but invisible in dim light. A red flower, for example, disappears as the dusk deepens. Common examples of moth flowers are datura, morning glory, tobacco, yucca and most orchids. Most of the moths that visit such flowers do not alight on the blooms, but hover before them, probing into them for nectar with their long tongues. This is especially true of the hummingbird moths (family Sphingidae). Night-blooming flowers attract moths not only by their pale coloration but also by heavy perfume.

There are a number of flowers that are especially adapted to attract flies. In contrast to the brightly colored flowers that attract bees and butterflies, the fly flowers are not very colorful and their "perfumes" resemble decaying flesh or dung. While these flowers are not colorful, some of them have interesting markings and shapes and so are often grown in gardens or greenhouses. One of these is the starfish "cactus" (*Stapelia*), which, as the name suggests, has a bloom shaped like a starfish. It smells like carrion. Among the fly flowers is found the world's largest bloom, the Rafflesia of Malaysia, which attracts flies by its odorous "perfume." Included in this group of flowers also are the Dutchman's pipes, which have strangely shaped flowers within which flies are trapped, dusted with pollen and then released.

Still other flowers avail themselves of beetles for pollination. Most of these flowers are white or greenish and depend on perfumes to attract their beetle visitors. Among these flowers are the magnolia, water lily, California poppy, elder, dogwood and arum. Flowers which specialize in beetles often have unique adaptations. For example, many of them hide their seeds and other flower parts inside protective coverings, since beetles are prone to gnaw away at any edible plant structure. Most of the beetle flowers occur in the tropics. One giant arum (*Amorphophallus titanum*) found in Sumatra generates heat at the time of blooming, presumably to volatilize its carrionlike odor. Here in our own country are found several plants of this same family. One of these is the common little jack-in-the-pulpit (*Arisaema triphyllum*), which attracts small flies into its vaselike spathe for the purpose of pollination. Most of the large, tropical arums, however, are beetle pollinated. The so-called dragon lily or black calla (*Dracunculus vulgaris*) is a large exotic arum from the Nile region that is often grown in American gardens and greenhouses. It is very large, often being 2 feet tall. The inside of the spathe is tinted deep purple and an odor reminiscent of dead fish is generated within it. Dr. J. D. Meeuse once collected 162 beetles that had entered one such flower, which testifies to the effectiveness of its "perfume." These beetles belonged to many different families. The voodoo lily (*Sauromatum guttatum*) from India and Pakistan is another showy arum grown in greenhouses and homes. Like other tropical arums it generates heat at the time of blooming to volatilize its odor. The heat is apparently produced by *calorigen*, a hormone secreted in the male flower parts. This arum, like most others, attracts beetles. It is believed that beetle-pollinated flowers were the first ones to use insects for carrying their pollen, and later colorful, nectar-bearing blooms developed to attract other flying insects.

Plants also protect their flowers from certain crawling insects that steal nectar and pollen but are of no value in pollination. Common examples of such insects are ants which feed upon pollen and nectar but are of little

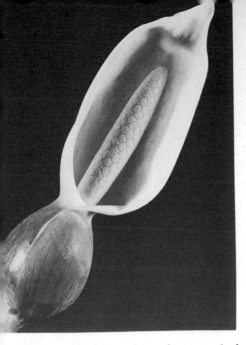

Small insects are attracted down into the bulbous cavity at the base of this arum bloom. Here they are trapped and bring about pollination.

help in pollination, since they crawl about on one plant and do not fly from flower to flower. To protect their wares from such plunderers, plants have evolved a number of techniques. For example, the fire pink and a number of other plants have their stems covered with sticky hairs that make it almost impossible for ants to reach the blooms. Other plants, such as the common toadflax, have their nectar hidden in deep nectaries where only long-tongued insects can reach it. Of special interest is the technique used by the snapdragon bloom. Its lower lip is pressed tightly against the upper lip and only a heavy-bodied insect, such as a bumblebee, can open the bloom and enter it.

Many flowers have adaptations to prevent crawling insects, such as ants, from obtaining their pollen and nectar. Crawling insects are of little value in pollination. In the case of this snapdragon bloom, only a heavy-bodied insect, such as a bumblebee, can force its way in.

The corollas of many flowers, such as this *Cymbidium* orchid, have guide marks to steer flying insects to the nectar glands deep in the blooms.

A flower advertises its wares in ways parallel to those used by man. Just as we erect signs advertising commercial products, so do flowers appeal to insects through colorful blooms with contrasting markings. In many cases the flowers go to great extremes to make it easy for their visitors to find their store of nectar. Flowers such as the foxglove and some orchids have their throats marked with lines leading into the deep flower tube where the nectar is to be found. These markings guide the insects. Many flowers have their lower petals formed into enlarged landing platforms for the convenience of flying insects. There are also many "target" flowers that are shaped and marked in ways to guide insects to a landing. If you will examine a number of pansy blooms, you will see that they are designed to attract the eye to their centers where the pool of nectar is to be found. Note also in the case of narcissus that the margin of the central corolla tube is tinted in a contrasting color to guide insects to it. We may appreciate the beauty of flowers, but their forms and colorations must, first and last, attract insects. It was for that purpose alone that flowers were evolved.

There are a number of instances where a very close working arrangement prevails between plants and insects to secure pollination and the production of seed. Probably the most remarkable of these involves the yucca and the yucca moth (*Pronuba yuccasella*). Yucca are common on the southern portions of the Great Plains, where they are conspicuous features of the landscape. Some kinds are also grown in gardens. They belong to the lily family and their blooms are large and white but are not attractive to most insects. Only the small white *Pronuba* moth is adapted to their pollination, and this moth shows no interest in any other bloom. The female moth has special appendages on her mouthparts with which she collects a ball of pollen and places it upon the stigma. This assures her that the flower is properly pollinated and that seed will be produced. The *Pronuba* moth also plunges her ovipositor into the yucca ovary and deposits several eggs. As the seeds develop, the *Pronuba* larvae feed upon them and grow. By the time that the larvae are mature most of the seeds will have been consumed. Only rarely, however, are all the seeds destroyed, and the plant is able to produce enough seeds to feed the *Pronuba* larvae and to perpetuate the yucca species. Here is a classic example of symbiosis, a case where two organisms cooperate to their mutual benefit. Without the moth the yucca would not be pollinated, and the yucca is the sole host plant of the moth larvae. One could not exist without the other.

In the case of the yucca and the *Pronuba* moth, the moth is a voluntary cooperator in the ritual of pollination, but there are many other instances where insects must be tricked into aiding in pollination. There are so many cases that space will permit the discussion of only a few outstanding examples. One such example is that of the epiphytic orchid (*Epidendrum tampensis*) that grows upon trees in the Everglades. The attractive little blooms of these orchids have their pollen enclosed in small containers (*pollinia*). In the act of probing into the flower for nectar a moth's eyes come in contact with the pollinia which adhere to them. When the moth flies away the attached pollinia are carried along and are rubbed off upon the stigmatic surface of the next orchid visited. The moth

Only the *Pronuba* moth is able to pollinate the flower of the yucca. The female *Pronuba* moth has special mouthparts in which she collects balls of pollen which she places upon the stigma. She then inserts her eggs in the ovary where her larvae will develop, feeding upon the seeds.

is thus the unwilling vehicle by which the pollen is carried from one orchid to another to bring about cross-pollination. A number of other orchids employ this same trick, including the coral-root orchids (*Corallorrhiza* and *Habenaria*) which are found in many places in the more northern parts of the United States. There is another orchid (*Ophrys*) found growing along the Mediterranean and in various European countries that employs an underhanded trick. The blooms of this orchid resemble rather closely the females of *Scolia* wasps. When an amorous male wasp sees one of these orchids and attempts to copulate with it, a pollinium is attached to it and this is later rubbed off on another orchid. Thus is the male wasp tricked into pollinating the orchid. A somewhat similar trick is used by an Australian orchid which emits an odor resembling that of a female ichneumon wasp (*Lissopimpla semipunctata*). The male wasp is attracted and attempts to mate with it. In South America there is an orchid (*Catasetum*) that shoots its adhesive pollinia like bullets so that they become attached to the thorax of a visiting moth.

Here in our own country, the grass pink orchid (*Calopogon pulchellue*) employs another trick. The upper lip of this attractive little orchid is held erect and is colored to attract bees. When a bee alights upon it, however, its weight causes the lip to flop down so that the bee's back comes in contact with the lower lip where pollinia are cemented to the bee's back. This orchid contains no nectar but the bees seem not to learn by experience, so a bee that has been tricked by one orchid and has pollinia cemented to its back soon alights upon another orchid where its pollinia become detached. These orchids achieve pollination without the use of nectar or any other reward for the bees.

Another native orchid, the lady's slipper (*Cypripedium*), employs yet another trick. The lower lip or "petal" of this pretty orchid is greatly enlarged and formed into a bulbous structure having an opening in the top. Within this hollow cavity are found the orchid's sex organs. Bees are attracted into the bulbous cavity where escape is somewhat difficult. As the bee crawls about it eventually finds that it can force its way out of a slit at the back of the flower. In escaping, however, it is smeared with pollen. When another lady's slipper is visited, the pollen is rubbed off on the stigma within the bulbous "petal."

Of all the techniques employed by flowers to secure cross-pollination, that used by the common milkweed is probably the most remarkable. Since milkweed is common almost everywhere, its pollination can be easily observed. If you will examine one of the small individual blooms, you will find that there is a central column surrounded by five nectaries. When a bee or other insect visits such a bloom and imbibes the nectar, its legs come to rest at the bottoms of U-shaped slits surrounding the central column. When the bee is ready to leave the flower, its legs are pulled up through the slits where tiny wishbone-shaped structures are attached to them. There is a bag of pollen attached to each prong of the wishbone. When the bee visits another milkweed bloom one or more of the wishbones and their attached pollinia are apt to be rubbed off onto the central column, which is actually the stigma. If a number of bees, wasps or butterflies are collected in a field of milkweeds, the legs of almost every one will be found to have attached pollinia. Sometimes the insects are loaded down with them. If many of the blooms are examined it will be found that many small flies have been trapped with their feet anchored in the slits. Such insects are not strong enough to extricate their legs and so they die, victims of the flowers' pollinating mechanism.

The Dutchman's pipe (*Aristolochia*) also traps insects for their aid in pollination, but the technique used is different from that of the orchids and milkweeds. These are mostly flowers of the tropics, but some kinds

Milkweed flowers attach their pollinia to the legs of insects which carry them to other milkweed flowers.

The Dutchman's pipe (*Aristolochia*) traps small flies in a bulbous rear chamber (cutaway view) where they bring about pollination before being released.

are grown here in our own country. The largest and most unusual kinds are called "pelican flowers" because of the shapes of their blooms. These blooms are deep-throated and beyond the expanded front part of the bloom there is a narrow, curved neck opening into a bulbous expansion. Small flies are attracted into the bloom by odors which often resemble decaying flesh. Within the narrow neck of the flower tube there are backward-directed hairs that prevent the escape of the flies once they have entered the expanded portion at the back of the flower. Here the small flies buzz about. In time, which may be several days, the flower releases pollen and the flies become well dusted with it. Then, as if by a miracle, the hairs which have so far prevented the escape of the flies, now wither and the flies are able to leave their prison. The foolish flies, however, have not learned by their experience, so they enter other pelican flowers carrying the adhering pollen. Within the flower they are again trapped but the pollen they carry is dusted off upon the stigma, bringing about pollination. This certainly seems to be a roundabout means of achieving the desired result, but it seems to work. Sometimes so many flies are trapped by large *Aristolochia* blooms that their unhappy buzzing can be heard several yards away.

A number of flowers have evolved mechanical devices as aids to pollination. One of the more interesting of these is that used by salvia or sage (*Salvia*). This common garden flower has a deep throat with its nectar glands located at the far end. The lower lip of the flower tube is formed into a convenient landing platform for flying insects such as bees. When a bee alights upon this platform and pushes into the bloom, its head comes in contact with the lower ends of two levers. The upper extensions of these levers are long and curved and have pollen-filled anthers attached to their ends. As the bee pushes into the bloom, its head presses against the lower extensions of these two levers, causing the anthers to swing downward and smear pollen on its back. When the bee visits another salvia bloom, this pollen is trapped upon the stigma which extends outward above the flower tube.

In order to prevent self-pollination flowers have evolved a number of interesting devices. One of these is illustrated by the common iris. When a visiting bee alights she crawls into the flower over a path covered with hairlike papillae. These were apparently evolved to aid the insects in forcing their way into the bloom. As the bee pushes into the flower to reach the nectar deep within, her back rubs against a membranous flap and any pollen adhering to her back from previously visited blooms is rubbed off onto the sensitive outer surface. After the bee pushes on into the flower to sip her fill of nectar, her back comes in contact with the pollen-covered stamens. Now, as she withdraws, the membranous flap swings outward preventing the newly acquired pollen from being rubbed off upon the sensitive outer surface. Thus, it is only when the bee is in the act of entering the iris bloom that the sensitive surface of the stigma can be dusted with pollen. In this manner the flower is assured that it will only be pollinated by pollen from other flowers.

Catalpa blooms and some others use a somewhat different technique. In this case the stigma is forked with one lip curving upward and the other downward. When a bee enters the bloom any pollen on its back is rubbed off upon the open lips of the stigma. While the bee is in the flower imbibing nectar, the lips of the stigma rapidly close, pressing tightly together. When the bee withdraws there is no way that the new pollen dusted on its back within the flower can come in contact with the sensitive surface of the forked stigma.

Pollination of flowers is often an intricate and ingenious process—one that required many millions of years of evolution to develop. Perhaps nowhere in nature are the ways of evolution better exemplified.

chapter fifteen

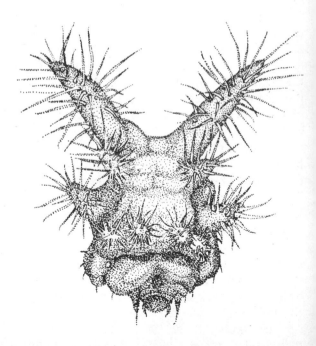

Chemical Warfare

CONSIDERING the fact that their enemies are legion, insects must have effective methods of defense. Some escape enemies by speed of movement, others construct cases or shelters in which they conceal themselves. Some burrow within the tissues of plants where enemies have difficulty in attacking them, yet others tunnel in the earth. Many defenseless insects employ methods of camouflage—thus concealing coloration or form. Many leaf-inhabiting insects are green, some caterpillars mimic twigs, while the larva of the orange-dog swallowtail (*Papilio cresphontes*) resembles a bird dropping on a leaf. The fore wings of *Catocala* moths resemble the bark of trees upon which they often rest with their colorful hind wings concealed beneath the camouflaged fore wings. Insect camouflage often takes strange forms. The little trash-carriers (family Hemerobiidae) attach the dry remains of their past meals or plant debris to their backs as a means of concealment.

Not all insects, however, are satisfied with such passive roles and have evolved more aggressive and positive methods of escaping enemies. These methods involve the use of stings and poisonous or repellent secretions. This, in a manner of speaking, is chemical warfare and the great majority of the insects that use this means of defense are brightly or strikingly colored. Such warning colors are a necessity, especially to those insects that protect themselves with stings, poison spines or ill-tasting bodies. A

273

The caterpillars of some moths mimic twigs, thus camouflaging themselves. Other caterpillars use poison spines or repulsive secretions.

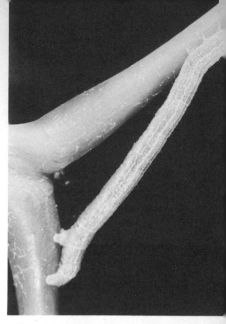

dead insect, even though it has stung its assassin, has received no benefit from its defense mechanism. The only benefit that can come from such an encounter is the memory of the experience in the mind of the assassin. Here is where distinctive coloration enters the picture. An animal or a man that has been stung by a red and black wasp is very apt to remember the experience for a long while and avoid red and black wasps. Warning colors advertise the fact that the insect is dangerous. This is a defense principle found throughout the animal world and, to a lesser extent, in the plant world. Many poisonous seeds are gaily colored, as are some of the most deadly of marine animals. That this principle actually has value has been proven by a number of observations. Dr. A. D. Imms, of England, records an instance where 4,490 beetles were captured by starlings and fed to their young. Among these were beetles of many kinds but, significantly, there were only two ladybird beetles which are ill-tasting and brightly colored. Many ladybird beetles discharge droplets of repellent material from various parts of their bodies when they are disturbed. The source of this material is especially at the joints of the legs and the bases of the wing covers. Stink glands are found also in other beetles and in the stinkbugs (family Pentatomidae). Some tropical stinkbugs, such as species found on cacao in Trinidad, emit such powerful aromas that if several of them are placed in a jar they will be immobilized within a few minutes. In the case of the blister beetles and oil beetles (family Meloidae) an oily substance called *cantharidin* is secreted and

Stink bugs (family Pentatomidae) protect themselves by pungent secretions that make them distasteful to most enemies.

is so powerful that when one of these insects crawls over tender skin a series of blisters results. At one time this material was extracted and used in medicine. In the Kalahari Desert region of Africa, there is a beetle (*Diamphidia locusta*) whose larvae contain an extremely toxic saponin that is used by natives as an arrow poison. Some members of the family Chrysopidae, known as stink flies, emit a repulsive odor when handled, which probably protects them from predators. It is believed that the body of the monarch butterfly contains a substance which makes it disagreeable to birds.

All of us are familiar with the tobacco-spitting habits of grasshoppers. Just what actual protective value this brown material has is an open question but it does make the handling of grasshoppers disagreeable, at least to humans. There are some species of grasshoppers that discharge a repellent liquid from glands on the thorax or other parts of the body. In Africa there is a colorful grasshopper (*Zonocerus*) that has a vile odor and is known as the "stinking grasshopper." While many ants protect themselves by squirting formic acid on adversaries up to distances of more than a foot, there is an African ant (*Megaloponera foetens*) that, like the African grasshopper, emits a nauseating odor that can be detected for many yards.

While many, perhaps most, of the repellents secreted by insects serve as protection against birds, some insects use these substances against their insect enemies. One of the most remarkable instances of this is the use of repellent or glue-like materials by certain tropical termites, especially those of the genera *Nasutitermes* and *Coptotermes*. These protective materials are ejected from nozzlelike projections from the fronts of the soldier termites' heads and are used chiefly against ants.

The spittle bugs (family Cercopidae) create masses of slimy froth within which they live and suck the juices of plants. Apparently this affords them protection.

While the defense technique used by the spittle bugs (family Cercopidae) is not strictly of a chemical nature, it is close enough to fall in this category. The young or nymphs of these small insects live on plants where they feed by sucking plant juices. They live within a mass of froth which is of their own making and which appears to afford them protection. There are extensions of the plates at the tip of the abdomen of a spittle-bug and these form a space within which spiracles or breathing pores open. A waxy secretion is emitted from the anus and air from the spiracles is blown into it causing it to foam up. The result is the mass of froth or foam within which the bugs live. Actually, the basic substance composing this foam comes from the Malpighian tubes or excretory organs and more or less resembles silk in its chemical nature.

Of special interest are the repellent glands of larval spicebush swallowtail butterflies (*Papilio troilus*). These glands are located just back of the head on top of the first body segment and consist of two reversible sacs which can be pushed out like the fingers of a rubber glove being turned wrong side out. They are bright orange in color and, when fully extruded, are about a half inch long. They are called *osmeteria* and give off a very pungent, spicelike odor, which is probably effective in repelling birds and, perhaps, other enemies. If this material gets on a person's hands they must be well washed in soap to eliminate it. In Trinidad there is another swallowtail (*Papilio anchisiades*) whose osmeteria emit an odor resembling decaying flesh. These caterpillars are gregarious, feeding

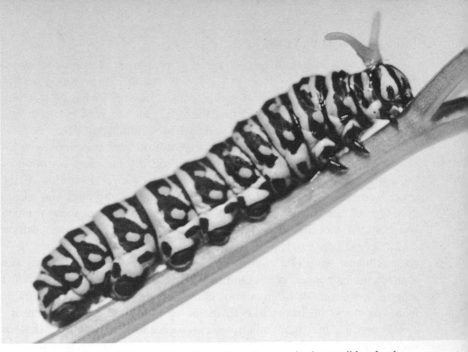

Spicebush swallowtail larvae (*Papilio troilus*) have paired eversible glands on the tops of their first body segments. When pushed out, these glands give off a repulsive smell.

upon citrus during the night. Before dawn they crawl down the limbs in single file and congregate on the trunk where they spend the day in a group. If one of these groups is disturbed their collective odor is over-powering.

Tropical butterflies of another family (Heliconidae) emit repellent odors in the adult stage. These long-winged butterflies roost in clusters at night and probably derive benefit from their smell. Most of the species of these butterflies are inhabitants of the true tropics, but one species, the zebra butterfly (*Heliconius charithonius*), is common in the Everglades area of Florida. I have seen them in large numbers along the Gumbo Limbo Trail in the 'Glades. These butterflies are all strikingly marked which is probably a type of warning coloration.

A number of other insects secrete various chemical substances which apparently have protective functions. For instance, the caterpillar of a certain moth (*Notodonta concinnula*) emits hydrochloric acid and the caterpillar of another moth (*Dicranura vinula*) ejects relatively large amounts of formic acid. Some fungus gnat larvae (family Mycetophilidae) spin webs for the capture of insects and secrete droplets of oxalic acid to kill the captured prey. One of our native ground beetles (*Calo-*

soma promines), when disturbed, ejects a spray from the tip of its abdomen. When tested in captivity it was found that this spray was powerful enough to repel a blue jay that was intent on making a meal of it. Upon chemical analysis it was found that the substance secreted by the beetle was salicylaldehyde, a substance secreted by a number of other beetles.

Some substances secreted by insects have protective functions without themselves being poisonous or repulsive. Probably the most common of these substances are wastes secreted by insects of several families of the order Homoptera. These include species of aphids, mealybugs and whiteflies. One of these is the woolly apple aphid (*Eriosoma lanigerum*) which secretes long wax filaments. Another case is that of the cottony cushion scale (*Icerya purchasi*), a serious pest of citrus. Still another example is cottony maple scale (*Pulvinaria vitis*) that secretes masses of white wax that resembles popped corn. One of the mealybugs (*Walkeriana ovilla*) secretes long, slender filaments around the edge of its body that enable winds to carry the insect like thistle-down. Some of the wax-secreting aphids produce wax filaments up to two inches in length. One of these is the woolly alder aphid (*Prociphilus tessellatus*). Such waxy secretions apparently are disagreeable to most enemies. Many scale insects, on the other hand produce hard shells formed of a mixture of waxes and resins underneath which they live in comparative security. Some of these scale insects are serious orchard pests. Another scale insect is the lac insect (*Laccifera*) of India and other tropical areas that secretes stick lac from which shellac is obtained. To the living insects this material serves as a protective covering.

The woolly alder aphid (*Prociphilus tessellatus*) secretes strands of wax which make it distasteful to most enemies.

Io moth caterpillars (*Automeris io*) are covered with poisonous spines that cause severe irritation if they come in contact with human skin. They are bright green in color.

While many insects fend off their enemies by ill-smelling or mildly poisonous secretions, as does the common skunk, there are others that have developed more effective methods of chemical defense. The stinging caterpillars, for example, bear poisonous spines that have been known to make hospitalization necessary. There are about 50 different species of caterpillars that are actually poisonous. Most of these are either strikingly colored or strange looking. As a matter of policy, it is usually a good idea to handle any unknown caterpillar with care, especially if it is covered with spines or hair. One of the more common of the venomous kinds is the larva of the io moth (*Automeris io*). This caterpillar when full grown is about 2 inches long and is green. It is covered with numerous sharp spines. If the tender skin of the arm comes in contact with these needle-sharp spines, there is an immediate stinging sensation followed by swelling, though not all people are equally sensitive. Even more poisonous is the saddle-back caterpillar (*Sibine stimulea*), a very pretty little critter which is green and has an orange "saddle" upon its back. On both front and hind portions of the body there are fleshy tubercles bearing many sharp spines. The caterpillars feed upon a wide variety of trees and shrubs and most sting cases are reported in late summer when they are full grown and about ready to spin cocoons. They seem to be more abundant during some years than others.

Closely related to the saddle-back is the puss moth (*Megalopyge opercularis*), whose larva is covered with soft brown hair. This caterpillar

The puss-moth caterpillar (*Megalopyge opercularis*) looks quite harmless, but hidden beneath its brown fur are very poisonous spines. They should be avoided.

Hickory horned devil caterpillars (*Citheronia regalis*) are nearly five inches long and very fearsome looking. They are quite harmless, probably receiving protection from their appearance. The adult is the attractive regal moth.

appears to be quite harmless, but hidden beneath the silky hair are numerous spines filled with venom. If these pierce the skin the venom enters the wound and causes considerable discomfort and pain. The sting of another species (*M. lanata*), which occurs in Panama, often causes pain and swelling. In instances where the wrist has been stung, the entire arm swells up, and there may be accompanying nausea and vomiting. In addition to the stinging caterpillars mentioned above there are others with urticarial or irritating hairs that cause discomfort to some people. In justice to the insects we should say, however, that there are many colorful or vicious-looking caterpillars that are completely harmless. For instance, one of the most fearsome of all caterpillars is the larva of the large and attractive regal moth (*Citheronia regalis*). The full-grown caterpillar of this moth is nearly 5 inches long and bears many spiny horns. Its appearance is so frightening that it is called the "hickory horned devil." It feeds upon hickory and other trees.

There are also a number of insects that defend themselves by biting and injecting a venom through their beaks. One of these is the so-called kissing bug (*Triatoma sanguisuga*) that often bites people, causing intense pain. In South America these bugs also transmit Chagas disease. Some other members of the bug clan will also bite if carelessly handled. For example, the giant water bugs (*Belostoma*), which range in size up to several inches, can inflict painful bites. In their native habitat in ponds and streams their beaks are used to kill and suck the blood of fish, frogs and even snakes. Other aquatic bugs (family Notonectidae), the backswimmers, can also bite and the result is about equal to that of a bee sting.

Of all the defensive techniques used by insects, however, the use of stings is probably the most effective. Of all the insects, only the members of the order Hymenoptera make use of this method. These include the wasps, hornets, bees and ants and it is only the females that sting since stings are actually ovipositors or egg-laying tubes that have been modified into hypodermic mechanisms for injecting toxic or narcotic substances into enemies or prey. The sting of the honeybee may be taken as a typical example of this mechanism. A bee's sting is located at the tip of its abdomen and consists of a needlelike shaft to which is attached a bulblike poison sac. The sting actually is made up of three parts: there is a hollow structure called the *sheath* and two slender *lancets* or *darts* which slide freely upon tracks on the lower surface of the sheath. The sheath actually has two functions; it is used to open the wound in the skin and it holds the darts or lancets in position for penetration. Poison or venom is introduced into the wound in the victim's skin through a passage formed between the sheath and the two lancets. The sting may be pushed out or withdrawn at will.

Associated with the stinging mechanism are three sets of glands. One set secretes lubricating material, another the poison and the other an alkaline substance. In the act of stinging, the secretion for the poison gland is mixed with that of the alkaline glands to form the highly toxic venom. While the large poison sac is not muscular and does not pump its contents out through the sting, there are two pouchlike lobes within it. When the lancets or darts are pushed outward, their pressure against the lobes forces the poison out through the passage and into the wound. When the lancets are withdrawn the pouches collapse and are then ready for the next injection of poison. Thus, the bee's stinging apparatus consists of a highly efficient pumping mechanism. Just what the relationship is between the poison glands and alkaline glands is not clear. Some authorities believe that the function of the alkaline secretion is that of neutralizing the acid or poison secretion remaining in the duct after the act of stinging. The sting of the honeybee is barbed and cannot be withdrawn after stinging. The bee simply pulls the entire mechanism out of its body and flies away to die. Thus, it is able to sting only once and sacrifices its life in the process. In other bees and wasps, as well as in ants, the stings are withdrawn and the insects can sting many times.

The venoms injected by stinging insects are complete organic substances whose chemical natures are but little understood. When introduced into animal bodies they cause various reactions; they may affect the red blood cells, act on the nervous system, cause swelling of tissues or produce anaphylactic or allergic relations. Some people are especially sensitive to bee or other insect stings and may be made very ill or even die as a result.

There are many cases where serious reactions occurred. For example, there was the case of a farm worker who was stung on the head by several wasps. He became seriously ill and was pronounced dead within about fifteen minutes. In another case, a 15-year-old boy was stung three times on the neck, back and finger by wasps. He had been stung previously without ill effects, but on this occasion, he became seriously ill. His life was saved only by prompt medical attention without which he would probably have died. There is a great deal of difference between the venoms secreted by various insects, and a person who is sensitive to the stings

Many ants, like bees and wasps, are equipped with venomous stings. Shown here is the imported fire ant (*Solenopsis saevissima richteri*), a native of South America, that is now found in many parts of the Southeast. Many people are especially sensitive to fire ant venom.

of one may be only mildly bothered by other insect stings. Beekeepers who work with honeybees develop an immunity or tolerance to the venom so that swelling no longer occurs. I can speak from personal experience. When I first began working with honeybees I was very sensitive and often had mild reactions. Eventually, however, I developed a tolerance so that their stings no longer bothered me, but unfortunately, there is never a tolerance built up against the pain of a sting, and that is something that must be endured as long as one works with bees. One of the most effective treatments for bee and wasp stings seems to be injections of Benadryl and calcium lactate.

While persons who are supersensitive to bee and wasp stings are not common, stings should not be taken lightly and should always be avoided whenever possible. It is an interesting and significant fact that more people are killed each year in the United States by arthropod bites and stings than by snake bites. During a recent five-year period there were 215 deaths recorded from venomous animals. Of this number, 71 were caused by poisonous snakes, 5 by scorpions, 52 by bees, 33 by wasps and yellow-jackets and 39 by spiders (including those by the black widow). There were no deaths reported from centipedes or tarantulas and only one death from an ant sting.

The mounds of the imported fire ant may be three feet high. Their interiors consist of honeycombed passages within which the teeming colony lives.

There are many wasps that use their venom to kill or paralyze prey. For instance the mud-daubers and other hunting wasps use their venoms to paralyze spiders and insects for their young so that they can serve as fresh food. While such wasps normally use their stings on prey, this does not mean that they will not sting in their own defense. The sting of the great tarantula hawk wasp, for example, is extremely painful.

In addition to the ordinary wasps, the wingless mutillid wasps (*Dasymutilla*) which are often called "velvet ants" can sting severely. These insects are often seen running about on the ground. They are reddish in color and covered with fine hair. Some of the larger species are called "mule killers."

There are a number of ants, also, that sting viciously. One of these is the harvester ant (*Pogonomyrmex*) that constructs conical, gravel mounds, especially on the Great Plains. One of the most painful of the stinging ants is the imported fire ant (*Solenopsis saevissima richteri*). Some people are very sensitive to the stings of these ants. Ants, in many cases, grasp the skin with their mandibles in order to anchor themselves for the insertion of their stings. Some stinging ants cannot sting at all unless they can grasp the skin.

chapter sixteen

Of Size and Strength

INSECTS vary in size from almost microscopic to gigantic, having wingspreads of nearly 2 feet. The prehistoric dragonfly (*Meganeura*), as we have seen, measured nearly 30 inches across. Some modern, tropical walking sticks measure 15 inches long, while the Atlas moth of India (*Attacus edwardsi*) has a wing spread of up to 17 inches! We usually think of insects as being quite small, and while it is true that some insects are smaller than the largest protozoa, many butterflies and moths have greater wing spreads than some birds. Many tropical beetles are considerably larger and weigh more than mice or rats. For instance, the African goliath beetle (*Goliathus regius*) measures from 4 to 5 inches in length and is quite heavy and bulky. It apparently feeds upon bananas which it peels with its snout. It is probable that this great beetle is the heaviest of all insects as well as the most powerful. It is said that if a door key is placed between the neck and thorax of one of these huge insects the key will be bent if the insect chooses to move! There is some danger in handling one of these beetles since fingers may be injured if they are accidentally placed between the wing covers and the body.

Another large beetle is the Hercules beetle (*Dynastes hercules*) of tropical America that measures more than 6 inches long. This beetle is not as bulky as the African goliath beetle since part of its total length consists of two hornlike projections, one from the top of the thorax and one

Among the rhinoceros beetles are found the world's largest and heaviest insects. This 4-inch species occurs in Japan.

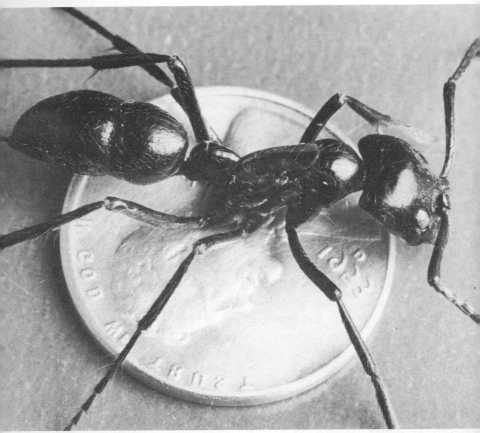

This ant (*Dinoponera grandis*) is one of the largest in the world. It is found in Brazil.

from the top of the head. The Hercules beetle is harmless, but I have heard of one instance in Central America where an automobile windshield was broken when one struck it at night.

There is a large grasshopper (*Cyrtacanthacris rubella*) in Africa that captures and kills mice. Here in our own country, I have seen giant water bugs (*Belostoma*) capture and kill 8-inch water snakes and small fish. By contrast, there are some minute British beetles (family Trichopterygidae) that measure only one-hundredth of an inch and could easily crawl through the eye of a fine needle. The fairy flies mentioned in a previous chapter are in about this same size range.

In the matter of strength, insects often accomplish seemingly impossible feats. I once saw a harvester ant worker lifting a pebble up out of its tunnel, and when both ant and pebble were weighed, it was found that the ant had lifted 52 times its own weight. At this rate a man should be able to lift nearly four tons! And with his teeth! It has been found that if a harness having an attached weight is placed on a beetle it can lift about 850 times its own weight! By comparison, a man could lift about 62 tons on his back! Consider what an elephant could do if it had the comparative strength of a beetle.

Ants can lift and carry relatively large objects. The harvester ant (*Pogonomyrmex*) can lift a stone weighing more than 50 times its own weight.

With respect to the loads an insect can pull, the weakest insect can usually pull five times its own weight while the average insect can pull over twenty times its own weight. By comparison, a horse can pull only 0.5 to 0.83 of its own weight, and man about 0.86. Insects can be placed on special dynamometers and their pulling abilities very accurately measured. On such an apparatus it was found that a betsy beetle (*Passalus*) could pull about 7.5 times its weight, while small beetles did somewhat better. The most powerful insect in the world is probably the large goliath beetle mentioned earlier, but I have no actual figures on its strength. A bumblebee can pull 16.1 times its weight, while the worker honeybee can pull 20.2. We might mention by comparison that an elephant working the teak forest of Burma can drag a log weighing four tons and a snail weighing less than one ounce can pull a pound weight over a smooth

By means of a body-lift, a beetle can raise enormous weights. Some beetles can lift, on such an apparatus, up to 850 times their own weight. By comparison, an elephant should be able to lift a small ship!

surface. It should be mentioned that there are many different methods of testing strength, so figures from different sources may not always be in agreement.

With respect to jumping abilities, the insects also accomplish many remarkable feats. The tiny springtail can hop about 8 inches. A flea, with legs only one-twentieth of an inch long, can broadjump about a foot and highjump nearly 8 inches. Thus, in theory, a flea, if it were enlarged to the size of a man, would be able to broadjump about 700 feet and highjump 450 feet. Probably the champion insect jumper is the grasshopper, which can broadjump about 30 inches. With the same capability a man would be able to hop the length of two football fields! A man makes a poor showing, relatively, when pitted against the insects—he can broadjump only 26 feet and highjump only about 7 feet. Remember, too, that these human records were made by Olympic champions and not by ordinary men. Also by comparison, we might mention that a jack rabbit can broadjump 23.3 feet and highjump 7 feet and a kangaroo can broadjump 32 feet and highjump 9 feet.

People often jump to the conclusion that since insects can seemingly achieve such fantastic feats of strength, they must have muscles of amazing power. Among the best examples of insect muscles are those found in the hind legs of the grasshopper, and these muscles are also quite easily studied. Weights can be attached to them and their power determined. The hind leg of a grasshopper is almost perfectly adapted to the purpose for which it is used—that of suddenly propelling the insect through the air from a resting position. It consists of a thigh or femur that is swollen with muscles and of a shin or tibia armed with sharp spines and hinged to the end of the thigh. When the grasshopper is resting on the ground the tibia is folded against the thigh, but when alarmed the insect suddenly activates its hind legs, which propel it into the air, often to distances of up to 20 times its body length. In what position the grasshopper alights is of little concern to it, since it is light enough to be uninjured by the fall. Unless the insect takes to flight, it has no control over its body while in the air.

If the lateral wall of a grasshopper's thigh is carefully dissected away, the interior structure can be easily studied, especially in a large specimen. Extending back from its point of attachment on the head of the tibia is a large, transparent extensor tendon having numerous muscle fibers attached along the sides. These fibers extend diagonally to the inner wall of the exoskeleton. When these muscle fibers contract, their combined force causes the tendon to pull the tibia outward. There is another opposing, or flexor, tendon attached to the head of the tibia below the hinge or pivot point. This latter tendon is much smaller and shorter than the extensor tendon and it also has attached muscle fibers. From this it can be seen that the extensor mechanism is larger and much more powerful than the flexor mechanism since very little strength is required to fold the tibia back against the femur after the insect has hopped. Thus, as in all muscles, whether they be of man or insect, there are always two opposing sets of muscles attached to the skeleton and to the movable part or limb. In the case of the insect, the muscles are anchored to the inner walls of the exoskeleton or shell giving them great leverage.

Jumping is a reflex action in which the tibias are suddenly snapped outward but the insect can also move its hind legs slowly while walking. The actual control of the grasshopper's jumping legs lies in a rather complex system of nerves. There are nerves extending from the leg muscles to the ventral nerve trunk and to the brain. On the ventral nerve trunk there are several enlarged nerve centers or ganglia. The third nerve center controls the jumping legs. Two sets of nerves extend from this ganglion and connect to the leg muscles. One set of nerves controls the slow movements of the leg, as while walking, the other controls the rapid movements of the leg, as in jumping. Also within the third ganglion there is a complicated switching arrangement which directs the nervous impulses to the muscles of the leg moving the leg slowly or cocking the tibia against the femur and tripping the large muscles which snap the tibia outward when the insect jumps. The actual process of jumping is very rapid, requiring only one-thirtieth of a second, but tremendous power is generated considering the size of the legs and their contained muscles. In a large grasshopper the extensor tendon involved in the jumping act is attached only about a millimeter from the pivot or hinge, thus great power must be exerted by the muscles to obtain sufficient leverage to propel the insect through the air. Actually, this leverage is about 40 to 1. In the act of jumping, one of these extensor muscles develops about 20,000 grams per gram of muscle. By comparison, human muscle develops only about 2,000 grams per gram of muscle. Thus, even though the tendon of a grasshopper's hind leg are anchored in such a way that its leverage is low, great power is exerted because of the relatively great power of the muscles. As a matter of fact, a large grasshopper can lift about 20 grams with its leg. These muscles are so powerful that, if the leg is held so that it cannot move, the muscles will often break and the leg be severed if the jumping reflex is stimulated.

From the above it is obvious that insect muscles appear to have greater power than those of vertebrates. Let us see if this is so. The absolute power of a muscle is determined by measuring the weight it will lift per a given area of cross-section. In other words, the length of the muscle has nothing to do with its strength. A tall man is no stronger than a short man. Due largely to the *manner* in which insect's muscles are attached— not the muscles themselves—they actually exert more power than equal weights of human or other vertebrate muscle. Vertebrate muscles are usually spindle-shaped and attached at their ends. In the case of the muscles of the grasshopper leg, the muscle fibers are all short and each one extends from the wall of the exoskeleton to the tendon. There are about 3,500 of these fibers and each one has a number of connecting nerves. As a result, when a nervous impulse to jump arises, every fiber is almost simultaneously activated and the tendon is pulled with tremendous force. Thus, even though the muscles of insects are no more powerful per given weight than those of vertebrates, they work much more efficiently.

If you have ever tried to pry open the shell of a clam or oyster, you will agree that the muscles which hold the shells together are very strong, indeed. Clam and oyster muscles demonstrate very nicely the principle that long muscles are not necessary for great strength. If we compare the strengths of muscles of some common animals, we find that there is actually only little differene between them. The absolute power of a muscle is determined by weight in kilograms that it can lift per square centimeter of cross-section. When measured in this manner, the absolute power of human muscle is from 6 to 10 kilograms, of frog muscle 3 kilograms and of grasshopper (*Locusta*) leg muscle 4.7 kilograms. There is, therefore, no correlation between absolute muscular power and animal size, and the apparently greater strength of muscles of small animals is an illusion.

There is, however, a crucial difference between the potential strength of a large animal and of a small one. If we were to drop an elephant from the top of a tall building it would be crushed to a pulp, but if we dropped a flea it would fall to the ground uninjured. On the other hand, a pollen grain would float away in the wind. Why? It is a matter of mathematics, that is, the comparison between outside dimensions and volume.

If, for example, we have a block of wood measuring one inch on all sides we find that it contains one cubic inch of wood. Now if we double the outside dimensions to 2 inches on all sides we will then have increased its volume, not to 2 inches, but to 4. If we again double the size of the block so that it measures four inches on all sides, it will then contain 64 cubic inches. From this it is obvious that the volume increases much faster than the outside dimensions. This is true whether the object be a block of wood or the body of an animal. Now suppose we were able to stimulate a beetle so that it continued to grow to enormous size, what would happen? As the beetle grew larger it would increase in weight and in strength but its weight would increase much faster than its strength. This is because, as we have seen, the strength of a muscle depends on the area of its cross-section and not on its length. As the beetle continues to increase in size it becomes heavier and heavier and more strength is needed for it to move about. Eventually a point is reached where all its strength is required for movement leaving none for anything else. Beetles, like most other insects, have hard outer shells or exoskeletons that are well adapted to a small insect but too cumbersome for a large insect. This is one of the reasons that gigantic insects were never evolved. Another, and perhaps even more important, reason is that the respiratory system of insects does not work efficiently in a large animal. Thus, in spite of the tales of huge insects in books of science fiction, the members of the insect clan seem destined to remain forever in the category of small creatures. After millions of years their size seems to have become stabilized. While we regard all insects as being small animals it may never have occurred to you that among them is found the greatest size range of any animal group, even greater than the difference in size between the mouse and the elephant. Insects come in assorted sizes ranging from microscopic to the larger beetles and moths of the tropics. An elephant is only 100 times taller than a mouse, but an Atlas moth is more than 1,000 times the size of a fairy fly.

Another important comparison point between animal strength and size is the ability of each creature to expend energy. A muscle, even though it is very powerful, is not of much value to its possessor unless it can do useful work or expend energy. When an animal is at rest it is still expending energy. The amount of energy an animal expends while at rest is called its basal metabolic rate, or the rate at which it consumes or burns up food materials. Muscular exertion increases this rate. In the case of a human athlete this rate may increase up to 20 times the basal rate but he can maintain this rate for only a short time. By contrast, a locust in flight increases its metabolic rate by 50 times and a honeybee by 52 times. In spite of the high metabolic rates of these insects they can maintain them for many hours. Only certain birds, such as hummingbirds, can even approach such energy output.

chapter seventeen

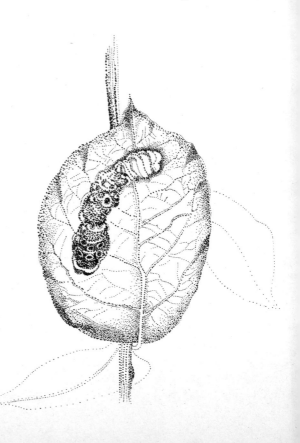

Of Light and Color

LIGHT plays an important role in the lives of most insects just as it does in ours. The majority of insects are especially active during the daylight hours, becoming inactive in darkness. Their lives are governed by the 24-hour cycle which, of course, is the period of one revolution of the earth. Over millions of years insects' lives have been adjusted to this rhythm and they are thus in tune with the cosmic forces that govern the lives of almost all living things.

In the case of plants there are short-day plants, long-day plants and day-neutral plants. The short-day plants are adapted to bloom in early spring or in autumn when the periods of daylight are short. Examples of such plants are dogwood, aster, ragweed and goldenrod. On the other hand, the long-day plants bloom only in midsummer during the season of maximum sunshine. Examples are red clover, althea, larkspur and spinach. Many plants and trees may be considered as being day-neutral since they will flower anytime. Some examples are cotton, buckwheat, snapdragon and many flowering trees. For most plants there is a rather definite time to bloom.

The lives of many insects, too, are governed by the length of the daylight hours. One such insect is the aphid or plant louse. During the summer these insects reproduce by giving birth to living young. Most of these individuals are females and do not mate; they reproduce themselves asexually by producing living young all summer, generation after generation. This continues until the approach of autumn when days become shorter. At this time a generation of males and females is produced that mate and lay eggs. These eggs, however, do not hatch but remain dormant or in a state of *diapause* until spring. With the coming of spring the eggs hatch and the summer reproductive cycle begins again. The aphid may thus be considered to be a long-day insect. Laboratory rearing of the vetch aphid in England has shed some interesting light on the effect of day-length on the life cycles of aphids. There it was found that if vetch aphid colonies were kept in constant 16-hour or long-day conditions, they continued to reproduce asexually indefinitely. The egg-laying generation was not produced until the day-length was shortened to 12 hours. Thus, it is not the approach of autumn with its cooler weather that triggers the production of the egg-laying generation but the arrival of shorter days.

Research on the silkworm in Japan has revealed even better information on the way day-length influences the life cycles of insects. This research was done on the commercial silkworm (*Bombyx mori*) which, as it turned out, is a long-day insect. When the silkworms were reared under artificial lights so that the length of the "days" could be varied it was found that as long as they were reared under short-day conditions the moths continued to lay eggs that hatched at once. If, however, the caterpillars were reared, under long-day conditions (long photoperiods) the eggs did not hatch but entered a state of suspended development or diapause. This is the state or condition in which silkworm eggs pass the winter. It was found that the eggs only resumed development when they had been subjected to temperatures near the freezing point for about 40 days. It was found also that day length or photoperiod had no effect on the larger larvae or the moths. It was only the eggs which were affected. In further research it was found that the mechanism causing diapause in the eggs lay in a hormone or chemical regulator secreted by a nerve center or ganglion in the head of the female moth. This hormone is passed on to the eggs and controls their development. Thus we have a clue to the reason why insect eggs laid by the late summer generation do not go ahead and hatch but go into an inactive state or condition of diapause in which winter is passed.

While much more research has been carried out on plants than on insects relative to their responses to day length, evidence is accumulating that many of the seasonal activities of insects are influenced by variations in the hours of sunlight. It has been known for a long while, of course, that certain insects, especially honeybees, have built-in clocks and can be trained to come to food at definite times of the day. Some insects, such as ants, orientate themselves by means of sun-compass responses. This is well known and has been discussed previously. Many insects are attracted to light. This is especially true of the moths but these insects are not all equally attracted to light of the same wave length or color. There are also variations in the times of night when they are most active. Some moths are crepuscular in habit, preferring the hours of dusk as their time of greatest activity. This is especially true of the hummingbird moths. Other moths like the darkness and are most active later at night. By contrast, those insects that are diurnal (daylight-loving) are not usually attracted to artificial lights.

Many insects follow 24-hour activity rhythms that correspond more or less to the normal hours of light and darkness. But the biological clocks built into insects' bodies do not usually follow exactly a 24-hour cycle. For this reason a new term has recently been introduced. The periodic cycle through which an animal passes is now called its *circadian rhythm* (about daily). For instance, many insects will follow their normal cycles of quiescence and activity when placed in a dark room where all physical conditions are constant. They will, in many cases, follow their normal routines for several days just as though they were in their natural habitats. As long as environmental conditions such as temperature and humidity are kept within reasonable bounds the insects will follow their normal solar time cycles.

A great deal of research effort has been devoted to attempts to adapt insects and other animals to daily cycles other than the normal 24-hour cycle. For instance, the American cockroach (*Periplaneta*) is active during the hours of darkness and inactive in daylight. An attempt was made to adapt these insects to a "day" consisting of two hours of light and six hours of darkness. They followed the abnormal "day" for awhile and then, in a manner of speaking, went berserk and followed no daily rhythm at all. When the cockroaches were kept under the 8-hour day conditions for ten days they seemed unable to revert to their normal daily rhythm of about 12 hours of activity and 12 hours of inactivity. Further research has shown that the American cockroach has a built-in clock in the form of glandular secretions from cells of the nerve ganglion lying just beneath the esophagus. The change from light to darkness causes these cells to secrete a hormone which stimulates the insect's activity. However, there are only certain possible times when the secretion of hormones can be stimulated, and if the light is turned off during the period when secretion is possible, the next period of hormone secretion will come from four or six hours sooner than normal. From this it is obvious that the matter is not a simple one. Dr. Janet Harker of Cambridge University recently performed an interesting experiment. She chilled a cockroach's head gland to stop the biological clock and then, by a delicate surgical technique, transplanted this gland into another roach whose activity rhythm had been stopped by exposure to continuous light. In the new roach the gland caused a daily activity rhythm retimed to the number of hours the gland had been chilled. In other words, the built-in clock within the cockroach's head is stopped or slowed down by low temperature, but starts up again when the animal is warmed. As a general rule, low temperatures tend to slow up biological clocks while high temperatures speed them up.

While small temperature fluctuations do not usually have much effect on daily cycles of activity, there are some cases where relatively small variations in temperatures are important. For example, in the case of one of the harvester ants (*Messer*) the period of greatest activity at low temperature is at mid-day. As temperatures rise, however, the times of greatest activity shift to later in the afternoon and, finally, to night.

While most of the research on biological clocks and circadian rhythms has been done on plants, there is a large amount of most interesting information accumulating on various animals. This is especially true of crabs, snails, fish and salamanders.

The colors of insects, like their reactions to light, are often related to their habits. Insects that dwell in darkness are usually pale in color. Examples are termites and boring grubs. Cave-inhabiting beetles and other insects usually lack pigmentation. Normally ground beetles (Carabidae) are black, but the cave species are nearly white. I have collected such beetles deep in the caves of Tennessee. On the other hand, many insects that dwell in the desert are pale as though they had been bleached by the desert sun. Species of tiger beetles that inhabit the sandy zone of ocean beaches are also of pale color. These pale shades are either of physiological origin or are the result of natural selection since pale coloration may have protective value in concealment in habitats where pastel shades prevail.

Color is a light phenomenon. Without light the eye perceives no color. Colorful insects, butterflies, beetles and dragonflies, are found every-

Many insects, such as this caterpillar of the orange-dog swallowtail (*Papilio cresphontes*), obtain protection by coloration. These caterpillars resemble bird droppings on leaves.

This caterpillar feeds upon daisy petals and camouflages itself by attaching petal fragments to its back.

where, but nowhere are their hues so brilliant and striking as in the sun-dominated forests of the tropics. The world's most beautiful butterflies are found in the hot, humid jungles where both plant and animal life runs riot with color. Through the Amazon region flit great *Morpho* butterflies dressed in iridescent, sky-blue colors. Whether the striking coloration of tropical insects is the result of heat, humidity or abundant sunshine is an unsettled question, but the fact remains that that is where the butterfly collector finds his most beautiful specimens.

The colors of insects are produced by two basic methods; they result either from the microscopic structure of the surface tissues or from the presence of actual pigments. Probably the most beautiful insect colors are the result of structural coloration. The best examples of this are found among the butterflies. If a scale from a butterfly wing is examined under high magnification it will be found that its surface is covered with fine lines or striations. When light strikes these striations it is broken up into prismatic colors just as in the case of *diffraction gratings* used in physics laboratories. In the case of the beautiful, blue *Morpho* butterfly there are

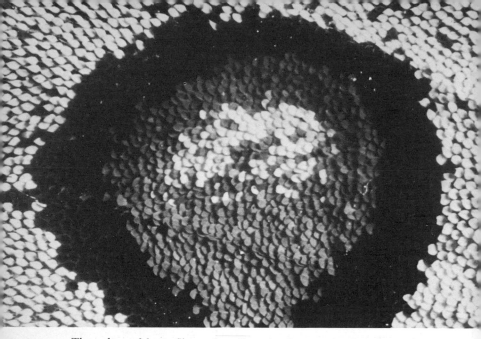

The colors of butterflies and moths arise from scales that cover the wings. This close-up shows a small portion of a *Parnassus* butterfly wing. (see next picture)

It is believed that the colors of butterfly scales result from fine striations that break up the light rays. If you look closely you can see these striations on the greatly enlarged scales.

about 1,050 striae per millimeter. When light strikes the scales of a butterfly the striae break the light up into its component colors just as does a prism and the color transmitted to the eye depends upon the angle at which the light hits the scale. At a low angle the color will be purple. As the angle of the incident light rises the color changes to red, orange, yellow and finally green. Since the scales on the butterfly's wings are not all set at exactly the same angle and are curved, their transmitted colors blend or overlap and the eye sees an iridescent color of one hue. This hue is, however, more or less changeable depending on the angle at which it is held.

In addition to the striations on the surfaces of the scales, there are laminations or layers within them that also break up the light rays. These laminations are probably of more importance in color production than the surface striations. As might be supposed, these layers are very thin, being in the range of from 0.3 microns to 1.5 microns (a micron is 0.001 millimeter). As a result of the combined effect of these scale structures a wide range of colors are produced including violet, blue-green, copper, silver and gold. The colors of many birds' plumage are a result of structural coloration. Colors of this type may be seen in blue jays, humming-birds and others.

In many insects, especially butterflies, the colors are due to a combination of structural coloration and pigmental coloration. In the case of the *Morpho* butterfly there is a layer of black or deep brown pigment within the scales that reflects or intensifies the beautiful blue prismatic color produced by the surface structure. In the case of the bird-winged butterfly (*Battus*) of Indo-Australia, there is an underlying yellow pigment that combines with the structural blue to produce a green coloration. However, authorities are not all in agreement as to several of the details of color production; some authorities discount the importance of the surface striations of the scales in color production.

In the case of other insects such as the tiger beetles (*Cicindelidae*), metallic wood-boring beetles (*Buprestidae*) and others, their pretty metallic colors are due to extremely thin layers or laminations. In this respect their color is produced in much the same manner as in the metals, such as gold and copper, which they resemble. In the case of the metals, light rays can penetrate to only very short distances but this distance is enough to break up the light rays into prismatic colors. Thus, the reflected light from gold is yellow and that from copper is coppery.

Some blue coloration in insects such as that of dragonflies is due to finely divided particles within a transparent layer. This is called "Tyndall blue" and is a result of light passing through a transparent medium having one index of refraction and in which there are particles having another index of refraction. The larger the particles are, the lighter blue is the color. The blue of the sky and the blue color of smoke is also due to the Tyndall effect.

The colors of many insects are the result of actual pigments or coloring materials within their tissues. These are of several types. Black, brown and sometimes yellow are due to a complex substance called *melanin* that requires the presence of oxygen for its deposition. This oxygen comes from the tracheal system and not from the air that is in contact with the surface of the insects' bodies. Newly emerged insects, such as beetles, are usually of pale coloration but become darker within a few hours. This is the result of the production of a color-forming substance called *chromagin* and the presence of oxygen. Some authorities believe that the production of melanin is related to the breakdown of metabolic waste products since it occurs, especially in some insects, at points where muscles are attached. It has also been found that dark, melanic races of some moths occur in industrial areas where fumes presumably affect their metabolism. Whether this is a direct effect or the result of eating plants having high contents of such metals as lead and manganese is still an unanswered question.

Probably the most common pigments in plants are those of the *carotenoid* class. These include carotene and xanthophyll and they are either yellow or orange in color. They are present in tree leaves and, at summer's end, give them their yellow or orange hues. When plants are eaten by insects the carotenoid pigments are absorbed and contribute their colors to the insects. Leaf-eating insects such as potato beetles and caterpillars absorb carotenoids with the result that their blood is yellow. Xanthophyll, on the other hand, is not absorbed to any extent by most insects but it is present in the tissues of the larvae of the yellow butterflies (*Pieridae*).

Pigments of another type are common in plants, these are the *anthocyanins* that range in color from scarlet to red, purple and blue. These same pigments give many flowers their brilliant colors and contribute their share to the coloration of autumn leaves. Beets contain large amounts of anthocyanin. These pigments are but little absorbed by most insects but they do give a vermilion color to certain aphids.

The green colors of many insects such as mantids and katydids are often believed to be the result of feeding upon chlorophyll-bearing plants, but this is apparently not so. The green coloration of these insects is caused by a pigment closely related, in chemical nature, to the bile pigments of mammals. Some green caterpillars apparently do get their color from chlorophyll absorbed from the plants they eat. The white colors of insects are not caused by the presence of actual pigment but by light-scattering structures.

While colors of most insects are fixed and do not change, there are a few cases where insects can change color like chameleons. For instance, a tropical walking stick (*Dixippus*) becomes dark at night and pale during the day. This change is caused by a clumping together of brown and orange pigment particles within the epidermal cells. However, if one of these insects is kept in complete darkness it will still follow its light and dark cycles for several weeks.

If the insects are kept in complete darkness from the time of hatching they do not exhibit the normal light and dark rhythm. Periods of illumination are required for the initiation of the diurnal cycle of color change. This cycle, like the other cycles or rhythms discussed previously, are apparently controlled by secretions of glands in the insects' heads, and these secretions, in turn, are initiated through stimulation through the eyes.

In the case of the migratory locust (*Locusta migratoria*) the insects adapt their coloration to their backgrounds. Possible colors range from dirty white to yellow, brown or black and these colors depend largely upon the light intensity. When these locusts enter the migratory phase their colors change to black with orange markings, these colors apparently being associated with intense muscular activity. It is interesting also that if locusts in the colorful, migratory phase are kept in isolation they revert to the lighter color of the non-migratory phase. When these locusts are fed on succulent food in a moist atmosphere they develop a green coloration.

Some butterflies have a seasonal coloration. In other words, there are differences in color between those of the spring generation and those of later generations. For example, the common violet-tip angle-wing (*Polygonia interrogationis*) has two forms, one occurring in spring and the other in autumn. It is thus said to be *dimorphic*. In some other butterflies, darker individuals are produced when reared under conditions of high humidity. There are also, in some cases, differences in the coloration of the same species of butterflies depending on whether they occur on islands, on mountains or in coastal areas. Insect coloration is dependent on many environmental factors.

While most insects are either repelled or attracted by light there are a number of others that produce light. Such light is called *bioluminescence* and there are many other creatures besides insects that produce it. If you have ever cruised through tropical seas you have no doubt seen the sparkling of the water as the ship passed through the sea at night. These "sparks" are flashes of light given off by protozoa or single-celled animals (*dinoflagellates*) that luminesce when disturbed. Again, if you have spent much time in deep forests at night you may, perhaps, have encountered fox fire, an eerie glow resulting from luminous fungi that live in rotten wood. In addition to these fungi there are luminous toadstools that shine with a ghostly light. In the depths of the sea, especially, are found many creatures that make their own light. These animals dwell in a realm of eternal darkness so any light there must be produced by them. There are also luminous bacteria that live on meat and dead fish.

In certain caves in New Zealand, located about 200 miles north of Wellington, large numbers of gnat larvae (*Arachnocampa luminosa*) live attached to the ceiling. The larvae dangle sticky lines and lure small flies and midges to their dooms. These larvae live in the caves in such large numbers that the ceiling is ablaze with their combined glow.

Most remarkable and best known, however, are the light-producing beetles that occur in many parts of the world. Most of these belong to the family Lampyridae, the lightning bugs or fireflies, of which there are more than 1,500 species in the world. Not all of them produce light, however. During the daylight hours these elongate beetles hide quietly among vegetation, but the hours of dusk and early night is their favorite period of activity, and it is then that they light their lanterns. Most kinds prefer damp situations such as lowlands and marshes and such places often twinkle with their flashes on summer evenings. If you will watch

Fireflies have light generating organs on the ventral surfaces of their abdomens that produce cold light. The flashes emitted by the males are more brilliant than those of the females. These flashes of light are mating signals.

closely you will notice that their flashes are always upward. This is because the beetles always rise as they begin flashing. Also, if you search among the grasses and lower vegetation you will see other, smaller flashes. There are the females whose flashes are aimed at attracting the males. The flashing of fireflies is thus a part of their mating behavior. These beetles use their flashes like code signals and the periods of their flashes are more or less characteristic for the species.

In the eastern United States the common species is *Photinus pyralis;* the male of this species flashes at intervals of about six seconds. The female gives an answering flash about two seconds later. If all goes well the male descends to her. Rather careful observations have been made on the courting behavior of a species found in Michigan (*Pyractomena dispersa*). The observations were made recently by James E. Lloyd, who found that these males give four or five yellow flashes, their rate being affected by the temperature. At 55°F. there were 3.1 flashes per second. The flashing males flew from a few inches to a yard above the ground, the flashes illuminating large areas beneath them. When a flashing male received an answering flash from a female, he dropped to the ground close to her. It was found, also, that the females would respond to the flashing of a male as far away as 15 feet. Mr. Lloyd also simulated the males' flashes by means of a small pocket flashlight and found that the females would not respond unless there were two or more pulses and that these had to be quite precisely timed. This research and others have shown that each species of firefly has its own system of flashing and that the females will respond only to flashes of males of the same species. An important part of the recognition lies in the time interval between the flash of the male and the answering flash of the female.

This brings up a deadly trick played by females of *Photuris pennsylvanica* on males of another firefly (*Photinus scintillans*). The males are attracted to the females of the other species, who at once devour them!

The eggs of fireflies are laid on damp ground and hatch in about three weeks. The larvae live among dead leaves or vegetation and feed upon snails, slugs or larval insects. Light-producing organs appear in about two weeks and, about a week later, these become functional. About two years are required for maturity.

The light-producing organs of fireflies are located on the posterior portion of the abdomen. This organ, which can be seen as a white or yellowish area, is richly supplied with trachea and is under direct control of the nervous system. The chemistry of the firefly's light organ has been quite carefully studied and it is now known that adenosine triphosphate (ATP) supplies the energy for the reaction between luciferin and an enzyme called luciferase. Abundant oxygen is a necessity. The light produced by fireflies is cold light; that is, it is about 98 percent efficient. An electric light bulb, however, dissipates most of its energy in the form of useless heat.

Closely related to the fireflies are beetles of the family Phengodidae, but in this case it is only the females that emit light. Even more inter-

This is the adult male beetle of *Phengodes*. The female is a glow-worm and never develops wings. Species found in the tropics are called railroad worms since they have rows of greenish lights along their sides and red "headlights."

esting is the fact that, while the males acquire wings the females retain their larval character, mating and laying eggs in that state. Probably the only insects that produce lights of two colors are larval beetles (*Phrixothrix*) of the American tropics; they also belong to the Phengodidae family. These insects are known as railroad worms and have 11 pairs of green lights along the sides of their bodies, in addition to a pair of red lights on the head. When the larva is in the act of crawling about it looks like a railroad train with green lights flashing along its sides and a pair of red headlights.

Probably the insects that produce the most brilliant flashes of light are tropical click beetles called fire beetles (*Pyrophorus*). The best-known species is the *Cucubano* (*P. luminosa*) of the West Indies. Other species occur in tropical South America. These beetles, some of which are two inches long, emit brilliant flashes of greenish light and are sometimes used by ladies as hair ornaments. The light-generating organs are located on the top of the prothorax and are in the form of two spots. Here in the United States we have a similar click beetle, the eyed elator (*Alaus oculatus*), which also has eye-spots on its prothorax but does not produce light.

chapter eighteen

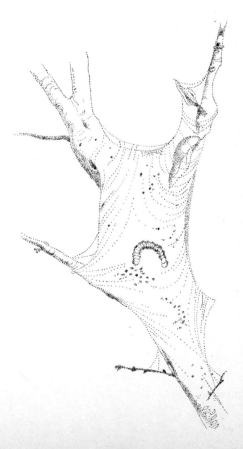

Insects and the Future

I F we consider numbers only, we are now living in the age of insects, since there are far more insects, both in the number of individuals and in the number of species, than all other animals combined. Man is in the small minority. Yet man, with his increasing technology, is exerting more and more influence upon his environment or the world in which he lives. There was a time, not too long ago, when our ancestors had to accept the world as they found it. Today, man alters the world to fit his special needs.

From the beginning of human history man has been in almost constant battle with the insect legions. Insects have destroyed his food and, as parasites, have sucked his blood. Too, these same insects have transmitted some of his most serious diseases including malaria, yellow fever, bubonic plague and typhus. It is only in recent years, since the discovery of effective insecticides, that these diseases have decreased somewhat in importance. Each year the world's chemists are developing newer and more effective insecticides to combat pestiferous insects. Some of these materials are so specific that they are effective against only one insect or insect group.

When the effectiveness of DDT as an insecticide was first discovered during World War II it was believed that it would result in the complete elimination of the housefly and perhaps other insect pests. But the amaz-

311

ing ability of houseflies and other insects to survive against great odds had been ignored. For a few years, housefly populations decreased greatly and it appeared that the battle had been finally won. But it soon became evident that houseflies had developed a resistance or tolerance to DDT and similar insecticides and that they could live and multiply in spite of them. Other pest insects had also developed resistance to insecticides. So the chemists returned to their laboratories and began looking for insecticides of other, more effective, kinds. This is where we find ourselves today. The insects have, seemingly, won the first round.

The insect tribes are very old and, during their long history, have survived in a world that has, at one time or another, been beset by almost every conceivable calamity. During the various ancient ice ages, arctic cold periodically crept down from the poles, and deep layers of glacial ice covered large portions of the continents. During the cold periods, insect populations were pushed southward but, when the ice receded, the insects moved northward again and repopulated the areas from which they had been driven. At other times, hot lava, flowing from volcanoes, spread over the land, and mountains sank beneath the seas and then slowly rose again. Some of the continents, too, were submerged for long periods. Various animal groups flourished in the world for a time and then disappeared, leaving only their fossilized remains as proof that they had ever existed. The insects lived on, gradually becoming better and better fitted to the lives they lived. The insect tribe has been a stable one that has changed very slowly. This is evident when one examines the ancient specimens preserved in amber. Even though these fossil insects are many millions of years old they resemble very closely the ones we see today.

Probably no other group of land animals has followed such a long path across vast stretches of time as have the insects. If we compare them with the mammal group, to which we belong, we find many differences, of course, but the most interesting difference lies in the development of their brains and in the way they function. Insects live by inherited knowledge that, for lack of a better word, we call "instinct." Instinct has its limitations, but "life by instinct" has served insects admirably for a long while. It has been tried and proven in the world's great evolutionary laboratory.

There are two ways by which an animal can carry out its work; it may live and work by skills inherited from its ancestors as do the mason wasps or it may learn its "trade" as an individual as we do. The bee, toiling in the summer sun to gather nectar for the colony, works by instinct. A man learns his special skill or trade as he grows up and then carries out his work, but his first loyalty is to his family and himself and not always to his society as a whole. The worker honeybee stings viciously in defense of her colony, but the fact that the act of stinging will kill her is of no consequence to her; she acts by instinct. By contrast, a man might weigh his chances of survival and allow selfish interests to interfere with his duty to the society to which he belongs. None of us, of course, would wish to change places with the bee but, perhaps in the long run, at least in this case, instinctive behavior does have its advantages.

We are just now beginning to understand and appreciate the complexity of the lives of social insects, the bees, wasps and ants. We have already learned much about honeybees, partly because of their economic importance to us and partly because they are easily studied. But we have much to learn concerning these and other social insects. What of such "wild" social insects as the famous leaf-cutting ants that cultivate underground fungus gardens? These amazing insects have been studied but little, yet it is probable that further detailed studies of them will reveal much remarkable information regarding their ways of life.

On previous pages we have learned something about the complex lives of the "agricultural" insects, the seed-harvesting and mushroom-growing ants as well as of the fungus growing termites of Africa, and of the honeybee. Many millions of years were needed for the habits of these insects to be developed. Man, with his superior mentality, took comparatively but a second to learn how to cultivate wild plants to supply his food. I cannot help but wonder, if we could peer a million years into the future, what would we find? It is probable that there would still be insects, since a million years more or less is but a short span of time to creatures that have already existed for nearly 400 million years. And what about man —will he still be dominating the earth, having at last mastered the complex problems of sociology and of learning how to control his environment? By that time man will certainly have learned how to control his insect enemies or have already eradicated them. Hopefully, not all the interesting forms of insect life will have been completely eliminated. It would, indeed, be a great tragedy if all the more interesting and unusual insects were to go the way of the dodo and the passenger pigeon. Many millions of years were required to evolve them, but man, ever in more direct competition with wild nature, may destroy them all.

By the year 1,000,000 A.D. what will insect life be like, assuming, of course, that man has not eradicated them all? While human civilizations will certainly have changed greatly, it is safe to say that insects will be about the same as the ones we see today. There will, of course, be different species since in the course of a million years some changes will certainly have occurred. They will probably average about the same size, or perhaps be somewhat smaller, since miniaturization in insect evolution has been the trend for millions of years. Probably the days of giant insects are long past. Among the social insects—ants, bees and wasps—there will probably be some minor changes in habits. For example, by that time, it is possible that the seed-gathering harvester ants will have "learned" to plant seeds and grow their own crops as do the fungus growing ants today.

At any event, considerable change will have taken place among almost all insects, and the technical descriptions of present-day species will then be obsolete. No form of life remains the same forever, though some kinds, for some reason or other, change faster than others. Insect life down the eons has been something like a slowly flowing stream of cold molasses. While continually on the move, it seems to be standing still when observed for a brief period. An insect described in great detail today may differ in some of its structural details a few thousand years from now.

It is perhaps strange that we have been able to perfect complex space ships and send them on long journeys to distant planets to seek out the secrets of space before many important facts regarding our own world have been answered. This, of course, does not mean that such projects are not worthwhile, since man is dedicated to acquiring knowledge of all his surroundings and not merely of the world he lives on. The skies are a challenge and man will never rest until he has probed their secrets. Still, the ocean depths are almost as unknown as is the surface of the moon at present, and there is unexplored terrain here on our planet where there may be, and probably are, many unknown insects as well as other animals and forms of plant life.

The insect world is a fascinating place—and many, even more astonishing creatures remain to be discovered. Such possibilities challenge the mind of man, luring him into unceasing study of the miniature world of the insect clan.

Index

Acacias, 250-253
Acherontia atropos, 46
Acheta, 54
Acheta assimilis, 55, 58
Acrobatic ant, 197-198, 250
Adenosine triphosphate (ATP), 308
Aedes, 48, 71
Aedes pandani, 113
Aedomyia, 105
Aeschna, 71
Aeschna grandis, 139
African dragonfly, 113
African goliath beetle, 287, 290
Air plants, 113
Alabama argillacea, 86
Alaus oculatus, 309
Aleppo oak gall, 243
Alexander, Richard D., 47
Algae, 98
Alimentary canal, 17-20
Allaptus, 67
Amber, insects preserved in, 6, 233
Amblycorypha oblongifolia, 58
Amblycorypha uhleri, 58
Ambrosia beetles, 160-162, 229
Ambush bugs, 127-129
American cockroach, 17, 299-300
Amitermes meridionalis, 238
Ammophila, 42-43, 125
Amorphophallus titanum, 264
Anaxipha exigua, 58
Angular-winged katydid, 58
Anisoptera, 110-113
Anoplura, 11
Antennae, 27, 42, 49

Antlions, 11, 131-134
"Ant-rice," 147
Ants, 11, 143-160
    flowers and, 264-265
    honey of, 221-223
    migration of, 89-92
    mounds of, 145, 149
    navigation of, 31-32, 93, 299
    odor sense of, 28-29
    paper-making, 197-198
    protecting of aphids by, 137
    queen, 65, 90-91, 153, 159, 160
    self-defense of, 275, 285
    sounds of, 48, 158-159
    tent-making, 200-202
    testing intelligence of, 41-42
    time sense of, 40
Anurida maritima, 96
Aphids, 11, 198, 223, 244, 297-298
Aphilanthops laticinctus, 125
Apis, see Honeybee
Apis mellifera, 208-210, 215-216
Apis mellifera carnica, 39
Apis mellifera ligustica, 39
Aquatic insects, 95-115
    hydrophobe hairs in, 103
    reproduction of, 98
    tracheal system of, 103-104
Aquatic pyralids, 230
Arachnocampa luminosa, 306
Arisaema triphyllum, 264
Aristolochia, 269-270
Armitermes, 235
Army ants, 89-92
Arrow plant, 257-258

315

Arthropoda (Arthropods), 9, 15
Asilidae, 141
Assassin bugs, 125-126
Atemeles, 233
Athripsodes ancylus, 184
Atlanticus, 58
Atlas moth, 287
Atta, 48, 153-160
Atta texana, 153
Attacus edwardsi, 287
Attaphila fungicola, 159-160
Australian ladybird beetle, 137
Austrophlebia, 71
Automeris io, 279
Azteca, 198
Azteca muelleri, 254-255

Backswimmers, 67, 103, 109-110, 126-127, 281
Bagworm moths, 204-205
Bald-faced hornet, 188-192
Basal metabolic rate of insects, 294-295
Basidiomycetes, 158
Bates, H. W., 154
Battus, 303
Beaver louse, 12
Bee milk, *see* Royal jelly
Bees, 11, 27
  color and, 29-30
  as pollinators, 261-262, 268-269, 271
  wings of, 49, 65-66
Beeswax, 216-217
Beetles, 5, 23, 96
  aquatic, 103, 108-109
  colors of, 300
  fungi-cultivating, 160-162
  light-producing, 306-309
  number of species of, 11
  parasitic, 233
  pollinating, 264
  predaceous, 135-138
  self-defense of, 274-278
  sounds of, 47
  strength of, 289, 290
  wings of, 9, 66, 67, 71
  in wood, 225-227
Belostoma, 102, 281, 289
Belostomatidae, 127
Belt, T., 154-155, 252, 253
Beltian bodies, 253
Bembex wasp, 43
Betsy-beetle, 47, 290
Biology of insects, 9
  blood circulation, 16-17
  digestive system, 17-20
  "ears," 49, 50
  exoskeleton, 13-15
  heart, 16
  hydrostatic organs, 102
  muscles, 13-14, 61, 68, 291-293
  nervous system, 20
  respiratory system, 15-16, 103-104
  silk-producing organs, 199-200
Bioluminescence, 306-309

Bird lice, 11
Birds:
  colors of, 303
  migration of, 77
  songs of, 45-46
Bird-winged butterfly, 303
Black blow-fly, 30
Black flies, 104
Black witch moth, 85-86
Black field cricket, 54, 55, 58
Black-horned tree cricket, 56
Blister beetles, 135-136, 374-375
Blood worms, 17, 100
Blow-flies, 18, 30
Blue burglar wasps, 125, 167-168
Bodies of insects, 9, 68
Bombardier beetles, 137
Bombus, see Bumblebees
Bombyx mori, 198-199, 298
Boring beetles, 225
Brachinus, 137
Brachycentridae, 185
Brachygastra (Nectarina) lecheguana, 220-221
Brachystola, 46
Brain, 20
"Brine flies," 96
Bromatia, 158, 163
Bromeliads, 113
Brown lacewings, 134
Brues, Charles T., 97-98
Bumblebees:
  flight of, 68, 71
  nesting habits of, 218-220
  as pollinators, 262
  pulling ability of, 290
Buprestidae, 228-229, 303
Bush cricket, 58
Bush katydid, 50
Butterflies, 11
  breeding of, 79, 83, 92
  color and, 29
  colors of, 300-303, 305-306
  egg-laying of, 27
  light and, 30
  metamorphosis of, 21-23
  migrating of, 78-85, 92
  as pollinators, 263
  self-defense of, 276-277
  tagging, 79-81
  wings of, 23, 65, 66, 71, 75
"Butterfly Town, U.S.A.," 82

Caddisflies (Trichoptera), 12
  as craftsmen, 110, 165, 174, 177-185
  egg-laying of, 176-177
  environment of, 97, 175
  evolution of, 175
  gills of, 104, 179
  number of species of, 11
  silk-making, 199
Calcium lactate, 284
Callichroma splendidum, 226-227
Calliphora, 18

Callirhytis seminator, 243
Calopogon pulchellue, 268
Calosoma, 137
Calosoma promines, 277-288
Camponotus, 202-203
Camponotus herculeanus pennsylvanicus, 232-233
Camponotus inflatus, 221
Camponotus mus, 48
Cancer, gall formation and, 242
Cantharidin, 274-275
Carabidae, 137-138
Carpenter ants, 151, 202, 232-233
Carpenter bees, 220, 230-232
Carpenter moths, 230
Caryomyia, 244
Caseflies, see Caddisflies
Cassia, 84, 255
Cataglyphis albicans, 32
Catchfly, 256
Caterpillars:
    blood circulation of, 16
    defined, 21
    molting by, 15
    muscles of, 14
    self-defense of, 279-281
    tent-making, 203-205
Catocala, 273
Catopsilia florella, 85
Catopsilia (Phoebis) eubule, 84
Caudell, A. N., 203
Cecidomyia poculum, 244
Cecidomyiidae, 243
Cecropia trees, 253-255
Cedars, 204-205
Cerambycidae, 226-228
Cercopidae, 276
Chagas' disease, 126, 281
Chalybion, 125
Chalybion caerulium, 167-168
Chaoborus, 100, 102
Chemical regulators for cell growth, 21
Chemical warfare of insects, 273-285
Chemotropism, 27-29
Chimney-case caddisflies, 185
Chinch bugs, 11
Chinese mantis, 130
Chironomidae, 17, 97, 100, 104
Chitin, 4, 13
Chortophaga, 15
Chromagin, 304
Chrysalides, 21, 23
Chrysobothris femorata, 229
Chrysomelidae, 19-20
Chrysopidae, 134-135, 275
Cicada killer, 121-123
Cicadas, 11, 23, 58-61
Cicindelidae, 136, 303
Circadian rhythm, defined, 299, 300
Citheronia regalis, 281
Clausen, Lucy, 48
Cloudless sulphur butterfly, 84
Coccinella, 71

Coccinellidae, 136-137
Cockroaches, 5, 11, 65, 299-300
    enzymes of, 18
    intelligence of, 42
Coleoptera, see Beetles
Collembola, see Springtails
Collophore, 107
Colobopsis, 256-257
Color perception, 29-30, 40
Colors of insects, 300-306
Communication:
    of ants, 28-29
    by dance, 33-39
    of honeybee, 33-40
    by sound, 40, 45, 47
    by wings, 48-49
Cone-headed katydid, 50, 52, 57-58
Compass termite, 238
Conidia, 162
Conocephalus, 52, 57-58
Copepods, 100
Coptotermes, 235, 275
Corallorrhiza, 268
Corethra, 100
Corixidae, 109-110
Cossidae, 230
Cottonwoods, galls on, 244
Cottonworms, 86
Cottony cushion scale, 278
Courtship habits:
    of predaceous insects, 141
    See also Mating calls; Reproduction
Crab spiders, 129
Crane flies, 106
Crematogaster lineolata, 197-198
Crematogaster pilosa, 250
Crickets, 11, 53-58
    ant loving, 151
    cages for, 54
    silk-secreting, 202-203
    songs of, 45, 54-58
Cuckoo wasps, 194
Cucubano, 309
Culex, 71, 102
Cynipid wasp, 243
Cynips gallae-tinctoriae, 243
Cypripedium, 268
Cyrtacanthacris rubella, 289

Damselflies, 11, 104, 110, 138-139
Danaus plexippus, see Monarch butterfly
Dance flies, courtship habits of, 141
Dances, 33-39
Dasymutilla, 285
Day-length, insects and, 297-300
DDT, 311-312
Death-watch beetle, 47
Deaths-head moth, 46
Deer bot fly, 72
Deer parasite, 65
Defense, 273-285
Dermaptera, 11
Dermestes, 19

Desert locusts, 71, 73, 86-88
Devil's darning needles, 110
"Devil's-flower," 131
Diamphida locusta, 275
Dicholcaspis eldoradensis, 242
Dickens, Charles, 54
Dicranura vinula, 277
Digestive system, 17-20
Digger wasps, 124-125
Dimorphic, defined, 305
Dinoflagellates, 306
Dione vanillae, 85
Dionea, 247-248
Diplolepis politus, 245
Diptera, 11, 66, 69, 73-75
Diseases, 126, 281, 311
Diving beetles, 108, 138
Dixippus, 305
Dobsonflies, 11
Dodd, F. P., 201
Dolbear, A. E., 57
Dolichoderus, 125-126, 198
Dolichovespula maculata, 188-192
Donacia, 105
"Doodlebugs," 132, 136
Dorylus, 89
Dorymyrmex, 152
Dracunculus vulgaris, 264
Dragonflies, 11, 110-113
   colors of, 304
   gills of, 104
   as hunters, 138-140
   locomotion in water of, 108
   mating of, 111-112, 140
   migration of, 89, 92
   naiads, 23
   sounds of, 47
   wings of, 66, 69-72
Driver ants, 89
Drosera, 248
Drosophila, 27
Dry-wood termites, 234
Dufour's gland, 28
Dutchman's pipes, 264, 269-270
Dynastes hercules, 287-289
Dytiscidae, 108

Earwigs, 11
Eciton, 89-92
Elmis, 105
Elophila, 230
Embiids, 199-200
Empidae, 141
Engraver beetles, 160, 229
Enzymes:
   in digestive system, 17, 18
   in fireflies, 308
   galls and, 242
   in nectar, 207, 209
Ephemeroptera, 11
Ephydridae, 96
Epidendrum tampensis, 267-268

Epipharynx, 46
Erebus odorata, 85-86
Eriosoma lanigerum, 278
Eristalis, 71
Eucalyptus trees, 82, 207
Eumenes, 125, 173-174
Eumenidae, 166
Eurosta solidaginis, 244
Evolution of insects, 3-5, 97, 98, 233-234, 312
   sounds, 47
   wings, 4-5, 63-64, 68
Excretory tubes, 19-20
Exodus, Book of, 86-87
Exoskeleton, 13-15
Exyra, 249-250
Eyed elator beetle, 309
Eyes, compound, 30-33

Fairy fly, 67, 107
Farmers, 143-163
Fibroin, 190
Field cricket, 54, 57
Fire ants, 151, 198, 285
Fire beetles, 309
Firebrats, 11
Fireflies, 138, 306-308
Flat-headed apple tree borer beetle, 229
Flat-headed borer beetle, 227
Fleas, 11, 12, 18, 291
Flesh flies, 250
Flies, 75
   courtship habits of, 141
   in leaves, 240
   parasitic, 140-141
   pollination and, 263-264, 270
   water and, 106
   wings of, 9
Flight, 63-75
   See also Wings
Flowers, 261-271
Fly maggot, 29
Forcipomyia, 71
Fork-tailed katydid, 58
Formic acid, 275
Formica, 41-42
Fossils, *see* Evolution of insects
Fungi, glowing, 306
Fungi-cultivating, 153-163

Gall-making insects, 225, 241-245
Galls:
   as source of honeydew, 223
   types of, 242-245
Ganglia, 20
Gelastocoridae, 110, 126
Gerridae, *see* Water striders
Giant water bugs, 127, 281, 289
Gills, 103-104
Glossina, 18
Gnats, 106, 277, 306
Gold, 151, 178-179
Goldenrod, 129, 244

Gouty oak gall, 243
Goliathus regius, 287, 290
"Grasshopper Constitution, The," 88
Grasshopper Glacier, 89
Grasshoppers, 5, 11, 141
  aquatic, 115
  excretory tubes in, 19
  in glacial ice, 89
  jumping ability of, 291-293
  nymphs, 23
  respiratory movements of, 15
  self-defense of, 275
  sound receptors of, 49
  wings of, 9, 66
Gravity, bees and, 36-39
Green-camouflaged mantis, 118
Ground beetles, 137-138
Ground cricket, 58
Grub, defined, 23
Gryllotalpa hexadactyla, 58
Gryllus, 54
Gulf fritillary butterfly, 85
Gyrinidae, 108-109
Gyrinus, 31

Habenaria, 268
Halobates, 96
Halteres, 73-75
Harker, Janet, 30
Harper, Francis, 115
Harvester ants, 143-153
  crickets and, 151
  food habits of, 29
  sting of, 285
  strength of, 289
  temperature and, 300
Heart, 16
Helianthus, 256
Heliconidae, 277
Helicopsychidae, 185
Hemerobiidae, 134, 273
Hemiptera, 11, 109, 125
Hemolymph, 17
Hercules beetle, 287-289
Hernandez, Francisco, 252
Hickory horned devil, 281
Hickory trees, 244, 281
Hilara, 141
Homoptera, 11, 19, 278
Honey, 219, 221
  Babylonian uses of, 208
  enzymes in, 209
  work in producing, 216
Honey ants, 242
Honeybees, 208-218
  alimentary canal of, 18, 19
  colors and, 29-30, 40
  flight range of, 73
  gall "nectar" and, 242
  honey dance of, 33-39, 215
  as nectar gatherers, 208-210, 215-217
  polarized light and, 32-33, 93

as pollen gatherers, 209-210, 215, 261-262
  pulling ability of, 290
  queen, 8, 39, 46, 210-214
  royal jelly of, 191, 211
  sensory organs of, 27-28
  sting of, 281-284
  time sense in, 40-41, 299
  units in eyes of, 31
  wings of, 71
Honeydew, 19
  as ant food, 197-198
  produced by galls, 242
Honey-guides, 217-218
Hormaphis hamamelidis, 244
Horned toads, 152
Hornets, 71, 188-192
Horsefly, 31, 71, 73
Housefly, 9, 27, 31, 49, 71
"House-renters," 172
Hover-fly, 71
Hummingbird moth, 71, 299
Hummingbirds, 30, 71
Hydrocampa, 105
Hydrochloric acid, 277
Hydrometridae, 106
Hydrophilidae, 108, 138
Hydrophobe hairs, 103
Hydropsychidae, 179-180
Hydroptilidae, 180
Hydrostatic organs, 102
Hydrotropism, 41
Hymenoptera, 11-12, 164-175, 187-205, 281-285
  See also Ants; Bees; Wasps
Hypermallus villosus, 228

Ichneumon wasp, 268
Idolum diabolicum, 131
Imms, A. D., 274
Imported fire ant, 198
Insecticides, 311-312
Instinct, 25-41, 312-313
  migratory, 77-93
Intelligence of insects, 41-43, 178
Io moth, 279
Isodontia, 250
Isoptera, 11, 233-239
Itonida anthici, 243

Jet propulsion, 108
Johnston's organ, 109
Junipers, bagworm moths and, 204

Kalotermes, 234
Kangaroo rats, 152
Kangaroos, 291
Katydids, 11, 49
  songs of, 45, 50-53, 58
  sound receptors of, 49
  temperature and, 57
"King hornet," 121-123
Kissing bug, 126, 281

Koo-tsabe fly, 96
Kymographs, 70

Laccifera, 278
Lacewings, 11, 134-135
Lactuca, 256
Ladybird beetles, 136-137, 274
Lampyridae, 138, 306-308
Large caddisflies, 180-181
Larra, 125
Laspeyresia saltitans, 258
Leaf beetles, 19-20, 105
Leaf gathering, 153-154, 156-158
Leaf shelters, 200-205
Leaf-cutter ant, 48
Leaf-folders, defined, 204
Leafhoppers, 11
Leaf-miners, 225, 239-241
Leaf-rollers, defined, 204
Leaf-rolling cricket, 202-203
Leaves as insect habitats, 239-241
Lepidoptera, 11, 175
Leptocella, 182-184
Leptoceridae, 182-184
Leptocerus, 184
Leucotermes, 48
Light, 297-309
    polarized, 32-33, 93
    produced by insects, 306-309
    reaction of insects to, 29-30, 40, 299
    time sense and, 298-300
Limnephilus, 181-182
Lindauer, Martin, 39
Lipoptena cervi, 65
Lissopimpla semipunctata, 268
Liver flukes, 89
Lizards, 31, 250
Lloyd, James E., 307
Locomotion in water, 105-108
Locusts, 60, 71, 73
    in glacial ice, 89
    migration of, 86-89, 92, 305
Long-horned beetles, 47, 226-228
Long-horned borer beetle, 226-227
Long-horned caddisflies, 182-184
Long-horned meadow grasshoppers, 115
Loyola crassus, 134-135
Lubber grasshopper, 46
Luciferase, 308
Lucilia, 29

McCook, Henry C., 151
Macrotermes, 235
Macrotermes bellicosus, 8
Macrotermes natalensis, 163, 238-239
Magnan, Antoine, 68
Mallophaga, 11
Malpighi, Marcello, 242
Malpighian tubes, 19-20
Mansonia, 105
Mantids (mantises; Mantidae), 11, 118
Mantis religiosa, 31, 129-151
Maple case-bearer, 240-241

Marellia, 115
Marine water strider, 106
Mason wasps, 18, 125, 166
Mating calls:
    of aquatic insects, 47
    of death-watch beetle, 48
    of katydids and crickets, 45, 50-53, 56
May beetles, 140-141
Mayflies, 11, 104
Meadow grasshopper, 52, 57-58
Meadow katydid, 50
Mealybugs, 233
Meeuse, J. D., 264
Megaloponera foetens, 275
Megaloprepus caerulatus, 110
Megalopyge lanata, 281
Megalopyge opercularis, 279-281
Meganeura, 66, 71, 72, 287
Melanin, 304
Melanoplus mexicanus mexicanus, 88, 89
Melanoplus spretus, 88-89
Meloidae, 135-136
Melophagus ovinus, 65
"Mellow-bugs," 109
Messor, 144-145, 300
Metabolic water, 19
Metallic wood-boring beetle, 228-229
Metamorphosis, 21-23
Mexican jumping beans, 258-259
Micro-caddisflies, 180
Microcentrum rhombifolium, 58
Midge flies, 71, 97, 104, 106
Migration, 77-93
Milkweed, 78-79, 268-269
Minims, 158-159
Mites, 9
Mockingbirds, 236-237
Mole cricket, 54, 58
Monarch butterfly:
    flight range of, 73
    migration of, 78-82, 92
    reproduction of, 79
    self-defense of, 275
    wings of, 71
Monobia quadridens, 232
Monomorium salomonis, 32
Morpho, 301-303
Mosaic vision, 30-31
Mosquitoes, 113
    breathing of, 102, 103, 105
    flight range of, 73
    sounds of, 48-49
    wings of, 71
Motes, 125
Moth balls, 27
Moths, 11
    chemotropic responses of, 28
    light and, 30, 299
    migration of, 85-86, 92
    as pollinators, 263, 266-268
    self-defense of, 277
    wings of, 65, 66
    as wood borers, 230

Mound-building termites, 235
Mud-dauber wasps, 25-27, 166-173, 285
Mule killers, 285
Müller, F., 254
Müllerian bodies, 254
Muscles, 13-14
  for flying, 68
  power of, 291-293
  for sound, 61
Mushrooms in ant nests, 158
Mutillids, 12, 285
Mycelium, 158
Mycetophilidae, 277
Mymaridae, 107
Myrmecocystus, 221-223
Myrmecophiles, 151, 159-160, 233
Myrmeleontidae, 131-134

Naphthalene, 27
Narcissus, 266
Nasutitermes, 235, 275
Navigation, 92-93
  by antennae, 42
  by Johnston's organ, 109
  by polarized light, 32-33
  by scent, 28-29, 81
  by sun, 31-32, 42
Nectar:
  defined, 209
  pollination and, 207, 261-271
  sugar content of, 207-208
Nemobius, 58
Neoconocephalus, 58
Neoconocephalus ensiger, 52
Neoconocephalus robustus, 52
Nepenthes, 249
Nepidae, 126-127
Nervous system, 20
Neuroptera, 11, 131-135
Noctuid moths (Noctuidae), 71, 86
Northern caddisflies, 181-182
Notodonta concinnula, 277
Notonectidae, see Backswimmers
Nymphula, 104, 230

Oak-apple gall, 243
Oak pruner beetle, 228
Oak trees, 228
  galls on, 242-243
Oblong-winged katydid, 58
Octopi, 95, 108
Odonata, 104, 111-113, 138-140
  labium of, 115
  species of, 11
  See also Damselflies; Dragonflies
Odors:
  of army ants, 90
  of flowers, 262-264
  of hunting, 119, 126
  of insects, 274-278
  of pitcher plants, 249
Odynerus, 125

Oecanthus, 56, 58
Oecetis, 184
Oecophylla, 200-202
Oil beetles, 274-275
Ommatidia, 31
Oncideres cingulata, 227
Ophrys, 268
Orange-dog swallowtail, 273
Orchelimum, 52, 58
Orchelimum bradleyi, 115
Orders of insects, 11
Organ-pipe wasp, 172-173
Orthoptera, 11, 45, 49
Osmeteria, 276
Ostia, 16-17
Oxygen, 98-100, 103-104, 304

Painted lady butterfly, 82-84
Palaeodictyoptera, 4
Pandanus, 113
Papaipema appassionata, 250
Paper-making insects, 187-198, 220-221
Papilio, 71
Papilio anchisiades, 276-277
Papilio cresphontes, 273
Papilio troilus, 276
Paraclemensia acerifoliella, 240-241
Parasites, 140-141
Parasol ants, 154
Paratenodera sinensis, 130
Paratylotropidia brunneri, 47
Parker, J. R., 88
Parrot pitcher plant, 250
Passalus, 47, 290
Pawpaw leaf, 203
Pears, sugar content of nectar in, 207
Pebble cases, 97
Pemphigus populi-transversus, 244
"Penny doctors," 136
Pentatomidae, 274
Pepsis, 118-121
Pessulus, 46
Petroleum flies, 96-97
Phaneroptera, 58
Phantom midge flies, 100
Pharyganeidae, 180-181
Pharynx, 46
Pheidole, 28-29, 145
Phengodidae, 308-309
Pheromones, 28, 29, 212-213
Philanisus plebejus, 97
Philopotamidae, 179
Photinus pyralis, 307
Photinus scintillans, 307
Photosynthesis in leaves, 239
Phototropism, 29-33
Photuris pennsylvanica, 307
Phrixothrix, 309
Phryganea interrupta, 176
Phymatidae, 127-129
Pieris, 71
Pillbugs, 9
Pine trees, 6, 261

Pine tree katydid, 58
Pitcher plants, 125, 248-250
Plagiotrochus punctatus, 243
Plant curiosities, 247-259
Plant feeding insects, 117
Plant lice (aphids), 11, 198, 223, 244, 297-298
Plecoptera, 11
Podura aquatica, 106-107
Pogonomyrmex, 143-151
Poisons:
    irritating gas, 137
    narcotic, 170
    paralyzing, 120, 122-123, 126
    in self-defense, 279-285
    venomous, 126, 127, 132
Polarized light, 32-33, 93
Polistes, 194
Pollen:
    collected by bees, 209-210, 230-231, 261-263
    insect attraction to, 261-271
    protein in, 209
Pollinators, 261-271
Polyembryony, defined, 140
Polygonia interrogationis, 305
Polyphemus, 198
Polyrhachis, 200
Potter wasp, 13, 125, 173-174
Praying mantis, 31, 129-131
Prociphilus tessellatus, 278
Pronuba yuccasella, 266-267
Propolis, 214
Protodonata, 5
Protozoans:
    luminous, 306
    in termites, 162, 234-235
Proventriculus, 17
Pseudomyrma, 250, 252-253
Psilopa petrolei, 96-97
Psithyrus, 220
Pterophylla camellifolia, 50, 58
Ptilocerus ochraceus, 125-126
Pulvinaria vitis, 278
Pupae, 21, 23
Pupation, blood in, 17
Puss moth, 279-281
Pyractomena dispersa, 307
Pyrgota, 140-141
Pyrophorus, 309

Queen ant, 65, 90-91, 153, 159, 160
Queen bumblebee, 218-220
Queen honeybee, 8, 39, 46, 210-214
Queen termites, 235-236
Queen wasps, 189-191, 196-197

Rafflesia, 264
Ranatra, 46, 102
Rats, 41-42
Rau, Nellie, 171
Rau, Phil, 171

Réaumur, René Ferchault de, 217
"Rear-horses," 130
Red admiral butterfly, 27
Regal moth, 281
Reproduction, 8-9
    of army ants, 90-91
    of *Atta*, 159
    of cicada killer, 122-123
    of cicadas, 59
    of dragonflies, 111-113
    egg-laying rate in, 8, 91
    of fairy flies, 67, 107
    of harvester ants, 153
    of honeybees, 8
    of monarch butterfly, 79
    of painted lady butterfly, 83
    of *Pepsis*, 121
    of water beetles, 108
Respiratory system:
    of aquatic insects, 103-104
    of nonaquatic insects, 15-16
Reticulitermes, 234-237
Rhinotermes, 235
Rhyacophila, 177
Rielia manticida, 131
Riffle beetles, 105
Robber-fly, 31, 141
Rocky Mountain locust, 88-89
Rose-leaf mantis, 131
Royal jelly, 191, 211-212

Saddle-back caterpillar, 279
Sagittaria (arrow-head), 105
Salicylaldehyde, 278
Salicylic acid, ants and, 40
Salivary glands, silk-secreting, 17, 19
Santschi, F., 32
Sarcophaga, 250
Sarracenia, 248-250
Saturniids, 199
Sauromatum guttatum, 264
Scale insects, 11
Scavenger flies, 250
Sceliphron, 125
Sceliphron caementarium, 166-167
Scent, navigation by, 28-29, 81
Schistocerca, 71
Schistocerca gregaria, 86-88
Schneirla, T. C., 41
Schwänzeltänze, 33
Sclerotin, 13
Scolia, 268
Scolytidae, 160, 229
Scudderia furcata, 58
Sea anemones, 95
Seaweed as insect food, 97
Sebastiania pringlei, 257, 258
Seine builders, 179-180
Self-defense, 273-285
Self-pollination, 262
    prevention of, 271

Sensory organs, 27
  antennae, 27, 42, 49
  "ears," 49, 50
  eyes, 30-31
  halteres, 73-75
  Johnston's organ, 109
Sericine, 199
17-year cicada, 13, 59-60
Sheep tick, 12, 65
Shield-back grasshopper, 58
Shinn, Alvin F., 172-173
Shore-flies, 96
Sibine stimulea, 279
Silene, 256
Silk secretion, 17, 19-20, 198-205, 240-241
Silken-tube spinners, 179
Silkworm, 198-199, 298
Silver water beetle, 108
Silverfish, 11, 20
Simulium, 104
Siphonaptera, *see* Fleas
Size of insects, 287-289, 294
Skertchly, S. B. J., 83
Smythe, P. H., 85
Snail-case caddisflies, 185
Snails, 92, 182, 290
Snake doctors, 110
Snapdragons, 265
Sniper-scope, 29
Snowy tree cricket, 56
Soldier-flies, 98
Solenopsis, 152
Solenopsis saevissima richteri, 198
Songs and sounds, 45-61
  of birds, 45-46
  of cicadas, 58, 59-61
  of crickets, 45, 54-58
  forced air and, 46
  list of, 57-58
  mating and, 45, 47, 48, 50-53, 56
  stridulation and, 46-48, 50-57, 61, 158
  tapping and, 47-48
  wing, 40, 46, 48-49, 51, 61
Species, number of, 3, 6
Sphecidae, 166-171
Sphecius speciosus, 121-123
Spicebush swallowtail butterfly, 276
Spiders, 9, 93, 129
Spiny rose gall, 245
Spiracles, 15, 46
Spittle bugs, 276
Spitzner, M. J. E., 33
Springtails (Collembola), 3, 4, 11, 20, 96, 107, 291
Squash bugs, 11
Stagmomantis carolina, 130
Stapelia, 264
Stenodictya lobala, 64
Stinging, 281-284
Stink flies, 275
Stinkbugs, 11, 274
Stoneflies, 11
Strength and abilities of insects, 289-295

Stridulation, 45-48, 50-58, 61, 158
Stroboscopic lights, 70
Subterranean termites, 234-237
Sucking lice, 11
Sugars, 207-208, 242
"Suicide missions," 86
Sulphur butterflies, 84-85
Sundew, 248
Sunflowers, 207, 256
Swallow-tail butterfly, 27
Sweet clover, 207
Sykes, W. H., 145
Symbiosis, 267
Syrinx, 46

Tachysphex, 124-125
Tachytes, 124-125
Tagging butterflies, 79-81
Tannic acid in galls, 242-243
Tarantula hawk wasps, 118-121, 285
Temperature:
  determination of, by insects, 56-57
  locust migration and, 87
  time sense and, 300
  wing-beat rate and, 71
Tenant wasps, 125, 172
Terias (Eurema) lisa, 85
Termitaries, 238-239
Termites, 234-239
  fungi-cultivating, 162-163
  number of species of, 11
  protozoa in, 162, 234-235
  self-defense of, 275
  tapping sounds of, 48, 235
Tettigoniidae, 49-50
Texas bush katydid, 58
Thalessa, 13
Thermacarus, 98
Thermal mites, 98
Thermotropism, 41
Thief ants, 152
Thigmotropism, 41
13-year cicada, 59
Thistles as insect food, 82
Thorax, 9, 68
Thoreau, Henry David, 54
Thread-legged bugs, 126
Thrips, 11
Thyridopteryx ephemeraeformis, 204
Thysanoptera, 11
Thysanura, 11
Ticks, 9
Tiger beetles, 136, 303
"Tippling Tommy," 162
Tipulidae, 106
Titanus giganteus, 226
Toad bugs, 110, 126
Toadflax, 265
Toadstools, luminous, 306
Town ants, 155
Townsend, C. H. T., 72
Tracheal system, 15
  of aquatic insects, 103-104

Trachymyrmex, 153, 160
Trash-carriers, 134, 273
"Traveling butterflies," 84
Tree crickets, 54, 56, 58
Tree frogs, 250
Triatoma, 126
Tribolium, 19
Trichoptera, *see* Caddisflies
Trichopterygidae, 289
Trophallaxis, 191, 194, 197
Tropisms, 27-33, 41
    defined, 27
True katydid, 50, 58
Trypetidae, 244
Trypoxylon, 125, 172
Tse-tse fly, 18
Turkeys, dragonflies and, 89
Twig-girdler, 227-228
Two-winged flies, *see* Diptera
Tyndall blue, 304
Typha (cattail), 105

Uhler's katydid, 58
Uralotermes permianum, 233-234
Urquhart, F. A., 79-81
Urticacae, 253-254

Vanessa cardui, 82-84
Vedalia beetle, 137
Ventral tube, 107
Venus fly-trap, 247-248
Vespula, 195-197
Vespula austriaca, 197
Vespula squamosa, 197
Vetch aphid, 298
Violet-tip angle-wing butterfly, 305
Von Frisch, Karl, 32, 33-39, 41
Von Ihering (entomologist), 254
Voodoo lily, 264

Walkeriana ovilla, 278
Walkingsticks, 11, 287
"Wasp years," 192
Wasps, 11
    gall-making, 242-243, 245
    hunting, 118-125, 250
    nectar-gathering, 220-221
    paper-making, 188-197
    parasitic, 140, 194, 197
    as pollinators, 268
    self-defense of, 285
    social behavior of, 193
    wingless (mutillids), 12, 285
Watch-winding cicada, 61

Water:
    insect conservation of, 18-19
    locomotion in, 105-108
    oxygen in, 98-100, 103-104
    surface tension of, 102-103
Water beetles, 31, 98, 101, 103, 108
Water boatmen, 103, 109-110
Water bugs, 11, 102, 127, 281, 289
Water lettuce (*Pistia*), 105
Water lily (*Nymphea*), 105, 115
Water measurers, 106
Water scorpions, 46, 102, 126-127
Water shrews, 103
Water springtail, 106-107
Water-tigers, 108, 138
Water-scavenger beetles, 107, 138
Water striders, 11, 96, 103, 105-106, 110, 126
Wenner, Adrian M., 40
Wheel bug, 126
Wheeler, William Morton, 250
Whirligig beetle, 31, 108-109
Wild lettuce, 256
Williams, C. B., 83, 89, 93
Williams, C. M., 72
Willows, sugar content of nectar in, 207
Wing-beat rate, 70-71
Wing-loading performance of honeybees, 210
Wings, 9
    of butterflies, 23, 65, 66, 71, 75
    evolution of, 4-5, 63-64, 68
    as fossils, 4, 64
    movement of, 68-70
    sounds made by, 40, 46, 48-49, 51, 55-56, 61
    in underwater propulsion, 107
    vibration rate of, 48-49, 52
Witch-hazel cone-gall, 244
Witch-hazel leaves, 244
Wood-boring beetles, 303
Woodpeckers, 127, 227
Wool-sower gall, 243
Woolly alder aphid, 278
Woolly apple aphid, 278
Wyeomyia smithii, 250

Xyleborus, 160-162
Xylocopa, 220
Xylocopa californica, 232
Xylocopa virginica, 232

Yellowjackets, 188, 196-197
Yellow-legged mud dauber, 166-173
Yerba de flecha, 257, 258
Yucca moths, 266-267

Zebra butterfly, 277
Zonocerus, 275
Zygoptera, 110